THE DARK
SACRAMENT

THE DARK SACRAMENT

EXORCISM IN MODERN IRELAND

DAVID M KIELY

CHRISTINA MCKENNA

Gill & Macmillan

Gill & Macmillan Ltd
Hume Avenue, Park West, Dublin 12
with associated companies throughout the world
www.gillmacmillan.ie
© David M Kiely and Christina McKenna 2006
ISBN-13: 978 07171 4003 9
ISBN-10: 0 7171 4003 2

All biblical quotes taken from the
King James Version, except those on pp 34, 372–4,
to be found in the Douay-Rheims Bible.

Design and print origination by David M Kiely
Printed by Creative Print and Design Wales

The paper used in this book comes from wood pulp
of managed forests. For every tree felled, at least one
tree is planted, thereby renewing natural resources.

A CIP catalogue record for this book is available from
the British Library.

1 3 5 4 2

Important Note

(Notes relating to the text are to be found on pp 387–410)

You are about to read nine true-life accounts of exorcism in present-day Ireland. When preparing *The Dark Sacrament* we conducted interviews with a great many people up and down the country. The principals in the nine cases we chose for inclusion are all very much alive, with but one exception: an elderly gentleman who passed away in 2003. In his case we relied on the excellent account supplied by the clergyman involved, as well as those of other key participants.

The names in this book are fictitious. From the outset we assured those interviewed that they would remain anonymous – if they so wished. All chose anonymity.

Among them are those who requested that we go even further, that we change important details, such as settings and minor participants, so that the originals could no longer be identified. Those individuals feared reprisals of one kind or another.

For these reasons the reader should note that we have, where possible, disguised the family circumstances of those concerned, e.g. the number of persons in a particular household, the gender of the offspring, etc. Similarly, settings are changed. While we may treat of events that actually occurred in, say, a market town in the midlands, the real name of that town is never used. We will have translated the events to a locality in another part of the island of Ireland, in order to safeguard the privacy of our contributors, be they lay or cleric. The alternative to 'naming names' was a text overburdened with the like of 'John W— lived in the town of T— .' This would have been less than satisfactory.

Moreover, in all cases we have placed the clergymen concerned in parishes other than their own.

We have also reconstructed certain scenes and conversations for the benefit of the narrative, while at the same time ensuring that such reconstruction remained faithful to the essence of the testimony given.

We approached our subject in a spirit of unbiased investigation. We were careful not to draw our own conclusions when examining the accounts of paranormal manifestation related by both victim and deliverer. To be sure, no one – including the witnesses themselves – can ever be certain that any single account is objective, and this fact we took into careful consideration when compiling this collection.

In the final analysis, it was a combination of trust and reason that prompted us to reject the one case history and embrace the other. It soon became apparent whose testimony was dependable, when set against those one could dismiss as fantasy. The nine cases we present are, to the best of our knowledge, reliable.

We cannot express strongly enough our gratitude and appreciation to the two groups of people who made this book possible.

Firstly, they are the exorcists: those men of God who gladly granted us the benefit of their knowledge and experience.

Secondly, they are the victims: those individuals who endured great hardship – in some cases over several years – when pursued by the paranormal. They gave freely and willingly of their time to speak to us, often for many hours and in the course of many sessions. They did this for the most altruistic and selfless reasons; their prime concern was to share with others their traumatic experiences. They did so in the understanding that others, being thus alerted to possible danger, would not have to suffer as they did.

We salute their courage.

David M Kiely and
Christina McKenna
Rostrevor, 2006

Darkness cannot put out the light.
It can only make God brighter.

Anonymous

Contents

Exorcism in Our Time

*My dear brothers, never forget, when you hear
the progress of enlightenment vaunted, that the
most exquisite of the Devil's wiles was persuading us that he doesn't exist.*

— Charles Baudelaire
'The Generous Gambler', 1864

THIS IS A DARK BOOK. It is also a book of enlightenment in a specific sense, because it attempts to throw a little light into the more obscure and secret areas of human experience. In doing so, it will challenge the reader's notions of this life, the afterlife, and – for want of a better expression – dimensions that lie beyond the physical. Broadly speaking, it deals with the paranormal.

It treats of the concept of Satan, also known as the Devil, and examines the possibility that he might, after all, be a real and unfabled entity.

Such a hypothesis will astonish the rationally minded; others will doubtless find it disturbing. Still others will consider it high time that the gloves came off and the 'great dragon' of Revelation was confronted head on.

There is one serious drawback in all this: very little is known about this elusive enemy. At one time, in another century, the Devil was as well defined as any adversary of flesh and blood. 'High on a throne of royal state,' John Milton wrote, 'Satan exalted sat . . . and princely counsel in his face yet shone, majestic, though in ruin.'

The words appear early on in *Paradise Lost*, the great epic in which the poet recounts events that followed the angel Lucifer's expulsion from heaven. The descriptions of hell sound strange in our ears, yet in Milton's own time – he published the poem in 1667 – his imagery would have been the accepted one. There are burning lakes and caverns, teeming with vast hosts of demon armies, all under the command of a rigid hierarchy of generals, chief among whom is Satan himself.

Few Christians living in the seventeenth century doubted the existence of hell and its rulers. There were many reminders in ecclesiastical art: paintings, sculpture, stained glass, the admonishments of the bestiary. Even the fearsome gargoyles set atop cathedrals were modelled on a fairly precise and generally prevailing picture of how demons *actually* looked; in the seventeenth century, all art was representational art. It was generally agreed that the Devil himself was a horned creature with a forked tail, who might sometimes appear as a serpent.

Before the Enlightenment

In our time, we regard all this as superstition, the infantile fantasies of a primitive society. We are to a certain degree justified in thinking this; the seventeenth century seems impossibly distant. Although William Harvey had established the circulation of the blood in 1628, his contemporaries still clung to antiquated nostrums. For example, most physicians held that a variety of ailments were attributable to 'humours', and that leeches – to 'let' blood – could assist in a multitude of cures. Sorcerers were feared. Across Europe, in Germany in particular, an unknown number of victims, perhaps tens of thousands, were tortured and put to death on suspicion of their being witches.

The so-called Great Hunt for witches in Britain and mainland Europe spanned two centuries, petering out in 1650. By then there were no more witches, real or imaginary, to burn.

Finally, and significantly, it should be remembered that until the Enlightenment, it was universally accepted that all illnesses – plague in particular – were punishments from God, and not a consequence of poor hygiene, as many surely were. And if the sicknesses were not the wrath of God, they were the work of the Devil, his demons, and his earthbound disciples.

In such a world of belief and unbelief, it is not surprising that evil entities were held responsible for mental disorders. Not until the late eighteenth century would it be thought otherwise, and the years leading up to the twentieth century saw the coming of age of the scientific approach to our place in the universe. It was a cosmology that no longer had any room for Lucifer and his nefarious associates. While the concept of heaven – or in any event an afterlife of some description – remained an article of Christian belief, the notion of hellfire and eternal damnation, with all the attendant medieval imagery, was no longer considered respectable. We felt we had outgrown such primitive thinking.

THE AGE OF SCIENCE

With the closure of the gates of hell came the opening up of entire branches of medical science: disciplines that could at last explain, in natural terms, what traditionally had been attributed to demonic influence. Even before the twentieth century, when men were attaching well-sounding labels to complexes of illnesses, it was decided that possession and oppression were nothing of the sort, but were symptomatic of 'schizophrenia' and other forms of psychosis. It was found that many such afflictions could be cured – and if not cured then at least held in check – by confinement to institutions, electroshock therapy, counselling and, in recent times, by an elaborate complex of medications.

There is nothing wrong with all this; indeed it would be very foolish to make light of such extraordinary achievements in the treatment of a diversity of mental disorders. But there is a difficulty. In the rush to embrace the new 'science' of psychiatry, the medical men were eager to jettison belief in evil forces, demonic oppression and affliction, and to ascribe natural causes to *all* mental diseases of unknown aetiology. It could be argued that they were, in effect, playing into the hands of the very Devil they wished to sideline.

In recent years, however, there has been a grudging reassessment of this position. While most psychiatrists are content with diagnosing mental illness in terms of abnormal brain function, chemical imbalances, and personality disorders brought about by nature or nurture, there are those who acknowledge that a small percentage of cases appear to challenge medical science. In short, they defy explanation – and indeed fall outside the known pathology of mental illness. Interesting in this regard is that many of these exceptional cases exhibit symptoms that have been traditionally associated with demonic influence.

MILLENNIUM FEVER AND THE DEVIL

In our time, the subject of demonic possession lay dormant until comparatively recently. To many it appeared that this 'sudden' interest in the occult had sprung from nowhere. They can point out that, before the 1960s, the Devil had no place in mainstream society. That was to change when, in 1966, Howard Stanton Levey gave himself out as Anton Szandor LaVey, and established the Church of Satan in San Francisco.

It is likely that LaVey, who died in 1997, was little more than a self-publicist who did not take his devil-worship seriously. Yet he began his 'movement' at a time when Timothy Leary, a Harvard lecturer in psychology, was experimenting with LSD and other 'mind-expanding' drugs. LaVey had little difficulty in attracting a following. With the founding of the Church of Satan, the Devil had left the shadows and gone above ground.

Perhaps the defining moment of this narco-satanism came in the summer of 1969 with the frenzied slaughter of Sharon Tate and others. The perpetrators were the Manson 'family' and evidently the crime had been satanically motivated. The Devil had arrived in America. Soon he would cross the Atlantic.

THE EXORCIST: SATAN ON CELLULOID

In 1971 William Peter Blatty's novel *The Exorcist* appeared, to be followed by a motion picture of the same name.

The effects of that single Hollywood production were seismic. Until 1973, the release date, exorcism was seldom spoken of in lay circles, much less experienced. That was to change, as long queues formed outside cinemas, and people emerged white faced, having seen director William Friedkin's stunning and altogether alarming dramatization of Blatty's book. The film was to spawn many imitators, and introduce an incredulous public to a subject that the churches had for centuries kept from all but a few.

It is a curious fact that from the moment the film was shown in Ireland, Britain and mainland Europe, there was a veritable epidemic of 'possession' symptoms presented by psychiatric patients, many consistent with those shown in *The Exorcist*. The simple explanation is, of course, that fakery was at work, and that those patients for whom attention-seeking was always an intrinsic part of their illness were doing no more than ratcheting up the pressure on their carers. In other words: the 'demonic possession' was a cry for help.

The principle of Occam's Razor, that the simplest explanation is usually the correct one, could certainly be applied with profit in most such cases. Yet a handful seem to fall outside the ambit of rationality, defying, as they do, reductionism. That of Anneliese

Michel is perhaps the most celebrated, and one of the more recent 'possession' motion pictures, *The Exorcism of Emily Rose*, was based loosely on her tragic circumstances.

A native of Würzburg, Germany, Anneliese began experiencing epileptic fits and 'demonic' attacks when she was eighteen. The bishop, Dr Josef Stangel, ordered the case to be investigated by an authority on such matters, who diagnosed possession. The bishop gave permission for an exorcism, to be performed by a Salvatorian priest with the assistance of a local pastor.

It was found that ten months of weekly exorcism could not banish the entities that had 'occupied' the young woman's body. They allegedly included Lucifer, Adolf Hitler, Emperor Nero and Cain. Such was the ordeal that Anneliese endured during the protracted exorcisms, that she eventually died. Too little attention had been given to Anneliese's anorexia, and possible anorexia nervosa, which may have hastened her end: at the last she was refusing all food and drink. A jury would find both the officiating clergymen and the girl's parents guilty of 'negligent homicide'; all four had, it was decided, allowed Anneliese to starve herself to death. Each was given a six-month custodial sentence, but this was mercifully suspended for three years.

That same year – 1976 – one of the most groundbreaking books on exorcism was published. Entitled *Hostage to the Devil: The Possession and Exorcism of Five Contemporary Americans*, it was written by Malachi Martin, a 'laicized' Catholic priest, a former Jesuit and a native of Ballylongford, County Kerry.

Dr Martin died in 1999 at the age of seventy-eight, and left a legacy of controversy. His detractors claimed that *Hostage* was a tissue of lies. Even the greatly respected psychiatrist and author, M Scott Peck, declares in his final book, *Glimpses of the Devil*, that Malachi Martin 'was perhaps the most bald-faced liar I have ever known.' It is a curious statement, given that Dr Peck was a great admirer and confidant of Dr Martin; he actually dedicated the book in question to the exorcist. Yet he went on to aver that: 'In everything that deeply mattered to me and my quest for the Devil, I knew him to speak only God's truth.'

Whatever the truth about his personal life and unorthodox activities, Malachi Martin's book had a profound effect on both Church and laity. Never before had the subject of exorcism been examined in public, and in such detail, by a professional exorcist, and one moreover who wrote with such verve and élan. *Hostage to the Devil* became a bestseller.

By this time, possession and exorcism were being openly debated around the world. This renewed interest had given rise to a frenzy of demon hunting, most especially among the more extreme evangelical movements. At prayer meetings across America, demons were being expelled from the 'possessed' as routinely as the collection plate was passed. The meetings were awe-inspiring, if not to say frightening, events, with hysterical people dropping to the floor, roaring and foaming at the mouth. Such 'deliverance ministries' had America in thrall. Before long, the rest of the world would follow suit. At the time of writing, the Ellel Ministries, a born-again group offering deliverance from 'unclean' spirits, is expanding rapidly. Begun in Lancaster in 1986, Ellel have a presence on four continents – Britain alone has four training centres. There is even a 'Pastors' School' in Siberia; ten years ago such a venture would have scarcely been conceivable.

The Church of England bishops have, of late, become increasingly concerned by the proliferation of such maverick exorcists and fundamentalist groups. Whether this reflects a jealous fear that others are encroaching on their turf, or a concern based on careful evaluation of such ministries, remains to be seen. The difference between the established churches and the newcomers is, inter alia, the length and comprehensiveness of training. Whereas the Anglicans require many years, Ellel training is accomplished in a matter of weeks. The courses are packaged slickly, and the language used owes less to the theology lecture hall and more to the business seminar. 'Satan's strategies and tactics' are examined with the enthusiasm of an advertising executive evaluating a competitor's latest pitch, and the trainee learns 'how demonic footholds can be established in a person's life and presents key principles by which the captives may be set free.'

It will hardly surprise that clerics of the old school are expressing their disquiet. Dr M Scott Peck once asked Malachi Martin his opinion of the exorcisms – or, more properly, the deliverances – performed with such aplomb by the charismatic 'healers'.

'They're generally just casting out their own fantasies,' he replied. 'But very occasionally, usually by accident, they do catch a real fish.'

THE RESTLESS DEAD AND EVIL SPIRITS

Ghosts are sometimes known as the 'restless dead'. It is important to establish that such entities are considered to be the 'souls' or 'spirits' of human beings. This is to distinguish them from non-human entities who have never drawn breath. It is such a broad area of investigation that it would be impossible to do more than touch upon it here. We do so in order to clear up a misconception: namely that all paranormal activity is somehow of demonic origin.

The exorcist will be at pains to point out that, while demonic oppression *may* accompany paranormal activity, there are many instances where it plainly does not. In such cases the exorcist must allow for the presence of an earthbound spirit, or spirits.

Such entities, also referred to as the 'unquiet dead', have been the subject of some interesting studies. In the mid-1800s, it was proposed that there are three categories of spirit, and each was assigned its own rung on the ladder of spiritual evolution. There were the 'low spirits', those trapped in the world of the living;

'second-degree spirits', who desire only to promote goodness on earth; and 'perfect spirits', those who have reached the pinnacle of their evolution. The three categories are, by and large, still accepted by modern psychic investigators.

The 'low spirits' are of particular interest to the exorcist. It is believed that, during their lifetimes, such entities were wedded to materiality and so failed to develop spiritually. For this reason they are unable to 'move on', choosing instead to oppress or disturb the living. At their most malign, they can be considered to be evil spirits; at their least harmful they are classified as poltergeists.

These theories were given currency in recent times by the notable British psychiatrist, Dr Kenneth McAll (1910–2001). He became interested in the powers of 'possession' while working in China as a missionary-surgeon. During the turbulent war years, he was confronted by phenomena which led him to an exploration of possession. He went on to dedicate his life to treating mental illness with reference to extraphysical causation.

Dr McAll's revolutionary thesis, introduced in his seminal work, *Healing the Family Tree*, was that many supposedly 'incurable' patients were the victims of ancestral control. By drawing up a family tree he claimed to be able to identify the ancestor who was adversely affecting his patient. He would then sever the bond between the ancestor and the patient by having a clergyman celebrate a service of Holy Communion. The ancestor would be delivered back to God, and the transgenerational hold consequently broken.

It was, in effect, a most unorthodox form of exorcism or deliverance. It is an important area insofar as it examines what one might call 'indirect' possession. Dr McAll concluded that the dead may become pawns in the struggle for the souls of the living, that souls in transition, or 'dislocated' souls, may become possessed by evil, so that they in their turn can possess the living, and so drive the living into despair, or worse.

'Evil symptoms and their inevitable fruit of despair, which leads to suicide,' he believed, 'bear the marks of the evil one battling with those who are sensitive to the uncommitted dead.'

Exorcism: some Definitions

Before going further, it may be useful to examine our definitions. As in the way of words, 'exorcise' has undergone a shift in meaning since earlier times. Its roots are in Greek: *exorkizein* literally means 'to out an oath'. To exorcise, then, is to place a demon on oath, and so command it by the power of God to depart and not trouble the afflicted again. In our time it is also acceptable to speak of the exorcism of places and inanimate objects, when obviously an oath is neither demanded nor sworn. Such exorcisms are common practice; for instance, a priest will exorcise all sacred vessels and paraphernalia before their employment in divine service.

The Catholic Church recognizes two distinct forms of exorcism: the solemn and the unofficial. Before performing a solemn exorcism a priest is obliged to obtain the permission of a bishop. There are sound reasons for this. In the first place, the rite must be enacted in the name of the Church, and it is used for the expulsion of evil spirits. This is dangerous territory, whether or not one holds with the existence of such entities. Done incorrectly, or by an individual not properly qualified or equipped to perform the rite, a solemn exorcism can end in disaster, for victim and exorcist alike. It is used only rarely.

It will be seen that such an undertaking requires that the priest *converse* with the entity. It is principally in this regard that the solemn exorcism differs from the informal.

An unofficial exorcism may be applied to a number of situations and circumstances. Moreover, it can be performed by religious and layperson alike. No permission is required and the exorcist does not act in the name of the Church, be that Roman Catholic or Protestant. Hence a Protestant minister can be said to perform an exorcism when delivering a place, or an individual who is beset by the so-called restless dead: the soul of a deceased person.

This is an important distinction. In short: *exorcism is used to expel both malignant and bothersome entities.*

Lastly, the term 'deliverance' is used today in a broad sense. Generally speaking, it applies both to Catholic and Protestant exorcism, and is the term of choice for most Protestant denominations, in particular those of the Reformed communions. The word, which appears frequently in these pages, is sometimes interchangeable with exorcism, especially when applied to the cleansing of a place. Within the Christian framework it is generally accepted that while both Protestant and Roman Catholic priests engage in a deliverance ministry, exorcism is largely a Catholic rite.

THE PARANORMAL AND THE DEMONIC

We have established that paranormal activity need not necessarily signal the presence of the demonic. One case examined in this book has no relation to evil: that of little 'Lucy' (pp 225–48), who saw a succession of apparitions. It is difficult to interpret the disturbances which the family experienced as an attempt by the Devil or other demons to influence the household.

That said, it will be seen that other cases began with ostensibly innocent occurrences, such as the case of the 'child Sarah' (pp 165–200), only to progressively develop into something more sinister. This appears to be a relatively common phenomenon, when so-called poltergeist activity makes way for malevolence. In his impressive study, entitled *But Deliver Us From Evil,*

Reverend John Richards goes some way towards explaining the phenomenon. At one point, he refers to the haunting known as the Epworth Poltergeist, which began in Doncaster in 1716 in the parental home of John Wesley, founder of the Methodist movement. John was thirteen at the time.

> It is difficult to say if there was anything demonic in the affair. Everyone, except the dog, seems to have become accustomed to the situation, which suggests that the early fear of the children was largely the fear of the unknown rather than the fear of evil. But it must be remembered that the Curé d'Ars was haunted by what ARG Owen calls, 'a strong resemblance to poltergeist activity.' These incidences are usually taken to have a predominantly spiritual significance because of the Curé's stature as a man of God and as an evangelist. When similar happenings occur in the home of John and [his younger brother] Charles Wesley it may not be without spiritual significance either. Even if no demon were involved, the Enemy would have been pleased if the intervention of the unknown had opened the door to fear which might distort and undermine the spiritual lives of the young boys; the greatest danger – then as now.

Richards's closing observation is an important one. Both John Wesley and his brother Charles went on to become Christian ministers, following as they did in their father's footsteps. Although there is little in the accounts of the haunting to suggest the presence at Epworth of a demon – much less one that required exorcising – there is likewise no evidence that would *preclude* a preternatural agency. At this long remove in time, nearly three hundred years after the events, it is of course impossible to determine the precise nature of the haunting. Nevertheless, the circumstances bring to mind words spoken by the Catholic priest whose brushes with evil can be followed on pages 137 to 164:

> Old Nick won't waste his time going for the sheep. He'll go for the shepherd instead. By weakening the shepherd he can get at the flock.

What better focus of attack for any aspiring demon than the home of three ministers, one already practising, two to come?

SOME CAUTIONARY TALES

'I don't understand why journalists are making such a fuss about this,' Father Daniel Corogeanu told the press in June 2005. 'Exorcism is a common practice in the Orthodox Church. Other priests use my methods.'

His 'methods' included crucifixion, the chaining of a young nun to a cross, after binding her and stuffing a rag into her mouth, to prevent her from crying out as she was made to suffer a slow and agonizing death. She died of thirst, compounded by shock and asphyxiation.

The scene of the botched exorcism was a convent in northwestern Romania, the victim: a twenty-three-old nun, Maricica Irina Cornici. Her death was the culmination of an unfortunate, short life that began in an orphanage, where the girl was systematically abused. Three months before she died she had visited the convent, found solace there and decided to join the community.

She began to hear voices – external locution – and display several of the other symptoms one associates with schizophrenia. Yet no physician was summoned; instead, the young woman was 'diagnosed' as a demoniac. Father Corogeanu, the spiritual head of the convent, undertook the task of exorcising her.

Two salient facts emerged during the subsequent murder trial. The convent in question, the Holy Trinity, was built in 2001 by a lawyer and had not been sanctified by the Orthodox Church. Nor was Corogeanu a qualified priest; he had never completed his studies. He had had his heart set on becoming a professional footballer, or a lawyer, but had chosen the religious life when denied a place at university.

For nine days, four nuns helped the 'exorcist' to restrain Maricica; this included chaining her to a cross while he said prayers over her.

When asked why he had not summoned medical help as a preliminary, the priest replied by saying: 'You cannot cast out the Devil with pills. You banish devils with fasting and prayer.'

In the wake of the tragedy, the bishop shut down the convent and had the community transferred elsewhere. It was thought at the time that Father Corogeanu would be sentenced to life imprisonment for the murder, and the four nuns who helped him given lengthy custodial sentences, but this seems unlikely. To prevent further abuses, the Orthodox Church in Romania has vowed to introduce psychological tests for men entering the monastic life.

The case must act as a warning to those unqualified 'exorcists' who meddle in spiritual matters, and to those who allow them to. Rogue preachers – some properly ordained, many not – find demonic influences at work in hitherto unsuspected places. If we are to believe their sometimes outrageous claims, demons are at the root of every human foible. Derek Prince, the Pentecostal minister who died in 2003, identified the demons of caffeine, compromise, cosmetics, criticism, fantasy, gossip, infidelity, masturbation, nicotine and sleepiness, while maintaining that the Devil is also behind Tourette's syndrome.

Frank and Ida Mae Hammond warn against not only the 'demons' of non-Christian religions but also the vile spirit of vegetarianism. (A cynic might point out that this west-Texan couple operate out of the biggest meat-producing state in America.)

The Hammonds speak of 'demon groupings', each embracing

a number of specific 'spirits'. The groupings include 'Bitterness', which embraces the demons of resentment, hatred, unforgiveness, violence, temper, anger, retaliation and murder.

There is also – most worryingly – the grouping termed 'Mental Illness'. It includes insanity, madness, mania, retardation, senility, schizophrenia, paranoia and hallucinations. Oddly enough, Frank and Ida Mae do not seem to share Derek Prince's 'demonization' of Tourette's syndrome.

Medical practitioners are understandably concerned by this trend, this willingness to see demons everywhere. It is even more alarming when self-styled clergymen perform 'exorcisms' and people die at their hands.

PROFILE OF A TRUE EXORCIST

According to the Catholic Encyclopaedia, an exorcist is 'in general, anyone who exorcises or professes to exorcise demons, in particular, one ordained by a bishop for this office, ordination to which is the second of the four minor orders of the Western Church.' All ordained priests are uniquely predisposed to effect deliverance.

In practice, however, very few men have what it takes to be a *successful* exorcist. Exorcists are special. One might even say that they are a unique body of men. In the course of our research we were privileged to meet a small number of them. Without exception we came away from such meetings with the sense of having shared the company of an extraordinary individual. Perhaps Emerson had such a man in mind when he wrote that 'the best effect of fine persons is felt after we have left their presence.'

The successful exorcists have one attribute in common: that of great humility. They never brag about 'their' prowess or achievements, never seek to impress. Each is at pains to establish that he is no more than a conduit, that he himself possesses no special 'gifts', be they of a spiritual or intellectual nature.

It is not hard to see a certain symmetry in this, once we accept the possibility of an evil force at work in the world, one intent on influencing the susceptible. To combat evil, then, there must be a proportionately vigorous application of good. Such virtue is hard earned, not given.

The Rubrics of the Catholic Church prescribe that an exorcist 'must be properly distinguished for his piety, prudence, and integrity of life,' (see APPENDIX ONE, p. 365). In his comprehensive study of evil, *Demons!: The Devil, Possession and Exorcism*, Dr Anthony Finlay sets out the qualifications necessary for a 'suitable' exorcist. 'In the face of often extraordinary situations,' he writes, 'rare attributes are required in an exorcist, strong and unwavering qualities which will strengthen the chances of success in the fearsome battle against so great an evil.'

Preparation is of crucial importance. Spiritual fortification through prayer would seem an obvious prerequisite, but Finlay also stresses the need to fast before attempting the ritual. He is careful, though, to differentiate between the scriptural idea of fasting and our modern equivalent. 'Fasting in the biblical sense', he points out, 'is not necessarily synonymous with the complete abstinence from food and drink, which itself would render the exorcist physically inadequate to the task.' Yet he goes on to assert that Christ's disciples – the fishermen and the others of modest means – were better candidates than most churchmen of our day, largely because the apostles, and those who came after them, gave excess a wide berth. In our time it is increasingly difficult to find clergymen who have not drifted far from first principles.

> We [priests] have become used to the comforts of society, and we find it difficult to give them up, even in such a cause as freeing someone from evil influences. How many of us throw away our worldly goods

EXORCISM IN OUR TIME

and follow Him, as Christ said was necessary? . . .
Simplicity in behaviour, frugality in manner, lack of
ostentation and of any kind of excess was His rule.
His disciples manifested these qualities and in this
respect were much more suited to confront evil in
possession of Man than we are today. How many of
us can claim to live up to the rule or vow, at least in
the Roman Catholic Church, of voluntary poverty
and scrupulous adherence to absolute obedience? It
is precisely in these areas that many clergy of today
are lacking. Days of prayer and fasting are regarded
as too onerous and as a result lip service only is
often given to the solemn occasion. We are not sufficiently prepared, with our desirable houses, cars,
housekeepers, secretaries, money in the bank or
schemes for making money, ambitions or whatever,
for the enormous task of casting out the Devil.

Finlay ends on a cautionary – and utterly chilling – note. He
reminds us that the Devil can see through the exorcist who is
unprepared, be it spiritually, mentally or physically.

He [Satan] knows that underneath the show of bra-
vado there is a soft underbelly, a weakness, a vulnerability which he can exploit. As a result he knows
he it is who will emerge the victor. The unfortunate
sufferer remains unchanged in all this – if he is lucky.
Often he is left worse off than before.

The Battle for Hearts and Minds

It was inevitable that a respected critic would emerge to debunk
the whole charade of the unqualified exorcist. In 2001, Michael
Cuneo, a Fordham University professor, published *American*

Exorcism (with the wry subtitle *Expelling Demons in the Land of Plenty*). It exposed the dubious practices of charismatic and evangelical preachers and their 'deliverance ministries'. In a devastating broadside, he turned his attention on one such typically American organization, the Faith Movement. He identifies it as belonging to the same culture as 'the tabloid television business, with its mock seriousness, its weepy sensationalism, its celebrity fawning – soul food for the bloated and the brokenhearted.' Or to the shopping mall: the 'community without contact, community contrived precisely to avoid contact.'

It is all too good to be true, he asserts, this fake American dream. It is 'living, strutting, pulsating caricature: One almost expects it at any moment to break into a Bugs Bunny cartoon.'

> The Faith Movement is . . . a collage of American clichés. The preacher as snake oil salesman or used car salesman; the preacher as Vegas showman. Miracle-workers in pink Cadillacs and pinkie rings, soul-savers in three-piece glitter suits and sixty-dollar haircuts. This is the world of the Faith Movement. Gushing emotionalism, grasping materialism, tears on demand, hustles blessed with a thousand ·'Amens'. The product of old-fashioned hucksterism, New Thought optimism, and Southern-fried born-againism, the Faith Movement is one of the fastest-growing enterprises on the American religious scene today – and also one of the most wildly controversial.

Cuneo reports that he was present at a great many deliverances of the sort, and was not impressed. He reports that in many cases the participants witnessed what they claimed to be paranormal manifestations, but that at no time did he himself share their experiences. He concludes that most – if not all – such banishments were either fraudulent or can more easily be explained in terms of psychiatric disturbance.

Cuneo had succeeded in polarizing the entire debate, leaving the general reader to ponder the question: Whom are we to believe? To many, the answer seems to lie midway between science and superstition. The aforementioned Dr M Scott Peck, who died in 2005, was perhaps the most notable among those who chose the middle ground.

In one of his earlier books, *People of the Lie*, the Harvard educated psychiatrist alludes briefly to two cases from his medical files, which forced him to reconsider his position on the preternatural. He recounts a particularly harrowing experience, during which a patient presented undeniable – for Peck at least – evidence of demonic possession. The disturbed young woman seemed to physically change before his very eyes. He recalls her face as wearing an expression 'that could be described only as Satanic. It was an incredibly contemptuous grin of utter hostile malevolence.' Later Peck tried to emulate that grin in his bathroom mirror, and found it impossible.

The change did not confine itself to the woman's face. Her entire body suddenly became serpentine. She writhed on the floor like a huge, vicious snake, and actually attempted to bite the members of his team. 'The eyes were hooded with lazy reptilian torpor,' he recalls, 'except when the reptile darted out in attack, at which moment the eyes would open wide with blazing hatred.'

In the face of such a monstrous metamorphosis, the psychiatrist was forced to concede the existence of an external entity present in his patient. 'I now know that Satan is real,' Dr Peck concluded in his book. 'I have met him.' He confessed also that, of the hundreds of cases he treated in the course of his professional life, a full five per cent of symptoms presented by patients could not be explained in terms of present-day medical science.

In the conclusion to his final book, *Glimpses of the Devil*, Peck summed up his convictions, arrived at in the course of treating a young woman he called Jersey. Her case alone had effected his conversion from sceptical psychiatrist to believer in an entity that was the very personification of evil. His new-found belief went beyond faith; Peck knew with certainty that such an entity existed, and furthermore had minor demons under his control.

> By the Devil, I mean a spirit that is powerful (it may be many places at the same time and manifest itself in a variety of distinctly paranormal ways), thoroughly malevolent (its only motivation seemed to be the destruction of human beings or the entire human race), deceitful and vain, capable of taking up a kind of residence within the mind, brain, soul, or body of susceptible and willing human beings – a spirit that had various names (among them Lucifer and Satan), that was real and did exist.

Exorcism and History

I interpret this hypothetical fall of man to be
the groping of newly conscious men to narratize
what has happened to them, the loss of divine
voices and assurances . . .

– Julian Jaynes
The Origin of Consciousness in the
Breakdown of the Bicameral Mind, 1976

IN ALL LIKELIHOOD the rites of exorcism are as old as civilization itself – and perhaps predate the first human settlements. The earliest recorded instance is in Sanskrit, and contained in one of the thousands of vedas, or teachings, that are intrinsic to Hinduism. This is the Atharvaveda, a collection of some six thousand verses written down by the sage Atharvan, at some time between 1,500 and 2,200 years before the birth of Christ. It is possible that the words were not those of Atharvan, but that he was the chief celebrant of these ceremonies. He was said to be the son of Lord Brahma, the chief Hindu god. The Atharvaveda is the oldest Indic text alluding to healing, and is part of a much earlier tradition, one transmitted orally for several centuries before being written down.

From the vedas one learns that two classes of priests were custodians of the 'sacred fire'. Of the two, the followers of Atharvan were largely the soothsayers of this fire-cult and performed propitiatory rites, while another class – the Angiras – were tasked with sorcery and exorcism. No details of those exorcisms have come down to us; we have only the assurance that 'evil spirits'

31

were expelled, thereby protecting the community from harm.

We do, however, have examples of the words used. The rituals – or 'charms' – were employed for all manner of purposes, from encouraging the growth of hair to curing leprosy. One such charm was used by the exorcist to drive out the classes of demon known as Rakshas and Pisâkas:

1. Do ye well offer within the fire this oblation with ghee, that destroys the phantom! Do thou, o Agni, burn from afar against the Rakshas, [but] our houses thou shalt not consume!
2. Rudra has broken your necks, ye Pisâkas: may he also break your ribs, ye phantoms! The plant whose power is everywhere has united you with Yama [death].
3. Exempt from danger, o Mitra and Varuna, may we here be; drive back with your flames the Atrin [devouring demons]! Neither helper nor support do they find; smiting one another, they go to death.

In neighbouring Tibet, in later centuries, arcane rites were carried out in the chapel of Mahakala – literally, 'the protector' – at Samye, the oldest monastery in the country. The chapel was kept locked for most of the year and only the chosen were allowed to enter. What occurred there at night was a mystery, but it was said that the monks would battle demons within its precincts; most nights screams could be heard emanating from within the walls, even though the place was uninhabited. Once a year the chapel's guardian would ceremoniously replace a crescent-shaped chopper and wooden chopping board, which had – very mysteriously – become worn from use.

Even today, the chopper or cleaver is still intrinsic to Buddhist ceremony. It has the symbolic use of slicing through ignorance or superstition – rather as Alexander the Great cut through the

Gordian Knot. In many ways, the chopper serves the same purpose as the dorje or the phurba, both being ritual daggers, and is employed in rituals of exorcism by priests and shamans. Many Buddhist exorcists also rely on a wooden staff embedded with metal rings. When the staff is shaken the rings set up a great cacophony, designed to frighten away evil entities.

But Buddhist exorcism relies also to a great extent on humour. An evil spirit is quite simply laughed at, held up to ridicule, and so made to depart in shame. This is achieved by friends or relatives of the afflicted person dressing up as demons, donning hideous masks, and acting out the demonic affliction.

Down the centuries the mask has been a feature of both Chinese and Japanese cultures, the latter being greatly influenced by Buddhism. For thousands of years the Japanese have held processions and ceremonies, during which fearsome masks were worn, each type of mask representing a certain class of demon. Such ritual was, and is, a prime example of imitative magic: by aping the demon a human being can appease it.

MESOPOTAMIA AND THE HOLY LAND

In the Middle East, the Babylonians of Mesopotamia were the principal practitioners of exorcism. During the period 1900–500 BC, magic was practised by a priestly sect called the Asipu. Their activities ran the gamut from hypnosis to magic, and included the casting out of troublesome spirits.

Christian demonology had its basis here, but it was another people, the Assyrians, who gave definition to belief in the preternatural. They had the 'official' religion of the priests, which coexisted comfortably with the demotic faith: the more primitive religion of the people. This 'underground' religion was the forerunner of European sorcery and magic. It was also the template for Satan: the Assyrians believed in a principal demon, or devil, who ruled over a vast hierarchy of lesser evil entities.

At about the same time, in nearby Israel and Judea, another Semitic race of people, the Israelites, were giving rise to prophets who had the ability to perform miracles, prefiguring the coming of Jesus. Angels and devils were everywhere. We learn from the Book of Tobit of an incident involving an entity named Azarias. He instructs Tobias in the roasting of a huge fish, for the purpose of exorcism:

> And the angel, answering, said to him: If thou put a little piece of its heart upon coals, the smoke thereof driveth away all kind of devils, either from man or from woman, so that they come no more to them.

But it is to the Talmud we must look for prime examples of Jewish exorcism. Noteworthy among the scourges of demons was Simon ben Yochai, a second-century rabbi 'learned in miracles', who is reputed to have performed feats of exorcism. One such involved the banishing of a female demon.

According to one source, Rabbi Simon was vexed that God had sent five angels to Hagar of Egypt, Abraham's maidservant, and not a single one to him. He saw his chance to summon an angel of his own when the king issued a decree which contravened Jewish religious practices. Simon set off to the palace to have it abrogated.

On the way he encountered a female spirit, or angel, who was perched atop the mast of a ship. She informed him that she had been sent so that he might perform a miracle. She would enter the stomach of the king's daughter, who would scream out in her agony: 'Bring me Rabbi Simon!' The rabbi would then whisper in the daughter's ear, causing the spirit to leave.

All went according to plan. The girl was possessed by the spirit, and duly requested that Rabbi Simon exorcise her. He whispered as instructed, the spirit departed, and shattered every glass vessel in the palace at her parting. So impressed was the king that he at once tore up his decree.

It is a curious tale, and is in all likelihood apocryphal. Yet it seems to show an ambivalent attitude to spirits in ancient Palestine. There is confusion as to what constitutes an angel. At no time is Rabbi Simon's angel considered to be evil; she is, after all, sent by God. She arranges her own demonic infestation so that Simon must exorcise her and thus impress the king. Such symbiosis between the divine and the preternatural has echoes in Christian theology: for instance, God's plan must of necessity include Satan in order to bring about the 'Fall', which in turn is reversed by Christ, who was betrayed by Judas Iscariot, thereby completing the circle.

There are many more allusions in the Talmud, the Torah, and the Old Testament to demons and how to combat them, yet it is not until the writing of the New Testament that exorcism is treated in any great detail. Scripture makes it clear that with the coming of Christ, Satan's days as ruler of the earth are numbered. Matthew also points out that Jesus could differentiate between the mentally ill and the demoniac.

> And his fame went throughout all Syria: and they brought unto him all sick people that were taken with divers diseases and torments, and those which were possessed with devils, and those which were lunatick, and those that had the palsy; and he healed them (4:24).

'My Name is Legion'

The Jews had long been accustomed to prophets and magi in possession of ancient wisdom and the power to expel evil entities, but this new miracle worker seemed to them to have infinitely more power than those who had gone before him. News of truly remarkable supernatural feats began to filter back to the Phari-sees. Mark (5:1–20) gives an elaborate account of the notorious incident of the 'Gadarene swine', and the demon who told Jesus that his name was 'Legion'. Luke (8:26–39) offers a slightly more succinct version.

There was the celebrated episode involving the woman whom the church fathers in a later century would – erroneously – brand a harlot: 'And certain women, which had been healed of evil spir-its and infirmities, Mary called Magdalene, out of whom went seven devils' (Luke 8:2).

Wherever he went, Jesus performed the twin rituals of healing the sick and casting out demons. The two ministries seemed al-most to go hand in hand: 'And in that same hour he cured many of their infirmities and plagues, and of evil spirits' (Luke 7:21).

Scripture leaves us in no doubt that Jesus wished his disciples to continue the work of exorcism. Mark relates how the Lord trained the twelve apostles: 'And he called unto him the twelve, and began to send them forth by two and two; and gave them power over unclean spirits' (Mark 6:7). Further on: 'And they cast out many devils, and anointed with oil many that were sick, and healed them' (Mark 6:13).

In the Acts we learn that the apostles carried on a successful ministry after Jesus had left them. Paul's work is the best docu-mented.

As we have seen, neither Jesus nor the apostles were enact-ing truly exceptional rituals in the eyes of the people – or their priests. Exorcism was an accepted therapeutic practice in the an-cient world, from India to Mesopotamia, to Palestine, to Greece and Rome.

The ancients believed that all maladies were caused by wicked spirits invading the body; it followed that the removal of the spir-its would effect a cure. Thus, medicine and ancient folk wisdom recognized exorcism not necessarily as a magic operation but as a matter of therapy, a cure for sickness both spiritual and physical.

By the middle of the third century the Christian Church had established the formal office of exorcist as a minor order. The office is mentioned in a letter written to the bishop of Antioch by Pope Cornelius in AD 253, which coincidentally was the year of the pontiff's death; it is believed that he died in exile, having been banished to the port city of Cittavecchio by the Roman Emperor, Decius. The exile was complaining about the man who had taken his place as head of the Church, Novatian, the 'antipope': 'He knew that there were in this Church forty-six priests, seven deacons, seven subdeacons, forty-two acolytes, and fifty-two exorcists, lectors, and porters.'

It is worth remembering that at the time – when Christianity was little more than two centuries in existence – there could not have been over 30,000 believers in Rome. To have more than a score of exorcists serving this one community seems excessive.

St Patrick and other Exorcists

The year was AD 441. Attila the Hun was galloping into the Balkans with his brother Bleda at his side, to capture the city that would become Belgrade. The Saxon Revolt had left towns and cities throughout Britain aflame, their pro-Roman citizens fleeing before the German invasion. On a tall, conical mountain overlooking Clew Bay in Connacht, St Patrick was deep in prayer.

He had spent forty days and forty nights on the bleak summit. It was known to the Celts of Ireland as Eagle Mountain, and the home of the pagan deity Lugh. In time it would become Croagh Patrick.

The future patron saint was engaged in his second mission to convert this heathen nation to Christianity. He had succeeded well; already half the tribes had come over to the foreign God of Palestine, turning their backs on the ancient divinities of their forefathers. Patrick needed but one more small push to evangelize the Irish, and it was to this end that he had chosen the high mountain for his forty days of prayer and penance. Like Moses in the Sinai desert, he believed that the peak of a great mountain would bring him closer to God.

But Patrick was about to do battle with terrible entities ranged against him. The dark pagan gods were not about to yield this green land without a fight. They converged on the mountain and attempted to thwart Patrick in his mission.

First, they used temptation, as they had done with St Anthony on his mountain-top in the Egyptian desert. A procession of voluptuous Celtic women appeared, to dance nude about the holy man, offering him their bodies and all the carnal delights he had vowed to forgo. He remained steadfast in his prayers.

Next, they tried belligerence. They gathered about the mountain as vast flocks of black birds: ravens, rooks and crows. So many was their number that they dimmed the light of the sun. They came too as dragons, and lastly as snakes – if the oral tradition is to be believed. To no purpose. Patrick fought the snakes and won. He banished them, driving them into a cavern in the mountain known as Lugh na Deamhain, or 'Hollow of the Demons'.

In our enlightened times we know with certainty that snakes were never actually native to Ireland. At the close of the last Ice Age – about 10,000 years ago – the northeast of the country was still joined to Scotland by a land bridge, and Britain to continental Europe by the great plain that would become the North Sea. The slow migration of wildlife from the south was beginning. Some 2,000 years later, three species of snake had settled in England – but by that time the land bridge between Scotland and Ireland was no more. The reptiles would remain unknown in the island.

So what was it that St Patrick drove from our shores in AD 441? Some commentators suggest that the snake represented the old gods that Patrick's new religion supplanted. They advance the argument that the snake was commonly associated with Satan – *an Diabhal* – and that the Celtic gods were somewhat demonic in character.

But this is to ignore the fact that far and away the majority of Celtic deities were quite benign when compared, say, to the bloodthirsty gods of ancient Rome. Most Celtic gods were worshipped as protectors of home and hearth, and bringers of health, wealth and happiness. Crom Dubh, a fertility god, was regarded as a friend, a force to call upon in one's hour of need. Lugh was among the most benign of all. When Patrick ascended the mountain sacred to that divinity, Lughnassadh ('Lugh's Feast'), observed on the first day of August, was approaching. It was a time of celebration, a harvest feast.

There is, however, a consensus of belief among church scholars that Patrick did drive out something of importance that day on Eagle Mountain, and the evidence seems to point to evil spirits. This was only the first skirmish of his long war against the powers of evil. Patrick was Ireland's first Christian exorcist, and his legacy has endured for over fifteen hundred years.

IRELAND AFTER PATRICK

Patrick and the saints who came after him were always going to have a difficult struggle against the Celtic spirit world. This 'otherworld' was never far beneath the surface in pre-Christian Ireland. The gods were everywhere, not only in the forests where they might take the forms of living creatures, but in the home as well. Communication with the otherworld was therefore relatively easy.

Even the Irish board-games seem to have had a dual nature, further facilitating communion with the dark side. The games of Branfad and Brandubh were associated with the raven or crow, a bird sacred to the warrior goddess Morrigan. More sinister, how-ever, was the board-game known as Fidchell. It was played in much the same way as chess or draughts; but its original, and more important, function was to communicate with non-corporeal en-tities. It was therefore a forerunner of the ouija board.

The task of the early Christian missionaries was to supplant the indigenous beliefs with a monotheistic religion whose very setting – the Holy Land – would have seemed impossibly alien to the people. For this reason, they found it expedient to graft Chris-tianity onto an existing credo rather than try to entirely eradicate the old beliefs. And so it was that pagan sites became associ-ated with saints, whether real or imagined. The first churches and monasteries even incorporated pagan symbols and art. The Celtic belief system endured far into the first centuries of Christianity, in particular the notion that human consciousness occupied a posi-tion between two worlds: the material and the spiritual. At any time, the spiritual might intrude; it could also be summoned at will, its demons and all.

The Patrick mythology would have us believe that Christian-ity triumphed in heathen Ireland without a struggle, beyond the saint's skirmishes with court sorcerers. In fact, for close on two hundred years it was a battle for hegemony, engaged in fiercely by both sides. The pagan demons were not prepared to go quietly.

There were heroes in those days. Or so the surviving manu-scripts would suggest. One such demon battler was St Fursey. The year of his birth is not recorded but we do know that he died in France circa AD 650.

Born the son of Fintan, a prince of south Munster, he received his baptism in a monastery on the island of Inisquin, Lough Cor-rib. He eventually joined the community there, going on to found his own monastery on the lake shore.

On a journey to his father's princedom in Munster, Fursey was stricken with a serious illness, which laid him low and sent him into a coma. While in this state he received the first of the extraordinary visions that would characterize his ministry. He saw angels who, in turn, battled demons for possession of Fursey's soul. Good triumphed, but not before the saint had a vision of the fires of hell. On his return to consciousness his fellow-monks observed that Fursey had developed actual burn marks over much of his body: scars that remained with him for the rest of his days.

The saint set out on a mission through Ireland, exorcising demons wherever he found them. He was to preach and exorcise in Wales and East Anglia, before settling in Normandy in 648. He became bishop of Lagny, near Paris. On his death, his body lay unburied for thirty days and was visited by thousands of pilgrims, many of whom claimed that the corpse showed no decay. A litany attributed to him is in the Trinity College Dublin collection of manuscripts.

Yet, for all the old saints Ireland is said to have produced, and for all their wondrous deeds, there is but meagre evidence that they physically engaged, much less overcame, the forces of evil. For historical evidence of exorcism in Ireland we must turn our attention to later centuries. In doing so, we must also briefly examine the traditional alliance between the Devil and witchcraft.

WITCHCRAFT AND EXORCISM

Practitioners of Wicca, or witchcraft, are adamant that their religion is a benign one, that it is no more than a nature religion. Its gods are those of the earth, sea, sky and forest. They will argue that, of all the thousands of adherents in these islands, the percentage who use their powers for evil is negligible – no more, they contend, than the percentage of Christians who subvert the message of Jesus for improper ends.

This is unquestionably true. Yet for centuries witches were pursued mercilessly for no better reason than suspicion of diabolic collusion. This was due in part to the witch's devotion to the so-called 'horned god of the forest', a deity who unfortunately bore more than a passing resemblance to the Devil of Christendom. There was more. Witches were said to worship Satan himself during their infamous sabbats, gatherings at which the Devil was sometimes present in person. He was known to 'brand' a new recruit with a mark, concealed on a part of the body not usually visible.

There is no doubt that witches, or 'wise women', played an important role in ancient societies. Where medical doctors were scarce, they provided cures for a variety of common ailments. In many parts of the developing world they still do.

But in doing so, such women were exposing themselves to danger. By openly demonstrating their powers, they were leaving themselves vulnerable to accusations of maleficence, in the event of an inexplicable malady suddenly besetting the community. If God had not poisoned the wells, sickened the livestock or sent pestilence, then surely the Adversary was responsible. At such times, the local witch, known for her occult arts, would become an easy target. In a patriarchal society it was deemed inappropriate that a woman should wield so much influence as did the witch.

THE IRISH WITCHES

The witch trials which raged throughout Europe from about the fourteenth century were somewhat more subdued in Ireland and England. In fact, only in the late sixteenth century did English law make it an offence to practise witchcraft. In Scotland it was otherwise.

Scottish witches bore the brunt of much of the frenzy. There was wholesale torture, hanging and burning alive, though not on the same, almost industrial, scale as was witnessed in France and

Germany. It is difficult to see in hindsight what the Devil had to do with all this, but as time went on, and the madness grew, wild accusations came to be levelled, chief among which was that of a witch having made a pact with Satan. How else but through diabolic abetment could a mere woman exercise power?

The first Irish witch trial took place in 1324: that of Dame Alice Kyteler of Kilkenny, a member of a prominent Anglo-Norman family. It was rumoured that she had already dispatched three husbands by poison when, at the urging of the Bishop of Ossory, she and her band of reputed sorcerers were arrested. The litany of accusations was lengthy and imaginative. Dame Alice and her cohorts were, it was alleged, guilty of every vice from the denying of Christ to seeking 'by their sorcery advice and responses from demons'.

They had, it was reported, sacrificed animals to the Devil; they had wrought spells, using mixtures containing 'certain horrible worms, various unspecified herbs, dead men's nails, the hair, brains, and shreds of the cerements of boys who were buried unbaptized, with other abominations, all of which they cooked, with various incantations, over a fire of oak-logs in a vessel made out of the skull of a decapitated thief.' Most damning of all, Dame Alice had her very own 'familiar' spirit:

> The said dame had a certain demon, an incubus, named Son of Art, or Robin son of Art, who had carnal knowledge of her, and from whom she admitted that she had received all her wealth. This incubus made its appearance under various forms, sometimes as a cat, or as a hairy black dog, or in the likeness of a negro (Æthiops), accompanied by two others who were larger and taller than he, and of whom one carried an iron rod.

But Dame Alice escaped punishment; she was well connected.

43

In her stead, her accomplices were pursued and punished. One such victim, Petronilla of Meath, was repeatedly flogged and tortured into confessing her guilt. Her 'crimes' included acting as a medium between Alice and a number of demons. At the behest of the bishop, Petronilla was burnt alive in Kilkenny on 3 November 1324. This is the first recorded witch-burning in Ireland.

THE WITCH OF YOUGHAL

From that time on, the country produced a small number of witch trials, noteworthy among which was that of Florence Newton, the 'Witch of Youghal'. She was accused in 1661 of casting a spell on a servant girl and causing the death of a boy. Apparently she felt no pain when, during her 'examination', an awl was plunged several times into her hand. When called to testify, a witness reported that Florence, like Dame Alice, had demonic 'familiars resorting to her in sundry shapes'.

A curious aspect of the testimony concerned the Lord's Prayer. It seems that Florence was incapable of reciting it. When asked to do so, 'she excused herself by the decay of Memory through old Age.'

The fate of the Youghal Witch is not known. It is likely that she was put to death; she was, after all, accused of murder. In total there are nine recorded witchcraft trials in seventeenth-century Ireland, only two of which resulted in the death of the accused. Later centuries would see even fewer trials.

Similarly, reports of exorcism in Ireland are concentrated in the seventeenth century. A notable case involved what was believed to be a fragment of the True Cross. The relic was preserved in the suitably named Holy Cross Abbey, near Thurles, and attracted a constant stream of pilgrims, for it was reputed to possess miraculous powers of healing. In 1609 a woman named Anastasia Sobechan, a native of Callan, County Kilkenny, came to the abbey and told the monks that she was the victim of magic spells.

The abbot, Reverend Bernard Foulow, had someone fetch a belt that had touched the relic of the True Cross, and placed it about Anastasia's waist. As soon as the belt touched her, she began to vomit up pieces of cloth, wood, sheep's wool and a variety of other foreign objects. This evacuation continued for a month, and there was no doubt in the abbot's mind that the power of the Cross had exorcised the evil.

A PRESBYTERIAN EXORCIST

Reverend Robert Blair, a Presbyterian minister, enjoyed a reputation as an exorcist from the time of his arrival in 1623 in the coastal town of Bangor, County Down. Blair recounts one instance where a wealthy parishioner, a Scot, called to his door and requested that they speak in the church. He was trembling. He told the minister that the Devil had appeared to him on a number of occasions, the first time offering him a purse of silver. The Scotsman made the Sign of the Cross, causing the Devil to vanish at once.

But Satan returned again and again, urging him 'to kill and slay' at random. The parishioner refused, and fled to Ireland. After the confession to Reverend Blair the Devil appeared again. He admonished the Scot for seeking the minister's help and promised him that, unless he murdered soon, the Devil would kill him on Hallowe'en.

The night arrived. The Scot went in desperation to the minister and Blair agreed to hold a vigil with him. They prayed together in the church the night long. The Devil failed to show, and the Scot in gratitude devoted the rest of his life to prayer, temperance and good works.

It was not an exorcism in the fullest sense but it enhanced Reverend Blair's reputation in the district. Soon after, he encountered many cases of religious hysteria. He described parishioners who suffered bouts of weeping and convulsions. He knew who was behind it: it was, he said, demons 'playing the ape, and counterfeiting the works of the Lord'.

At worship one particular Sunday, a member of the congregation went berserk. The woman, 'one of my charge, being a dull and ignorant person, made a noise and stretching of her body. Incontinent I was assisted to rebuke that lying spirit that disturbed the worship of God, charging the same not to disturb the congregation; and through God's mercy we met with no more of that work.'

News of the exorcism reached Archbishop James Ussher, the man responsible for the dating of Creation to the year 4004 BC. At his next meeting with the minister he congratulated Blair on a job well done.

These incidents, which Reverend Blair recorded in his autobiography, suggest that exorcism was still a haphazard affair until recent times, and could be carried out at a priest's own discretion without prior consultation with his bishop.

This was to change in 1641. In that year the solemn rite of exorcism, the Rituale Romanum or Roman Rite, became standardized in the Catholic Church. It would remain unchanged for over three centuries. In 1971, following on from the Second Vatican Council, Pope John XXIII overhauled the minor rites of ordination, which included that of exorcism. Then, in 1999, the Vatican again revised the ritual, shortening it and translating the Latin words into the vernacular.

ROME'S EXORCIST SPEAKS OUT

Those decisions were not well received. Father Gabriele Amorth, Rome's chief exorcist and author of *An Exorcist Tells His Story*, publicly expressed his disdain of the new rite and the Vatican

Curia that implemented the changes. 'They approved a new ritual which, for the exorcist, is a disaster,' he said. 'I continue to use the Rituale Romanum, which is still valid. If it were not, I would have to resign.'

The 1641 ritual was drawn up in a time that had witnessed an outbreak of witchcraft across Europe, one that spared few countries. As we have seen, an Irish witch was only rarely executed. Elsewhere, a conviction of witchcraft almost always carried the death penalty. In the few instances where clemency was shown, a priest might perform a ceremony of exorcism, to drive out the demon that was supposed to have taken possession of the witch. Or the priest might seek to nullify any 'pact' the accused had made with Satan.

Although the notion of pacts with the Devil vanished almost entirely in later centuries, pockets of belief and superstition persisted, especially in remote rural areas. In Germany, such superstition, or *Aberglaube*, relied on 'names of power' by which a demon might be brought to heel or warded off. As late as the last century, farmers would nail pieces of card above doors and stables before dawn on 6 January, Three Kings' Day. The letters CMB would be written on the cards, a reference to the magi: Caspar, Melchior and Balthazar. The ritual was intended to keep Satan – and his minions – away.

SATANISM AND THE BEAST

In England, in 1929, a flamboyant braggart named Aleister Crowley (1875–1947) published his *Confessions*, in which he all but admitted 'going over' to the Devil. His enemies – and he had made a great number – needed no such admission. Throughout his long career as a magician, scandal followed Crowley wherever he went, and he was accused of all manner of perversion, from satanism to human sacrifice. A newspaper famously called him 'the wickedest man in the world'; he himself rejoiced in the title of The Beast – the name by which his own mother knew him.

When he died in a boarding-house in Hastings, a hopeless drug-addict, he bequeathed to posterity a system of magic (or 'magick' as he preferred to call it) that was at the very least ambiguous in its dealings with the preternatural, the demonic.

But generally speaking, demonic possession, its prevention and cure, did not figure large in the early and middle decades of the twentieth century. There were isolated cases, most of which merited little more than a footnote in a news report.

That was to change. 'This is the dawning of the Age of Aquarius,' sang the chorus of the rock musical *Hair* in 1968, and we were invited to believe that we were entering a period of

> Harmony and understanding,
> Sympathy and trust abounding;
> No more falsehoods or derisions,
> Golden living, dreams of visions. . . .

It was a charming but dangerous naiveté. The reality would prove to be very different indeed.

DEMONS IN A TIME OF SCIENCE AND WONDERS

With the turn of the century – and the millennium – a paradox like no other in history arose. In the face of encroaching secularism and a flowering of science and technology, exorcism was more prominent than it had been for hundreds of years.

Even the pope was engaging in it. In September 2000, John Paul II cast a demon out of a nineteen-year-old Italian woman. She had attended a public audience with the pontiff in St Peter's Square.

She was brought to Father Gabriele Amorth, who tried twice to rid her of the evil that had taken control. He failed. It was a measure of Amorth's confidence in the pope that he allowed the woman to be brought before him. John Paul prayed over her for more than half an hour, and succeeded in banishing the demon – though only temporarily. At one point, the young woman, in a loud masculine voice, was heard to bellow: 'Not even the head of your Church can send me away!'

Catholics everywhere greeted the news with bemusement tinged with awe; when it became known that it was the *third* exorcism performed by that particular pope when in office, eyebrows were raised even more. For pontiffs are not supposed to soil their hands with the 'dirtier work' of the Church; they are expected to fulfil a more symbolic role.

The Holy Father's intervention served also to endorse a growing development within the twenty-first-century Christian Church: the recognition that Satan was at work with a vengeance, and battle had been joined.

Few could have imagined, half a century ago, that the third millennium of Christendom would be ushered in by the pope of Rome battling Christ's greatest adversary. The notion is unsettling for Christian and unbeliever alike. Satan ought not to have a place in our modern world.

Yet there are those who do not doubt that responsibility for many of the world's woes can be laid at the Devil's door. They argue that our species could not possibly visit so much evil on its fellow-creatures, alone and unaided. It is not part of our make-up, they contend; when men commit the most unspeakable crimes, they are going against human nature.

The debate – an important part of it in any case – is whether evil is innate, or whether demonic forces are at work in the world; forces that can turn ostensibly normal, rational individuals into monsters.

British author and former crime reporter Brian McConnell chooses to believe the latter. He writes:

The twenty-first century is . . . here, and more and more people are asking whether demonic possession exists. Who else but the demonically possessed could become cult leaders with one solution to life – mass murder and mass suicide; or serial killers; or Satanists; or sectarians slaughtering people in Northern Ireland because they belong to another religion; or religious people ethnically cleansing their fellow human beings in the former Yugoslavia; or tribal rivals committing genocide in holy places in Rwanda?

EXORCISM IN IRELAND

*In Carlow material things are taking over
from plain values, but for those interested in
material things, the reality is they only really
have a lend of what they have.*

– Tridentine Bishop Martin Pius Kelly
on the occasion of his exorcising
the entire town in December 2000

THE IRISH PEOPLE share an unusual belief with born-again Americans: they hold that Satan truly exists. Not in the sense by which the rest of the Christian world believes, viz. that the Devil is a convenient means to personify evil. The Irish – at least one third of the population – truly believe that Satan is a real entity.

It might be thought, then, that discussion of Satan would be widespread up and down the country. This is not the case. The Devil is seldom spoken of in urbane circles; he generally makes his appearance as a burlesque, in much the same way as do ghosts and goblins. Belief in him is relegated to the old ways of the country people. The Devil is synonymous with superstition.

Yet from time to time, inexplicable phenomena intrude upon our modern *Weltanschauung*: people and places present signs of paranormal oppression. And, in our urbane circles, the question arises: Can a case be made, after all, for the preternatural?

There is a stigma attached to admitting that such phenomena may have demonic origins. There hangs also a whiff of the unsavoury round about the ritual used for its banishment: the exorcism. Not for nothing do we call it 'the dark sacrament', given that many church authorities are reluctant to even admit that the ritual exists, much less that it is performed in the Ireland of today – the Ireland of great prosperity, a nation very much in tune with the modern world. Such matters are perceived as throwbacks to a darker, less enlightened age.

Yet exorcisms continue to be performed regardless, even if the Churches do not cry it from the steeples. At one time, a diocese would have its own exorcist. No longer. Whenever the need arises, a bishop will seek the advice of a priest experienced in the preternatural, and that priest need not be a specially ordained exorcist. At other times, the Catholic Church in particular will call upon the services of a foreign exorcist, sometimes from the Vatican, sometimes from Britain.

The calls for deliverance are going out with increasing frequency. It seems that 'evil' is on the rise. Few will deny that Irish society has become progressively more lawless, in the north especially but south of the border, too, to a frightening degree. We are witnessing crimes considered unthinkable even twenty years ago.

In May 2006, the Central Criminal Court found a Carlow man guilty of the horrendous and sustained sexual abuse of two nieces and a nephew, from 1993 to 2003. The forty-one-year-old had anally raped the girls, one of whom was only eight when her decade-long ordeal began. Mr Justice Carney handed down a custodial sentence of less than seven years.

The young and vulnerable are being preyed upon. So, too, are the elderly: old-age pensioners are being robbed in their homes, the robbery often accompanied by brutality. In January 2006 a twenty-seven-year-old entered the bedroom of a woman of seventy-two in Dromore, County Tyrone, at the ominous hour of 3 am. He viciously raped her, leaving her severely traumatized.

She was fortunate to survive such barbarousness, for there were precedents to the rape of elderly Irishwomen, some with lethal consequences. In the same Tyrone, in 1999, a nineteen-year-old raped his next-door neighbour, a woman of ninety-one, in her own bed. She died later of her horrific injuries, and the killer laughed and sneered when each detail of the vicious crime was read out in court. In December 2001 another nineteen-year-old savagely raped and strangled a nun in his native County Monaghan. She was sixty-nine and on her way to a friend's 100th birthday party.

An Erosion of Ethics?

Let us not forget that these crimes are being perpetrated in a First World country. We should know better than, say, a poor and 'emerging' African nation. Yet in traditional African societies, respect for the elderly is both a divinely and humanly imposed duty. In such societies it is not uncommon for young people to prostrate themselves before their elders, to doff their caps – and even to undo their sandal straps when speaking to the elderly. A complaint heard frequently is that Western values are eroding such traditional ethics. For an African, then, to assault and rob an elderly person is to be guilty of unconscionable evil.

So where does it come from, our Western neo-savagery? Are we perhaps witnessing signs of encroaching, external evil, or is this 'simply' deviant behaviour? There are those who attribute this descent into depravity to a moral bankruptcy in our society in general. Like Malachi Martin, they believe that it has created a breeding ground for extrinsic evil. In his preface to *Hostage to the Devil* he expressed a conviction that the general population is more prone than ever before to demonic attack.

> Our cultural desolation – a kind of agony of aim-
> lessness coupled with a dominant self-interest – is
> documented for us in the disintegration of our fami-
> lies. In the breakup of our educational system. In

the disappearance of publicly accepted norms of decency in language, dress and behaviour. In the lives of our youth, everywhere deformed by stunning violence and sudden death; by teenage pregnancy; by drug and alcohol addiction; by disease; by suicide; by fear.

Such pervasive cultural desolation, he concluded, 'is the most fertile ground one could possibly imagine for the causes of Possession to take root and flourish in almost unimpeded freedom.'

Dr Martin was writing of American society in 1992. His words might equally well apply to the Ireland of the new millennium.

Father Gabriele Amorth is in no doubt as to where blame should be apportioned. 'The majority of people have lost their faith due to a materialistic and hedonistic attitude,' he says. 'Barely twelve per cent of Rome's population now attend Mass.'

It is, to be sure, not unexpected that a priest should see a correlation between materialism and non-attendance at worship – indeed we would expect no less from an ordained minister of God. But Father Amorth goes further. He believes that apostasy is an open invitation to evil, and that Italy has reached the level of decadence of the Roman Empire at its worst. This has come about, he says, 'partly as a result of the misuse of the mass media . . . and partly because of Western consumerism and materialism, which have poisoned our society.' He expressed to us not only his sadness at this 'cultural desolation' but also his disappointment 'that the bishops do not believe in the Gospel, in the Church of Rome and its dispositions.'

And in our own country? In the 1970s, about ninety per cent of Catholics attended Mass each week; three decades on, that figure has been effectively halved. Like Father Amorth, many Irish churchmen view these sobering statistics with great concern. They are of the opinion that, where a belief or faith in God has been eroded, or is non-existent, the vacuum thus created will be filled by evil. The writer CS Lewis put it plainly when he stated: 'There is no neutral ground in the universe; every square inch, every split second, is claimed by God and counterclaimed by Satan.'

TRAINING THE EXORCISTS

The Catholic Church is fighting back. In February 2005 the Vatican took the unprecedented step of delivering courses on possession. Entitled 'Exorcism and Prayers of Liberation', the series of studies sought to remedy the clergy's problems when addressing 'such delicate themes'.

'The courses . . . deal with demonology, the presence of the notion of the Devil in sacred texts, and the pathology and medical treatment of people suffering from possession,' a Vatican spokesman said at the launch. 'The seminar will conclude with the testimony of two exorcists who will explain how to distinguish between someone who is ill and requiring medical care, and one who is possessed by demons.'

That last is crucial to any exploration of the preternatural and its manifestations. Some might argue that churchmen have no business interfering in psychiatric matters; others will contend that few psychiatrists have any true understanding of the spiritual. In practice, however, we found that there exists an admirable synergy between the Church and the medical profession, and that many enlightened psychiatrists have come to appreciate that there are times when a priest's intervention is needed. Dr Kenneth McAll told of an astonishing number of patients who were helped by prayer when they failed to respond to psychiatric treatment. He urged caution when approaching a diagnosis.

> When there is a suspicion that occult forces are at work in a person's life, a prerequisite of any subsequent treatment is a thorough medical examination.

Someone suspected of being under demonic control may in fact be suffering from depressive psychosis, schizophrenia or the effects of other organic psychoses. The person could be acutely neurotic, hidden aspects of his personality or an upsurge image from his deep unconscious could be the cause. Although all such diagnoses should be treated as psychiatric disorders, they do not exclude demonic control.

The nine cases which follow are broadly representative of a number that we examined in the course of our research. Several allude to general practitioners and psychiatrists whose diagnoses permitted the presence – in or about the patient – of forces beyond the physical, i.e. external entities. While many churchmen will applaud such open-mindedness, others will deem it prudent to join with experts, both lay and clerical, who warn against the application of exorcism in the treatment of certain medical conditions. One such is multiple personality disorder, also called dissociative identity disorder.

Those familiar with this condition will know that the symptoms that a patient presents can, at first blush, resemble those traditionally identified with demonic oppression. This fact cannot and should not be enough to justify an exorcism. The demonic is held to be present only when the patient displays behaviour or powers beyond the bounds of the natural. It must be stressed that expert opinion generally agrees that exorcism for multiple personality disorder is *therapeutically contraindicated*, and warns that various forms of harm may ensue if it is undertaken.

Caution and prudence must be our watchwords, in this and in all matters pertaining to the diagnosis of resident evil.

DEVILRY ON THE
DINGLE PENINSULA

ERIN FERGUSON knew at once she had taken the bend too sharply, but knew too late. She had made no allowance for the fresh fall of rain. Her car was skidding towards the white van, and there was nothing she could do to prevent it. She braced for the impact.

She must have blacked out. She came to, after what seemed like hours but could surely have only been seconds, brought round by an urgent rapping on her window. The face she saw through the glass startled her. It was a man's face; a man with eyes so dark and penetrating that her immediate impulse was to reverse the car swiftly and flee the scene. She was a lone female on a remote road miles from nowhere; the stranger might be anybody, capable of anything.

He continued to stare in at Erin, saying nothing. Should he not, she thought, be asking if I'm all right? Should he not be showing some concern? She tentatively reached out a hand to lock the door, but he got there before her and yanked it open.

'Are you okay?' He had spoken at last.

'I think so.'

It was a good way from the truth. Erin sat up in her seat, giving thanks that she had been wearing a seat-belt. She had muscle pain, neck pain, a raging headache. But nothing seemed to be broken. She angled the mirror, and her eyes widened at the sight of the bruise above her left eye. It was going to be a nasty, ugly bump.

Erin climbed out. She did not like the way the stranger's dark eyes flicked to her skirt as she smoothed it down.

Surprisingly, the damage to the van was slight. Her car had grazed the rear mudguard and spun out of control, to collide with the mossy face of the crag that ran down to the road.

The owner of the van introduced himself as Ed O'Gribben. Erin apologized for the damage and offered to cover his repair costs without involving her insurance company – her premium was high enough as it was. He said very little, simply nodded when appropriate, and continued to stare at her in his unsettling way. They exchanged details; he would be in touch as soon as he had an estimate.

Ed O'Gribben helped her to get her car back onto the road. There seemed to be very little wrong with it, and that was all to the good. Erin had no wish to remain on that isolated stretch of road a minute longer. It was more than the distress of the accident that bothered her; the man with the too-dark eyes unnerved her. She departed with a sense of relief. As she drove away, she could not have imagined that a year later, in June 1996, she and Ed O'Gribben would be exchanging rings and vows at the altar.

They had met 'by accident'; the elements had thrown them together. Perhaps that should have been a warning.

The first months of Erin's marriage were difficult. At Ed's insistence, she gave up her job as a legal secretary – in any case, commuting to and from work was becoming unsustainable. She was having to adjust to a whole new way of life. A city girl at heart, used to the bustle of Tralee, the twenty-six-year-old now found herself hopelessly isolated in the hinterlands of the Dingle Peninsula.

The house that 'came with' her husband – as Erin would joke in the beginning – was at least a century old. It was situated at the end of a long lane and looked as lonely and forgotten as the landscape it stood in. Imposing though it was at a distance, when seen at close quarters the two-storied granite building was downright shabby. The moss-caked roof was dilapidated enough, but there was moss also on the paving that led to the front doorstep; the window frames were peeling and decaying.

If the outside was disappointing, the interior was not much of an improvement. Erin was crestfallen when Ed showed her round; she just about managed to hide her dismay. The rooms were large, yet frugally appointed with heavy oak furniture. The carpets were threadbare. The windows, hung with dusty drapes from another age, admitted very little light. She was reminded of the gloomy atmosphere of a funeral home.

'I tried to put a brave face on it,' she tells us at our first meeting. 'A lick of paint and some cheery wallpaper would soon put things right, I said to myself. It was also heartening to see that there were radiators in every room.'

But the puzzling part was the cold. Why, she asked herself, was the house so cold when there was central heating? And why did every room reek of mildew?

Her husband was a successful contractor. He had made a point of telling her as much when they started going out together; he would proudly point out a school or development his company had built. Why, then, live in such near-squalor? Surely he could have carried out some improvements. Or, better still, tear the old house down and erect a new one. After all, the family land extended in all directions; the site was there already, so Ed could build with the minimum outlay.

But he had very different views on the subject.

'My ancestors built this place,' he declared one evening. He said it a little too gruffly for Erin's liking. They had just finished supper and he was preparing to look in on a client. (He seemed to be forever visiting some client or other.) 'It doesn't do to tamper with the past.'

'Ed, you're only thirty, for heaven's sake! You sound like an old man of eighty.'

He did not respond; only stared at her in that unsettling way of his, and left.

'And why do you need to go out so much?' she shouted after him as the back door slammed shut. 'Why am I always left alone with *her*?'

The 'her' was Ed's seventy-nine-year-old mother, the woman Erin called the Matriarch – but only to herself, under her breath. Ed had referred to her in their courting days, but always in an offhand way, as though his mother were no more than a minor part of his life.

The reality was otherwise, as Erin was to discover. Martha O'Gribben would command a principal role in the couple's marriage. She had made her acquaintance on her wedding day, when the bridal pair returned to the rambling old house on the Dingle Peninsula.

First, she discovered why Mrs O'Gribben had been unable to attend her son's nuptials: she was very frail and confined to bed with arthritis. This was news to Erin. She had not bargained for the role of a geriatric nurse; worse, her husband seemed to take for granted that it was a natural extension of her duties as wife and housekeeper.

All might have been well had Martha been kindly and considerate, as was Erin's own mother. But, frail though she was, the old lady nevertheless seemed intent on making her daughter-in-law's life as difficult as possible. She occupied a room on the ground floor, to the front of the house and, most disconcertingly, directly under the couple's bedroom.

Erin remained standing in the kitchen until the sound of Ed's jeep had died away. She sat down at the table again, buried her face in her hands and wept. Her tears flowed freely; there was no mascara to run, for she had stopped wearing much make-up of any kind. Make-up seemed at odds with the drabness of the house – like wearing a ball-gown to the office party. She desperately wanted to phone her family for a heart to heart. Gemma would understand. But she was reluctant to disenchant her younger sister; Gemma had such idealistic notions of marriage. And as for her widowed mother, she could hardly go upsetting her either. Her mother was so proud of the 'wonderful match' her elder daughter had made. Ed was the perfect son-in-law: wealthy, courteous and handsome.

'I should be happy,' Erin sighed to herself. 'By rights I should be happy.' But as she allowed her gaze to drift about the kitchen, lingering over the heavy cupboard with its display of decades-old, craquelured china, the distempered walls and ancient door, the overall dismalness of the place struck her. 'How did I get here?'

She got up and began clearing the table. But no sooner had she finished than she heard an all-too-familiar sound. It was the frantic banging of a walking stick against the radiator in the front room. It made her feel even more depressed. Mrs O'Gribben was demanding her attention.

'Yes, I'll be with you in a minute!'

She checked the clock; it was 9.15. Time for the bedtime ritual: time to metaphorically don her nurse's cap and do the necessary.

Erin recalls with dismaying clarity her first meeting with Martha O'Gribben. 'I remember having the same uneasiness I felt on the day I literally ran into Ed on that winding road,' she says. 'To be fair to Ed, my first misgivings seemed cockeyed. He was a thorough gentleman. He was always so attentive and loving when we were going out together. He'd make a fuss of me. He was like that as well during the first months we were married.'

To be sure, there were sides to him she neither liked nor understood, yet the good she saw in him outweighed the bad – or the mysterious. In lieu of the impossibility of perfection, Erin was willing to settle for less. As most women are wont to do, she had told herself.

But Mrs O'Gribben was a different story. There was no discernible warmth in the woman. Her manner was as cool as the hand she would offer in greeting. At first Erin felt sorry for her, interpreting the hostility in the old woman's eyes as the (somehow understandable) resentment of her new daughter-in-law. That, coupled with the antipathy of the bedridden towards the able-bodied. Yet as time wore on, she was to discover that the woman's hatred went deeper – deeper by far than anything she could have imagined.

Bang! The radiator was struck hard, its note reverberating through the house like a bell, and sending Erin's nerves a-twitching. *Bang!* Again.

'I'm coming!'

The radiator had been struck twice more before the 'nurse' could attend to the patient. She assisted Mrs O'Gribben with her ablutions, and gave her her medication and nightcap. These tasks had become so routine that Erin now performed them without a thought – and without a word. She had long given up on the small-talk and pleasantries; nor did she expect a word of gratitude for her trouble. Instead she awaited, as always, a complaint of some kind.

'This cocoa isn't hot enough!'

'Well, maybe if you drank it quicker, it wouldn't have time to go cold.'

'Maybe if you left it longer on the boil you mean.'

The daughter-in-law made no reply. She knew the script too well. Acquiescing seemed the best way to keep the peace. She took up the mug and headed for the door.

'I'll reheat it then. Be back in a minute.'

'And another thing: you're not allowed any callers to this house, d'you hear?' Mrs O'Gribben tightened her crocheted bed-jacket about her. 'This is still *my* house, not yours. And as long as I'm here, you'll do as I say.'

'I know,' said Erin with exasperation. 'You've been telling me that from the minute I got here.'

It was a repetition of so many of her evenings. When she was single, working in the office in Tralee, Erin's life was relatively uneventful. Yet, compared to her new situation, it seemed almost exciting. Thinking back on those days, as she frequently did, she wondered if she had not made a blunder.

For marriage to Ed, far from the expected idyll, had become a mind-numbing routine. Her only outing was to the nearest town twice a week to do the shopping. Even then, her time was not her own, because old Mrs O'Gribben could not be left unattended for long.

Gradually, the young Mrs O'Gribben began to withdraw into this curiously caged world. Her friends stopped ringing. No wonder; whenever she arranged to meet them, something would upset her plans; that something usually involved her mother-in-law, and Erin would have to cancel.

She rarely saw her husband. When he came in from work around five, somebody was sure to telephone, and he would be off again. Often she would fall asleep in the early hours while waiting for him, and wake in the morning to find that he had already left.

The house received few visitors. No neighbours dropped by for a chat, as was the case with Erin's mother. From one end of the week to another she only saw her in-laws.

'If I'm honest with myself,' she tells us, 'I'd have to say I'd have preferred no visitors at all rather than that lot.'

Ed's two younger brothers, Dan and Michael, were bachelors in their late twenties. They were plasterers by trade, and worked in the family business. Their sister Mary, the youngest sibling, worked in a crèche. From the outset, all three made no secret of their dislike for Erin. Mary especially was highly critical of any changes she would make in the house. Erin thought at first that her sister-in-law might be a sympathetic ally – she was, after all, the only girl in a family of boys – but Mary had other ideas. She seemed to resent the 'intruder' who had the audacity to make a claim on her oldest brother's affections.

Dan and Michael were 'odd' – Erin has no better word that describes them. They seemed incapable of holding a conversation, and when they tried to, could rarely maintain eye contact. For Erin, the effort to be friendly towards them was so taxing, she gave up altogether. They were shy, she concluded; it was as simple as that. She got used to being ignored and was relieved to see them exit by the front door after they had visited their mother. Avoidance rather than embarrassment, she reasoned, was best all round.

Father Lyons, however, was quite another matter. He was the parish priest, the only other visitor to the O'Gribben house, and for Erin a real enigma. A handsome man in his early forties, he did not fit the stereotype of the rural Irish priest. He seemed especially attentive to Mrs O'Gribben's needs and called several mornings each week, while on his rounds of the sick.

What disconcerted Erin most was the freedom with which the priest came and went. He never bothered knocking, but would materialize in the kitchen at any hour he pleased, grunt a greeting and disappear into the patient's room. Often he startled Erin by emerging from the mother's bedroom when she had no inkling he was even in the house.

The situation reached absurd heights one morning. Ed had left for work and Erin was dressing in the bedroom. She was intrigued to hear the upstairs toilet flush; it was at the end of the corridor. She peered out her door and was in time to see Father Lyons steal down the stairs. It was eight o'clock. What on earth, she wondered, was going on?

'That made me *so* indignant,' she says, and it is plain to see that it still rankles, almost a decade later. 'After all, I was Ed's wife, the "mistress of the house", even if oul' Martha had other ideas. I thought it was a bit rich of Father Lyons, treating the house as his own. It just wasn't on.'

But he was a priest, and Erin's upbringing dissuaded her from challenging him there and then. She was determined to do just that in the event it should happen again. It did, a day or two later. And Father Lyons's response astonished her.

'Oh, but I have my own key,' he said cheerily, as if that explained everything.

'Your own key. I don't understand.'

'It's very simple,' he said, as if speaking to a child. 'Ed had one made for me. Martha wanted me to have one.' He was no longer smiling and his voice had taken on a patronizing tone. 'After all, this is Mrs O'Gribben's home. If you don't want me to have a key, perhaps you should discuss it with her.'

Erin was gobsmacked. 'Oh no, that's all right,' she heard herself say. 'Do as you please, Father.'

'Good. As long as we know where we stand.' He rubbed his palms together and grinned. 'Now, a cup of tea would be lovely. Bring it down to the room, would you. Time to look in on the patient.'

He left Erin fuming. It was all she was going to take. She vowed that, before the week was out, she would tackle her husband about the intolerable situation.

'I knew I was as much to blame,' she says. 'I stood meekly by and allowed a bedridden old harridan to dictate my life, aided and abetted by a priest who showed no respect for another person's privacy. So right there and then, I swore I was going to have it out with Ed. I'd had enough – of him, his mother, and that stuck-up priest.'

But the confrontation was postponed. Two days following Erin's exchange with Father Lyons, the unexpected happened. Martha O'Gribben suffered a severe stroke and slipped into a coma.

She was removed without delay to the county hospital.

For the first time in seven months, Erin found herself quite alone in the old house. Ed and his siblings maintained a rotating bedside vigil and the priest had no reason to call. The young housewife was not unhappy being left by herself. She had applied to do a distance-learning course in the hospitality trade and was working on completing the first module of the two-year curriculum. She could study undisturbed and undistracted.

All the same, the house was having an unsettling effect on her. She put it down to the isolation; she could not help comparing it to Wuthering Heights or some other bleak old ancestral home of fiction. And she knew full well that West Kerry had lost some of the innocent charm she remembered from childhood. Crime had affected the locality just as much as elsewhere; out-of-the-way dwellings had become easy pickings for burglars. Before going to bed each night, she made certain that all windows and doors were secured. She even locked her bedroom door.

She slept well on those first two nights of solitude. Not so the third. That night she was to have her first brush with the paranormal.

At about two in the morning Erin was awakened by a frightful pounding on her bedroom door. It was terrifyingly loud; it was as though somebody was using their fists against it.

She switched on the light, thinking it was Ed, angered that his own bedroom door was bolted against him. Was he drunk? Trembling, Erin slipped out of bed.

'Wait now, Ed! I'm coming.'

Fumbling, she unlocked the door and yanked it open.

There was no one. The landing was disconcertingly deserted.

'Ed,' she called out hesitantly, 'is that you?'

No answer came. My God, she thought, what is going on? There was plainly someone in the house. The pounding on the door had sounded while she slept, but continued after it roused her. It was no dream. Every fear she had entertained while alone in the house was lining up to assail her. She thought of burglars, thieves, rapists, murderers. . . .

She was standing on the landing, wondering whether she should brave it down the stairs, when she noticed something odd. The door to old Mrs O'Gribben's room was slightly ajar, and the light was on. It had not been on in days, not since they had brought her to the hospital.

'Hello, who's there?' she called out. She was endeavouring to keep the fear out of her voice. 'You'd better come out or I'll call the Gardaí!'

She waited. There was no response.

The bedroom seemed the safest place at that moment. She dashed back in and slammed the door shut. She fumbled with the key; her fingers were trembling. She sat down on the bed and tried to reason things out.

'I'd only been in oul' Martha's room the day before,' she recalls. 'And I distinctly remembered locking it. There'd been no one in the house since then – no one. I was frantic; I got down on my knees and started to pray to try and calm myself. It helped.'

Eventually, Erin climbed back under the covers and switched off the light. The house was silent, reassuringly so. She drifted off.

Shortly after six she was awakened by the telephone on the locker. It was Ed, always the early riser. Yes, he had been at his mother's bedside all night. Why?

'Just wondered, Ed. Thought maybe you'd come back for something and didn't want to wake me.'

'No,' he said, half-stifling a yawn.

Erin decided to keep her unsettling experience to herself.

'How is she? Any change?'

'No, not really. But we lost her for a bit.'

'What? I don't understand. What do mean, "lost her"?'

'Around two. She stopped breathing. Only for a few minutes, thank God.' She thought she heard Father Lyons's voice in the background. 'Look, got to go. See you at lunchtime.'

The following night proved even more disturbing.

Ed had left her on her own again. She slept fitfully and awoke in the early hours. She had had a very vivid and distressing dream: old Mrs O'Gribben had appeared in the corner of the room, screaming at her, over and over.

'Get out of here!' she ordered. 'You're not wanted in this house!'

The dream seemed so real, almost as though Mrs O'Gribben had been there in the flesh; it had none of the vagueness and disjointedness one associates with ordinary dreams.

'It upset me no end,' Erin says. 'I kept thinking something must be wrong. It was like one of those premonitions people say they have. So I rang the hospital, and got Ed on the line.'

His mother had passed away a few minutes earlier.

Sitting in the kitchen, drinking cup after cup of tea, not daring to return to bed, and perchance to dream again, Erin was knitting together strands of evidence, and drawing a disquieting conclusion. Her 'Wuthering Heights' was haunted.

'I didn't want to admit it to myself before then,' she says, 'mainly because I always thought ghost stories were rubbish. Now I wasn't so sure. All those weird things that were happening: they were like something out of a ghost story.'

There was, however, a glaring inconsistency in Erin's theory. Ghost stories involve ghosts, the phantoms of the dead. Ed's mother, though terminally ill, was still alive when the alarming disturbances began. She wondered how it was possible for a *living* person to haunt her.

But Mrs O'Gribben was certainly dead now. Erin could not

bring herself to mourn her passing. Nevertheless she did her duty and attended the funeral service; it would have been the scandal of the parish had she not. Predictably, Father Lyons conducted the service, and equally predictably eulogized at length about the kind, generous and pious lady the deceased had been. One thing puzzled Erin: she was not the only person present who showed no grief. Neither Ed nor his siblings shed a tear. All seemed some- how relieved at their mother's passing.

She was missing something; she felt almost like an actor called upon at the last minute to stand in for a role – and nobody had given her the script to read.

On 18 January 1997, one month after Mrs O'Gribben's death, Erin discovered she was pregnant. She was overjoyed. All the dif- ficulties that had been plaguing her seemed to melt away. With her mother-in-law gone, and having the house to herself at last, she felt freer and happier than she had ever been.

Her difficult in-laws no longer had reason to visit, and she saw less of Father Lyons. The priest did not stop calling altogether, though. Twice a week he would collect Ed on 'parish business'. Both were members of the local GAA cumann and, every Tuesday and Thursday evening, Ed gave up his free time in order to coach the boys' under-12 football team.

As her pregnancy progressed, Erin became used to being left alone for most of the day and evening. The old house seemed somehow less intimidating; she felt that it was becoming *hers*. It no longer made her nervous. The two frightening episodes she had had concerning her mother-in-law – the pounding on the bedroom door and the nightmare – she put down to stress. It was a new year, she had made her resolutions, a baby was coming. The new mistress of the house felt better about everything.

Surveying *her* home early one morning, she made a decision: a clean sweep was called for. And the best place to start was the bedroom vacated by the scarcely lamented Martha O'Gribben. She would clear it out: perhaps turn it into a sitting-room or study.

There was something about the room that made her uneasy, even *sans* patient. It was not just the cold; that particular room had always been colder than the rest of the house; she had got used to that. There was something else. An odour: 'a dirty rotten odour, as though a toilet had never been cleaned in ages.' This noisome stench persisted even after everything – Mrs O'Gribben's effects, bed and bedding, the trappings of home nursing – had been disposed of.

'The strange thing about it,' Erin says, 'is that it didn't seem to fade, as smells normally do. I could stand in the hallway with the door to that room open and I wouldn't smell anything at all. But once I put my head in, it was overpowering.'

After that, it began to follow her.

'There was something really unnatural about it, because it would come and go at random all over the house, as if it was being switched on and off, almost like a light.'

At first Ed claimed he could smell nothing but eventually gave in.

'It's probably a blockage in the sewerage system,' he said.

Erin had her doubts. There were only two bathrooms, one upstairs, one down, both at the rear of the house. The smell had begun – and was still at its most pungent – in the mother's room. It had no en-suite; none of the bedrooms had.

It seemed to Erin that something was determined to thwart her attempts to set her own stamp upon the house. The smell was only the beginning. One evening, while in the kitchen writing up an essay, she felt certain she heard her name being called; but there was no one. On another occasion, she distinctly heard someone knocking on the back door, and was surprised to find no visitor on the step. Sometimes she would awaken in the middle of the night with a jolt, believing she had heard old Mrs O'Gribben's summons – the walking-stick being dragged across the radiator in the room below.

Again, Ed was not prepared to share her concerns.

'Maybe it's my mother wanting you out,' he said dismissively.

And Erin had the mad notion that he meant it too.

In October 1997, Mrs Erin O'Gribben gave birth to a healthy baby boy. Quentin was all a mother could wish for: a beautiful brown-eyed little bundle, who rarely cried and rarely disturbed his parents' sleep.

Ed turned out to be an attentive enough father; but, as Quentin's first birthday drew near, he made a rather strange announcement.

'We'll not be having a birthday party for him,' he said.

'What do you mean?'

'There'll be no parties in this house.'

'Why not?' She was puzzled. It seemed an odd thing to say. What was wrong with a birthday party?

'We've never had them. My father didn't like them, and neither did *his* father.'

'Are you telling me you never had a birthday party? None of you? Not even when you were kids?'

'That's right.'

'So it's a family tradition then.' Erin knew she sounded scathing but did not care. It was ridiculous.

But Ed simply glared at her, saying nothing. She hated it when he behaved that way. It made her feel as if *she* were being the unreasonable one.

'Okay, we'll go out to a restaurant,' she said, annoyed. 'Is that allowed?'

'Fine,' he said after a time. 'Yes, fine. You go ahead. I'll be working anyway.'

Father Lyons's car pulled into the yard then, and presently Ed took his leave. Erin was left once again holding the baby. It was a situation she had come to accept as normal.

Looking back now, she admits that there was a good deal wrong with her marriage. 'All the signs were there,' she says, 'but I chose to ignore them. You know how it is. I was young, idealistic. I thought I could change him and that things would work out. But I know now that you can't change anyone. Not really.'

But there were other, ominous, signs that there was something not altogether right about the house. Erin could not help but conclude that the signs had multiplied since Quentin's birth and in the months that followed. Nor was it her imagination; they were physical, concrete signs.

The bedroom on the ground floor – the old sickroom – seemed to be the focus. She had succeeded in clearing it out, but never actually got round to redecorating it. Time after time the coldness and foul smell put her off. She let the room be, promising herself to tackle it 'at some stage'. Quentin's approaching birthday seemed to be the incentive she needed. She unlocked the door – and was greeted by a very odd sight.

The windowsill and the floor below it were covered with dead, black flies. This was puzzling. After all, it was wintertime and the window was perpetually shut. On closer examination, Erin saw that some of the flies were incomplete. It was as if they had been chopped in two or – more worryingly – bitten in two. A shiver ran through her. She remembered, some years before, seeing the same phenomenon in a film: *The Amityville Horror*.

'I go cold thinking about it,' Erin says, 'and not just because of the chill in the room. It was only later that I remembered more about that film, about the awful smells and the flies. A long time later. If I'd remembered then, I'd have been out of there immediately and taking Quentin with me. The slaughter of a whole family was responsible for the evil in Amityville, and I suppose I realize now that murder doesn't always have to be physical; killing a person's spirit is just as evil – maybe worse.'

'I don't know what was going through my head half the time,' she confesses. 'I was beginning to think all kinds of things about the O'Gribbens. They were definitely dysfunctional; there was no love lost between them, that's for sure. I had the idea that they all really hated each other. I just didn't dare think about what might have gone on in their past. From what Ed told me, his father sounded like a right header. And as for the grandfather . . . I'd seen enough of the mother and the others to convince me they were all a bit loopy. Not dangerous, you understand; just loopy.'

She hurriedly hoovered up the flies, made the room a little more presentable, and left. It made her uneasy.

But the following week curiosity got the better of her, and she went to check the room again. This time, the smell was worse – and the flies had returned. There were more of them too: little black corpses on the sill, and more forming a semicircle below the window, as though somebody had spilled a canister of black peppercorns. Erin was repelled by the sight; she cleaned up quickly again and left.

'It went on for weeks,' she says. 'I'd hardly got rid of them but they'd appear again. I couldn't understand it; there was no rational explanation I could think of. I thought about spiders. But there weren't any, not in the winter. There shouldn't have been flies either – but there they were. They made me sick just to look at them. Horrible things!'

When finally the flies stopped appearing, their absence was compensated for by something equally bizarre.

Like most new parents, eager to capture each precious, never-to-be-repeated moment of their child's development, the O'Gribbens had taken countless photographs of their son. The sitting-room especially had become a showcase, with framed pictures everywhere. Erin's particular favourite showed Quentin in

Anascaul park on his birthday. She loved it so much that she had had several copies made. One medium-sized print held central position in a silver frame on the mantelshelf. A second, larger, version, hung on the wall.

Erin suspected nothing when, two days after the disappearance of the flies in the sickroom, she found the photo on the mantelpiece lying face down. She righted it without giving it much thought. Perhaps Ed had been looking at it, she told herself, and not replaced it properly.

But, inexplicably, the circumstances repeated themselves, on four more occasions.

'I asked him about it,' Erin tells us, 'but he said that he hardly ever went near the room – which was true – and I'd had no reason to doubt him. There was a TV in the sitting-room, but we rarely watched it. That would have been Ed's only reason for going in there. The room was for "visitors"; it was just the same in my mother's house.'

Both pictures became targets. Each time she entered the room she found the one on the mantelpiece lying face down, and the bigger one turned to face the wall. And each time she righted them, the following day she would find them disturbed again.

It was almost as if somebody was targeting her little son.

In October 2003, on the eve of Quentin's sixth birthday, Erin drove away from the old house on the Dingle Peninsula for the last time. She left behind the man who had masqueraded as her husband, who had vowed to love and cherish her, but whose vows had been a sham.

She shut the door on the priest who had proved to be a travesty of a priest: Father Lyons. And finally she bade adieu to her in-laws, asking God to forgive them all and praying that she would never set eyes on any one of them again. She had lived for seven years in the grip of depravity; she was determined to put as many miles as possible between the evil that was threatening her and her young son. So she chose Donegal.

She settled in a picturesque locality on the northwestern coast. Her smart, semi-detached bungalow is a world away from the decrepit farmhouse that was her home for too long. The sun is streaming through the patio doors of the living-room where we sit as she relates her story. The peach-and-white colour scheme is bright and uplifting. There is no whiff of mildew here, and it is hard to imagine the paranormal intruding on Erin's 'hideaway'.

She escaped, then: left it all behind her.

'That's what you would think,' she says with a shrug, 'but my story is far from over. When I stumbled on the horrific truth of what I had married into, all those weird happenings, the cold-ness, the foul smells, the flies, the strange noises in the house, my child's photo being upset, suddenly everything made an appalling kind of sense. You know there were times when I thought I was going mad. Little did I realize that I was the only sane one among a whole network of mad, evil people.'

It took Erin six years to come to terms with the full extent of that evil. In that time, the manifestations came and went, each one making way for a new one. In hindsight she sees that all were related, that each fresh outbreak of the paranormal should have been a warning to her.

To be sure, she had her suspicions almost from the beginning. In the five months preceding her departure, all were confirmed.

'Having Quentin and raising him almost single-handedly made me more conscious of a mother's role,' she says. 'I wanted to protect him at all costs, and it got to the point where I was not prepared to stand idly by and stay in my pretend marriage just for appearances' sake. I had a responsibility to get at the truth for my son's sake. When I began to face up to things, my world fell apart. It was just too bizarre to take in.'

Her husband's behaviour and habits ought to have alerted her, and they did, to some extent. Yet Erin made the mistake so many women do when they marry into a set of circumstances that are insufferable: she came to accept them, and grew to look upon them as normal.

It started with those evenings spent at the GAA cumann.

There were the children; always the children. Whenever Ed called Erin from the club, she would hear children in the background. Not playing football, as one would expect, but screaming and wailing. If she asked what was going on, he would say that someone had fallen down and hurt himself. The explanation did not ring true somehow; Erin had no recollection of Gaelic games inducing so many injuries.

Then there was her own child. She had indeed brought him up single-handedly. Ed took virtually no interest in Quentin; he seemed content to have merely produced an heir. He showed no tenderness towards the boy. He did not behave as Erin, in her naiveté, had expected a father to behave. She had grown to accept this as normal.

Likewise, Ed's brothers – Dan and Michael – seemed strangely reluctant to show affection for their little nephew. They brought no sweets, never spoke to him, complained when he cried. She had put this down to a lack of experience of children. This too she came to regard as normal, rural bachelor behaviour.

But one day, when Quentin was four, Erin came downstairs to hear voices coming from the 'sickroom', Mrs O'Gribben's old room. No one but herself ever went in there. She opened the door – and got the shock of her life. Quentin was sitting on the windowsill, and Dan was removing the boy's shirt.

'What the hell are you doing? Jesus Christ, what do you think you're doing?'

'Nothing.' He could not meet her eye. He stood up to leave and tried to brush past her. Quentin seemed not to be perturbed.

'I swear to God, Dan O'Gribben, if you ever so much as lay a hand on that boy again I'll report you to the police!'

A ghastly picture was taking shape. And Father Lyons seemed always to be part of that picture, whether in the foreground or behind the scenes. Right from the start he had made Erin feel uneasy. There were times when she felt that he truly resented her. She would catch him looking at her in a disconcerting way. Not sexually; more antagonistically. From time to time, he would ask her questions that she felt no priest had a right to ask. They were intrusive and made her uncomfortable.

'Everything all right on the family side of things now, Erin?' he enquired one evening in the summer of 2003. He was having a cup of tea in the kitchen, waiting while Ed was upstairs changing. The two were off to yet another 'parish meeting'.

'The family, Father? Oh, they're all grand I'd say. Mary calls now and again, but I haven't seen Michael lately. I think him and—'

'I didn't mean that, Erin. I meant the physical side of things. Between Ed and yourself.'

She was caught off guard. She reddened, unsure of what to say. She caught him looking at her queerly again.

'You know I run marriage guidance courses, so I'm well acquainted with the physical side of things,' he said without a trace of irony. 'You can always confide in me.'

Confiding in this man, who had consistently remained aloof from her, was the last thing Erin wished to do. But Ed saved the day, and her blushes, by appearing in the doorway. What happened next, however, unsettled her even further.

It was as if the men had rehearsed a scene together, she thought, or that Ed had overheard the priest discussing him. In any event he entered the kitchen and beamed at Father Lyons, ignoring her. The priest went immediately to him and clapped an arm around his shoulder. Erin half-expected them to embrace.

'You wouldn't want this good man running off with someone

else now, Erin, would you?' the priest said with a grin.

'I think that was the clincher for me,' she tells us. 'It's hard to put into words, but I think you know when a relationship is *wrong*. That night I really felt there was something very unhealthy about Ed and the priest. It was the way they looked at each other. It wasn't the sort of thing fellas who've known each other for years have. I knew by the way Father Lyons kept his arm around Ed's shoulder as they left. It was altogether too intimate for my taste.'

Erin believes it was at that moment that she put two and two together.

'All those nights they spent at the GAA and at parish meetings: how did I know if they were for real? My mind was racing that night. I went to bed and couldn't sleep. I couldn't get certain thoughts out of my head. I kept thinking of Ed, the priest, and those children. I was determined to get to the bottom of things.'

She was still awake hours later when she heard the priest's car coming round the back of the house. He was dropping Ed off, as he had done on a thousand occasions. Erin, driven mad by then with her suspicions, got up and went down the hall to Quentin's room. It overlooked the backyard. He was sleeping peacefully, as expected. Carefully she went and drew aside the curtain.

The moon was high, gibbous, its light bathing the yard. The paintwork of Father Lyons's black Mercedes gleamed. She saw the two men step out of car. Next thing she knew, they were locked in a passionate embrace.

Erin reeled back from the window in horror. She almost woke Quentin with her sobbing. She hurried back to the bedroom and bolted the door. In a few heartbreaking seconds her marriage had ended.

'What was that all about last night?' Ed demanded of the wronged wife next morning. 'Locking the door like that?'

'What, *you're* asking *me*?' She was furious. Lack of sleep seemed to have given her a courage she rarely had. She loathed confrontation with Ed. 'You're asking me about bolting the door? What were you doing with Lyons in the yard? I *saw* you.'

'Oh, that.' He said it with a shrug. His nonchalance astonished her. 'I thought you knew. Me and Frank have been lovers for years. And what of it?'

She could not believe what she was hearing.

'Sure wasn't it Frank who persuaded me to get married? Just to be on the safe side and to stop the gossip.'

So all those evening trips to the football club were just a sham. Erin tried to take it all in. She was weary. She felt on the verge of a nervous breakdown. But she pressed on; there were still some matters that needed clearing up. She was still thinking of the football club – and drawing frightening conclusions.

'My God, Ed, what have you been doing? The children . . . ?'

'What children?'

'I heard them in the background. Crying. When I phoned you at the club. What were you doing? Ed, what was going on there?'

He turned his back to her and crossed to the window. She waited. There was a part of her that wanted to run from the nightmare. But she knew that what she was experiencing was not a nightmare; it was real and it was happening to her. The only way to end it was to learn the truth.

'The truth, Ed – no matter how terrible. I have to know. You owe me and our son that at least.'

He turned back from the window, calmly took her by the arm and led her down the hallway to what was once his mother's bedroom. The foul smell had lessened over time but the coldness was as bone-chilling as ever. It was a dismal place.

'This is where it all started,' he said evenly. 'This is where I cried and screamed – just like the little brats that you heard on the phone.'

There was so much fury in his eyes, Erin feared for her own safety. 'Go on,' she managed to say. 'I'll try to understand.'

But he seemed not to want her understanding. Her patience and her attempt at empathy seemed to make him even angrier.

'Oh, you will, will you?' he roared, his face gone crimson. 'Well, here's the thing. My father raped me in here.' He pointed at the mildewed skirting-board. 'He raped me there on his dirty old bed, nearly every night from as far back as I can remember. Then when Dan and Mick and Mary came along, I got a break and he did the same to them. Then we started doing it with each other, because he liked to watch. And then—'

'Enough!' Erin screamed. 'Oh, Jesus Christ, *enough!*'

He laughed in her face. He adopted a mock female voice. '"The truth, Ed,"' he mimicked. '"The truth, no matter how terrible." Well, now you're getting the truth and you're going to hear every nasty, horrible, dirty little bit of it.'

She stood back against the wall, using it for support, as the monster that had taken the place of her husband continued his horrific confession – a confession that seemed to her to be more of a boast.

'God, I was so happy when the old bastard died,' he said. 'But I might have known it wouldn't last long. Then *she* started.'

He kicked the wall where his mother's bed had been.

'"Gentlemen friends" she called them. They came at all hours, and "had" all of us. Right here in this f***ing room. She used to wake us up and say, "Now go and be good to Mister so-an'-so. We need the money, now that Daddy's not here." So what do you expect me to do, now that I'm supposed to be a man? I take revenge, that's what I do. Because that's what men did to *me*. Those little brats you heard deserve it. As long as I'm alive I'll mess up every little bawling brat I see. I'll take—'

'Stop it, *stop it!*'

She ran from the room, to emerge into the hallway, distraught.

She heard him pull the door shut behind him.

'His anger was like this living thing that took hold of him,' Erin says. 'I could feel all the hate, going back years, all pouring out of him that day. Quentin was in the yard playing with one of his friends. They were on their summer holidays. Well, the last thing I wanted was for him to come in and see his daddy like that.'

Erin had to know about Quentin. In her mind's eye she was back in the sickroom, when the child was four, and his uncle Dan had brought him in there. She could still see his rough hands with their permanently dirty fingernails undoing the buttons on Quentin's shirt. She tried to form the question that she could not bring herself to ask. But Ed got there before her.

'No, I haven't touched Quentin, all right? Now, I've got things to do.' He strode from the house, slamming the front door behind him. Through the glass in the side panel she saw Quentin following his father's departure with curiosity.

'I think my heart was breaking at that moment,' she says.

Ed's confession gave Erin little relief. He had lied to her about everything, from the day they met. But at that moment she accepted what he said; her sanity depended on it.

Nonetheless her marriage was over. The following day she and Quentin moved out of the godforsaken old farmhouse and returned to her mother's home in Tralee. Only after a couple of months did Quentin feel confident enough to confide in his mother; his new surroundings and his caring grandmother dispelled his fear. Erin learned what she had feared the most. She becomes terribly upset when recalling this.

'You have no idea how horrible it was,' she says. 'I'd begun to guess the truth but it turns out it was worse than I'd dreamed of. They were all at it: every single one of those sick people. Ed had abused him, but so had his filthy brothers, Dan and Michael. And of course Father Lyons. I don't know how they managed it, right under my very nose! But I suppose people like that are clever. They're up to all the dirty tricks in the book.'

With her mother's help she arranged counselling for the boy in Tralee. She could not send him back to school; not in Dingle. Instead she decided she would keep him at home for a year, 'to have him under my wing; I didn't want to let him out of my sight.' She arranged for private tuition in September.

Meanwhile, she was determined that the O'Gribbens and their degenerate priest be brought to justice. She set about having them prosecuted. That proved unexpectedly difficult.

'I tried to get something done and alerted the powers that be, but I was thwarted at every turn. My letters would go missing or not get answered. I got tired of not being believed and of people thinking I was crazy.'

Then the calls started.

'They were anonymous at first, but pretty soon they began to turn nasty. They threatened that if I persisted with a prosecution I'd "be dealt with". God, even my own mother thought I was inventing things. I suppose it was inevitable that I would have a nervous breakdown. Thankfully I wasn't so bad that I had to go into hospital. I needed to be there for Quentin, so I had to keep going. I'd a good friend living here in Donegal. Linda and me met on holiday in the mid-eighties and we'd always kept in touch. Her phone calls kept me sane throughout it, and when me and Quentin came to stay with her for a while I fell in love with the place. That's when I decided to buy this house and make a clean break. I just wanted to get as far away from Kerry as was humanly possible without actually leaving the country.'

In June 2004, Erin moved into her new home. She put the past behind her as best she could. She distracted herself with interior decorating and getting Quentin settled. He seemed to be happy and even had made a friend: Little Connor from next door was a regular visitor. Linda was of tremendous help and a great boost to her self-confidence. She is an educational psychologist; as such she was a very necessary shoulder to lean on. She also introduced Erin to a whole new network of friends.

Her life was returning to normal. Quentin had never known a truly normal life and was consequently enjoying its pleasures for the first time. Anxiously, Erin watched the boy as he got through his day, quietly registering every little quirk of personality, every little deviation from 'acceptable' behaviour, every word or gesture that might signal a reaction to the abuse he had suffered. Linda told her what to look out for.

At the end of August, out of the blue, Erin got a phone call. At first, it seemed relatively innocuous: it was her solicitor in Tralee. He was working with Ed's solicitor, negotiating her divorce settlement, and was keeping her abreast of progress. But he had news as well. A month earlier, Father Francis Lyons had died in a car crash. Such a shame, the solicitor said, and so young: just forty-six. Erin feigned what she felt was the expected response.

'I remember feeling sick and angry at the same time when I put down the phone. And I remember saying over and over to myself: "God, the monster got away with it, the monster got away with it!" But, as I soon learned,' she says with a sigh, 'you might get away with things in this life but not in the next.'

The day after the upsetting phone call, a change took place.

It was as if, with the news of the priest's death, something dark and malefic was loosed. Erin's lovely home, her retreat from the bleak past, was to become the focus of an evil presence. And it would announce itself in an all-too-familiar way.

'It started with the smell again,' she says. 'When I came down the stairs the next morning to get breakfast, the strange smell from the old Dingle house was in the kitchen. It was faint, but it was there. I checked the bin, checked everywhere, but there was no telling where it was coming from. I knew it wasn't blocked drains, because these are new houses.'

Although mild at first, the stench seemed to grow stronger as each day passed. This was the first disquieting sign that something was not quite right. Linda suggested that it was perhaps a symptom of stress brought on by news of the priest's death. But when visitors to the house started to comment on it, she knew something was seriously wrong. Erin called in a plumber but he found nothing.

Soon she began to discern another odour, different from the first.

'It was like what you would get in a church. Not unpleasant; like the smell of incense and candle wax, not lighted candles, but ones that have been extinguished. The funny thing was I would only get it in Quentin's room and my own bedroom, and only at night-time.'

Erin might have left Dingle, but Dingle seemed bent on coming to her. A third manifestation arrived: the coldness. The chilling coldness that had plagued the house in Kerry started to creep into her new bungalow. It was September and still very mild outside; but inside the house it was near freezing. Sometimes she kept the radiators on all day, but to no effect. At night she piled both beds with extra blankets. It was the only way they could get to sleep.

She was reluctant to confide in anyone except Linda, not least because none of her new friends was aware of her past. She had mentioned Ed and Father Lyons and their gay relationship, but kept the unsavoury details concerning the incest and paedophilia to herself. She was careful of what she said, lest they thought she was deranged. After all, if her own family found her story simply too hard to believe, what might her new acquaintances think?

She could not run; she could not hide. She had fled and it had found her again. She felt helpless in the face of encroaching evil. Erin resolved that she would make a stand in Donegal. She was going to draw on the power of prayer.

'I knew the local priest here to see,' she says, 'but obviously I'd gone off the Catholic Church and all it represented. I hoped that prayer would work, and I made a point of praying with Quentin before he went to sleep.'

It worked. As the days passed and her prayers became more fervent, the stench and the bitter coldness began to abate. She was so relieved that she vowed to keep up her prayers. It was a matter of necessity.

The haunting of Erin, her son and her home was to progress as a discrete sequence of manifestations. First came the olfactory: the foul or intrusive smells. Next, the auditory: unaccountable sounds and disturbances. There followed prophetic dreams and daytime visions, before the haunting culminated, most frighteningly, in a combined assault on all the senses.

The manifestations could occur at any time, without warning. She remembers one particular afternoon. It was a Saturday; Quentin was off school. He was out the back, playing with little Connor from next door. Erin could keep an eye on him, or at least be assured of his whereabouts.

She had a mild headache, brought on by four loads of washing and spin-drying. She settled herself on the two-seater in the living-room, thinking that watching an episode of *Murder She Wrote* might help her to relax. Ten minutes into the programme she lost interest, lowered the sound, curled up on the sofa and closed her eyes.

After some minutes she could feel the headache easing; the lie-down was helping. She resolved to keep her eyes shut, even when she heard Quentin come in. Drowsy, she heard him slide back the glass connecting door to the living-room. He followed his usual pattern, and crossed to the sofa. Instinctively, Erin pulled up her legs to make room for him.

'That you, sweetie?' she asked, not bothering to look. 'Mummy's tired.' She stifled a yawn.

She felt the cushion yield as he sat down. The characters on television argued over the details of an LA murder as Erin tried to sleep.

After about ten minutes she heard Quentin get up and leave, go down to his room and shut the door. Unusual, she thought. Quentin never closed doors behind him – or drawers for that matter. Erin sensed that something was not as it should be. She went out into the corridor. His door was indeed shut. She thought he might not be feeling well. She knocked gently. There was no response.

'Quentin?'

It was most unlike him. She opened the door. The room was empty.

Erin stood perplexed. She decided she must indeed have nodded off. She went out to the back garden. He was nowhere to be seen.

'Quentin!' she called out loudly. 'Where are you, Quentin?'

There was no sign of him. She called again.

'He's in here with Connor, Erin.' Connor's mother was hanging out her washing. 'They're in the front room, playing. Did you want him home?'

'Thank God for that. How long's he been with you, Liz?'

'An hour, maybe more.'

Erin was stunned. It made no sense at all. At that moment Quentin appeared, excited.

'Mummy, come and see! Me and Connor built a castle.'

'Not now, sweetie. You need your tea.'

She waited until she got him indoors.

'Quentin, answer me truthfully now, okay? Did you come in here a few minutes ago when I was lying down? And go into your room?'

'No, Mummy.' He shook his head solemnly.

'Are you sure, sweetie? Mummy won't be at all cross if you did.'

Erin's heart was beating very fast; her mouth was dry.

Quentin was quiet for a time; then he said: 'It might've been the little boy maybe, Mummy.'

'What little boy?'

'I see him sometimes in the garden. But Connor can't see him. Then sometimes he's in the house and he's crying.' Quentin became earnest. 'And when I ask him why he's sad he goes away.'

'Does he run away?' Erin tried to smile to hide her mounting panic.

'No, he just goes into the wall. But he goes all blurry first.'

Erin could barely speak. She sat down heavily on the sofa and took Quentin on her knee.

'D'you know who he is, sweetie? I'll tell you who he is. He's a little angel that God sent. Now, the next time you see him, you must—'

'No, Mummy, he's not a little angel!' Quentin was adamant. 'He's got no wings.'

Erin smiled. 'That's because they're hidden under his shirt, sweetheart.'

Quentin's little face puckered with annoyance. 'No, Mummy,' he protested, 'he doesn't have any clothes on.'

Erin felt the colour drain from her face. She could not speak. She was barely aware of Quentin squirming out of her embrace and leaving her lap. He went to the shelf under the TV and took out his favourite wooden jigsaw. All angels – and devils – were instantly forgotten.

'I'll get the tea now,' she heard herself saying, and she went to the kitchen, much troubled.

That day saw the beginning in earnest of the renewed extraphysical assault on Erin. The new phase assured the return of many sleepless nights.

She began to experience unusually vivid dreams. Many were of a sexual nature; others – of diverse content – proved to be unerringly prophetic, and were all the more disturbing for that.

She dreamed of a wedding that, in the fluid way of dreams, turned into a funeral. Three weeks later her cousin's wedding echoed the dream in chilling detail: halfway through the wedding breakfast the groom's father suffered a fatal heart attack. Erin kept the dream, and its tragic mirroring in reality, to herself.

One of her more curious dreams involved a frail old priest on a beach. It resembled the beaches close to her new home, but a larger town was visible in the background. The priest was standing behind a red line he had just drawn in the sand. He carried a stick – or it might have been an old-fashioned cane, such as those wielded by teachers of another era to punish recalcitrant pupils. Repeatedly, the priest pointed at the sand with his cane.

'DON'T CROSS THE LINE!' he said, over and over.

Liz, Erin's next-door neighbour, appeared later on in the same dream.

It disturbed Erin. Priests rarely figured in her dreams. She had the nagging feeling that the old priest carried some hidden meaning, and that he was somehow linked to the recurrence of the manifestations. She could not keep it to herself. She decided to confide in Liz.

'Can you remember what he looked like?'

Erin described the priest as best she could. And the beach. She surprised herself with the amount of detail she had retained.

'It sounds like my uncle,' Liz laughed.

'How can that be? I've never met the man. How would I know what he looked like?'

'Beats me. But I'll show you a photo.'

She brought an album. Erin gasped, hardly able to believe her eyes. The old priest in the snapshot was the same man she had seen in her dream. Not only that; the picture had been taken on a beach.

'Father John Scully,' Liz said. 'I believe it was taken in Bundoran. He spent his last days in a retirement home there, run by the Augustinians. God, now let me see . . . He must be dead about fifteen years at least.'

Erin did not know what to think. This was the stuff of ghost stories. Until that day, she had never clapped eyes on Liz's family album. It seemed inconceivable, then, that an image from that album should come to vivid life in her dreams. Something was invading her senses and her subconscious mind. The implications were both profound and alarming. Liz saw her distress.

'Wouldn't pay much heed to it, Erin,' she said. 'If it makes you feel any better, I'm not surprised he was giving out to you about not crossing a line or whatever. He was a teacher in his day, and a holy terror from what I heard. Beat the life out of every child who sat in front of him. God forgive me, but I sometimes wonder how these people can call themselves men of God.'

'I know.' She wanted to say, 'Liz, you don't know the half of it,' but all at once the image of Father Scully reared up in her mind and she heard him reiterate his ominous words.

'DON'T CROSS THE LINE.'

Later, in her own home, she would mull over the possible significance of those words – and the fact that a priest had uttered them. Try as she might, she could not see how she was crossing any line. She had aborted her attempt to bring Father Lyons to justice, and his death certainly put paid to any prosecution. Nonetheless the dream must be important and have a bearing on her present circumstances; why else did it include an uncle of her next-door neighbour? It was all very puzzling.

Sleep became impossible for Erin. Like the American teenagers of Elm Street, she feared the dreams that might come, and their consequences.

'I was dreading night-time,' she says. 'I would put off going to bed for as long as I could. I knew it was stupid. I'd have to sleep eventually, and then I'd dream. I kept asking myself what I'd do if I dreamed about my own death. Or worse still, Quentin's. I was at my wit's end. Linda said I should go to see the doctor, so I did.'

She told him about the nightmares, but did not elaborate. He prescribed a short course of sleeping pills. The pills, he explained, would relax her but not prevent her dreaming. He recommended instead that she refrain from watching stimulating or violent television programmes before bedtime, and avoid alcohol late at night. Lastly, he suggested that she listen to soothing music while drifting off to sleep.

The doctor also advised a course of antidepressants. Erin declined.

'I couldn't tell him this but I knew it wasn't my mind that was being attacked,' she says. 'It was my "spiritual integrity". That's what I picked up later on. Linda called it that: my spiritual integrity. So medication wasn't going to help; I knew that. If I was really and truly honest with myself, I knew that the only thing that was going to help was an exorcism. But how do you find an exorcist in Donegal? Where do you even begin to look?'

The seeking of an exorcism was no precipitate decision on Erin's part. She had been considering it for many weeks; in fact, she had thought hard and long on exorcism at the time of the more traumatic paranormal episodes in Dingle. But she knew very little about it, beyond its lurid Hollywood portrayal. She did not even know if it were still being practised. This time, she resolved to find out.

Common sense told her to seek out the parish priest and ask his advice. But she was still nervous around priests; she had not yet set foot inside her local church. Events took a hand, however. The presence she calls her 'intruder' was to make up Erin's mind for her, and send her hurrying to the priest. It happened less than a week following her visit to the doctor.

At about 4 am she awoke to find herself pinned to the bed. Erin had always suffered from a mild claustrophobia. Her worst nightmare was finding herself a victim of an earthquake: awakening to discover that a ceiling, or an entire building, had collapsed on top of her, and the slow, agonizing death that would ensue. She could not believe that her nightmare had become real. She was being crushed by a paralyzing weight.

'God, it was awful,' she recalls with a grimace. 'I thought I was going to die. I couldn't move. And the cold was back – much worse than before. It was *so* cold in the room. I couldn't decide if it was the weight or the cold that was paralyzing me. The only part of me I could move was my head.'

There was a smell too: the same pungent odour she had experienced before. More than ever it resembled burnt candle wax.

She tried not to panic. It occurred to her that her intruder was immobilizing her for a reason, that she was being held against her will to prevent her accomplishing some action or other. She could not begin to guess what that action might be. Then she heard a child crying out, and that was explanation enough.

'It's Quentin, I thought. I was frantic. My whole body was numb. I couldn't budge. I remember screaming, and calling his name over and over. And then I called out for God to help me.'

In that instant, all changed. Time for Erin seemed suddenly to telescope itself; the normal laws of space and motion no longer applied. In the next instant, she was out in the corridor and running towards her son's room. To this day, she cannot fill the gap in her memory between being trapped on the bed and finding herself out in the corridor. There is no logical joining up; it remains a mystery for her.

But she found Quentin deep in sleep. There was nothing to suggest that his sleep had been disturbed.

Then she heard the sound again: that of a child crying. It was coming from *elsewhere* in the house. She stood still, trying not to breathe too loudly, trying to place its exact whereabouts.

The pieces of the puzzle were snapping into place. She was remembering the night in Dingle when she heard someone call her name. It was the voice of a little boy. She was remembering the little boy Quentin claimed to have seen. It was all starting to make sense – of a kind. She was remembering the wailing of children heard down the phone line. . . .

Of a sudden, the crying stopped. She returned to her own room, but remained uneasy. She was telling herself that she could not leave her son on his own. What if something were to happen to him? What if the 'intruder' were to turn his attention on Quentin? She would never forgive herself.

Erin went out into the corridor again. She was pulled up short. The sobbing had resumed. It was most definitely coming from some other part of the house, not from her son's room. The sobs of the phantom child were heart-wrenching: continuous, inconsolable, unutterably sad. As a mother, she felt moved to act, to rescue the child who was in such torment. But it was impossible to determine where the cries were coming from. One moment they would sound behind her, the next to her right or left. She would go in one direction and find that the sobbing had shifted. A line or two of a poem learned in childhood went through her head: *Little one! Oh, little one! I am searching everywhere.*

She gave it up. Her rational mind was telling her that she was chasing after ghosts. She went into Quentin's room, locked the door, and eased herself into bed beside him. He slept on, oblivious to the danger that Erin felt convinced was threatening him.

Through the locked bedroom door she continued to hear the heart-rending sobbing of the ghost child. Erin clasped Quentin to her and began to pray. Gradually, the weeping faded away, then ceased altogether.

At 8.30 am, having dropped off Quentin at school, she made an appointment to see the parish priest.

* * *

While walking the short distance to the parochial house, Erin was uneasy, for she was going against many years of unbelief. She could no longer recall when it was that doubt about God set in, but thought it must have been soon after she left school and began to make her 'way in the world' as her late father put it. Her Mass-going stopped being a weekly duty and settled down to become the Christmas and special-occasion observance of the lapsed Catholic – again to quote her father: 'hatchings, matchings and dispatchings'. Erin usually smiled at that, but not now.

And as for Quentin, she had not gone out of her way to bring him up in 'the faith'. She had always considered it to be slightly hypocritical to instil Christianity in the child when her own faith was weak, to say the least. Ed, however, had made a point of having Quentin accompany him to Mass each and every Sunday, with Father Lyons as the celebrant. They shared a pew with Ed's siblings; Quentin had assured her that he derived little from the Masses. In hindsight, this came as no surprise to Erin. Like her, Quentin had not seen the inside of a church since they fled the Dingle Peninsula.

She did not know what to expect from Father Maurice Higgins. A part of her told her that she was doing the right thing, but in her heart she had little faith in the enlisting of a priest. Faith was the key, she decided. She had lost whatever faith she had a long time before. As she looked into the well-kept gardens along the route she was taking, she wondered how many of her neighbours shared her lack of faith. She wondered how many of them paid lip-service to religious worship. God was a different matter, she thought. Erin had never lost her faith in God, her belief that the righteous would prevail, as they used to say. She asked herself how the priest would receive her.

He turned out to be a wiry man in his late sixties. He wore the tired, rheumy look of someone who had seen it all, done it all, and was not overly interested in seeing or doing much more of it. But he listened patiently, punctuating Erin's words from time to time with 'dearie, dear', tut-tutting and raising his eyes to heaven with a 'merciful God!' or a 'Lord save us!'

She could not tell him all; that much she had decided on, even before she reached the parochial house. She had asked herself what a fellow-priest would make of her husband's homosexual affair with Father Lyons. It was 2004; the wounds to the Church inflicted by the disclosure of clerical sex abuse were still very raw. On meeting the elderly priest, she decided that he was not ready for yet another scandal. It might turn him against her, and she desperately needed him on her side.

When she had finished he sat back in his armchair and said: 'Now, to be honest with you, Mrs . . . ah . . . ?'

'Ferguson.'

'Mrs Ferguson, to be honest with you, I'm not used to this kind of thing at all. All that exorcism business isn't done these days anyway. But what I could do is come and say a Mass with you and the boy, and anybody else you'd like to be there—'

'Oh no, Father; just me and Quentin. I don't want anyone to know.'

'I understand. That's all right. But I think a Mass should do it.' He got up and fetched a diary from a writing desk. 'The day after tomorrow, around eight in the evening?' He stood with his pen poised above the page.

'That would be very good, Father. I'm very grateful. Thank you so much.'

'That's all right, Mrs Ferguson. We'll do what we can and trust that it works. And if it doesn't then we'll try another way.'

Trust that it works? Erin had expected somewhat more from the priest. She knew very little about exorcism but had understood that it was the Church's most effective weapon against the paranormal. She also had been encouraged to place her trust in the extraordinary spiritual power of the Mass. The priest's words did not inspire confidence.

It seemed to her that Father Higgins was preparing her for failure.

He was as good as his word. He arrived at the appointed hour and celebrated a Mass in the living-room.

Erin was acutely aware of the effect he had on Quentin. The boy was nervous; he could not meet the priest's eye.

'I sensed what was going through his head,' she tells us. 'I'd prepared him as best I could for Father Higgins. "He's a nice old man," I told him. "He's coming to say prayers for us." I thought he'd be okay with all of it, but he wasn't. I know it was the collar that did it. As soon as he saw that, he went all nervous. I was hoping he wouldn't. It wasn't fair that Frank Lyons turned Quentin off all priests. But who could blame him?'

Father Higgins, for his part, did not seem to notice, or, if he did, paid no mind. Erin had the impression that he tolerated children but had no great affinity with them. After some minutes, however, the priest had to some extent won Quentin's confidence. It was enough for the ceremony.

It was not the first time that Erin had participated in a Mass celebrated in the home. The Station Mass, a survival from Penal times, was an important ritual in her native Kerry. She and her family had often been invited to attend such an event. It was regarded as a great privilege that the priest should grace one's home with the sacrament. Candles would be bought and the best linen brought out. The altar would be set up in the parlour with great solemnity, chairs arranged in the room. The priest would make a great show of bringing out the sacred vessels, and disposing the holy water and oil. The parlour would be thronged with the devout of the parish.

But on this occasion Erin made no such elaborate preparation, nor did she invite anybody else to participate. Father Higgins had asked her not to 'go to any trouble'. He came alone; she would assist, reading the responses from a printed sheet. The altar was simple: she used the drop-leaf table in the dining-room, draping the middle section in white linen.

The Mass progressed smoothly. At its close, Father Higgins blessed mother and son. Quentin seemed to have overcome his initial aversion to anything priestly; he had followed the ritual with great interest.

Lastly, the priest blessed the house, sprinkling holy water in each room while employing suitable prayers. Erin saw him frown when all was completed. Something was troubling him.

'I see you have no holy pictures in the house.'

'No,' said Erin, taken aback. She had never gone in much for the iconography of Catholicism, believing that her religion was a personal thing, not something to be validated through a display of imitation art.

'Oh, it's very important to have a picture or two of the Sacred Heart or the Blessed Mother herself,' Father Higgins assured her. He was stowing his consecrated objects in a small case. 'She's our protector from all harm, you know: the Virgin. He could never get near her.'

Erin did not much care for the sound of that 'he'; she did not have to ask whom the priest was referring to.

'Call into the house and I'll give you a picture,' he said, as he made ready to leave. 'Any time. I'll leave them with Peggy. That's my housekeeper, don't you know; so if you don't see my car outside, don't be put off.'

'I'll remember that, Father. Thank you very much. A cup of tea perhaps?'

'I'd love to, Mrs Ferguson, but I've another visit to do, so I'd just as soon get on. Thank you all the same.'

And he was gone. Erin hesitated for a long time at the door.

She freely admits that she expected a miracle that day, that her bungalow would be transformed, and it would feel different. In fact, it did.

'Call it imagination; I don't know,' she says. 'But there was a special feel to the place when I went back inside. Quentin seemed to feel it too, because he wasn't a bit nervous, like he was when the priest came. There was such a sort of *glow* of peace about the place.'

Best of all, the coldness that had plagued the house had retreated. That night, Erin slept better than she had in a long time. She awoke the next morning feeling refreshed and, in a sense, liberated.

The days passed. The glow of peace remained in Erin's home. Life returned to normal. Quentin seemed calmer too. Often she would watch him at play with the other children, and there was nothing about his behaviour that set him apart. On the contrary, the other boys accepted him readily. They might tease him about his 'funny' accent, but that was all. Linda looked in on them, and complimented Erin on how well both were faring.

Then the cracks began appearing in the new-found quietude. The first incident occurred ten days following the Station Mass. It was afternoon. Quentin had just come in, and gone to his room to change out of his school uniform. Erin, as usual, prepared a snack for him in the kitchen. He was taking longer then usual. She went to see what was keeping him, and found him struggling with his jumper: one arm in, one arm out.

'Here, let me,' she said, stooping to help him.

Quentin was sitting on the bed as Erin adjusted his jumper. But as she straightened, she found him looking over her shoulder, and wearing an expression she could not read.

'Mummy, who's that man behind you?' he asked. 'The man in black.'

Erin dared not look round. She could feel her scalp crawling, as if insects were moving over it. Quentin seemed unperturbed; she was beside herself with fright. There *was* someone behind her. The sense that alerts us to the presence of another in close proximity was telling her there was a third person in the room. Somebody was breathing on the back of her neck. She could feel her hair being gently disturbed with each gust of breath.

'Nonsense,' she managed to say, despite her disquietude, 'there's no one here but you and me, sweetheart.'

It was true. As she spoke, she could feel the presence behind her departing, almost as though somebody had gone out by the door, without making a sound. She could see Quentin following something with his eyes, and it horrified her. She could barely contain a scream. Her impulse was to bundle the child into her arms and get as far away from the house as possible. Instead she tousled his hair and took his hand.

'Here, come. Your tea's getting cold.'

In those few minutes, Erin's home had subtly changed. It was as though Father Higgins had never been, that no Mass had been said. She thought of the 'holy pictures' given to her by the priest's housekeeper, some of which she had placed in Quentin's very room. She asked herself why they were not doing the job the priest had promised they would. She wondered if her own luke-warm faith was not lessening their efficacy.

'I got really scared that day,' Erin confesses, 'but I prayed that it would be a one-off. Even though I had felt some kind of presence, I was willing to believe that it could just as easily have been my imagination. Children can have very colourful imaginations too, so I managed to convince myself that Father Higgins's Mass had worked, and I tried to get on with things as normal.'

But normality did not wish to come to Erin. That same evening the electricity started going haywire. Lights would dim and brighten again for no apparent reason; the power would go from

DEVILRY ON THE DINGLE PENINSULA

the fridge ten or twelve times a day; the electric shower would turn icy without warning. Often the television and Quentin's Play-Station would switch themselves off, much to his annoyance.

The erratic surges and power outages became so frequent that Erin learned to anticipate them; she knew instinctively when the lights would fail, and would go in search of candles and matches. She got an electrician in to inspect the wiring. He gave the house a clean bill of health. The wiring was new, he said; there should by rights be no disruptions. He muttered something about the 'local grid' and 'surge impedance', and left without charging her any more than his call-out fee.

The electricity was not the most ominous sign that the attacker had returned to the house in Donegal. Quentin reported seeing the strange, unclothed boy again.

'It made me go cold,' Erin says. 'I know kids sometimes have invisible friends but this wasn't like that. For me, the naked boy and the sobbing I heard that night were connected. Quentin told me he was playing with Connor in the back garden and he saw the boy come in the back door. He followed him, and found him in his room. He was kneeling beside the bed and praying. How was I going to explain to Quentin that him seeing this strange boy was somehow "normal" behaviour? That all children saw spirit children.'

A catalogue of events followed the apparition in quick succession. They left Erin in little doubt that she was dealing with the preternatural – as opposed to benign, or even neutral, forces. The foul odour and the freezing cold returned. The sobbing of the phantom child could be heard not only in the middle of the night but during the day as well. Often she would feel a presence behind her in the kitchen. And, in a ghastly echo of her experience in the old house in Dingle, something would pound loudly on her bedroom door.

She had lost faith in Father Higgins's Eucharist, but still clung onto the hope that prayers and holy pictures would keep the darkness away. That hope was to disappear when a final and terrifying manifestation intruded into her home.

'I'd just come back from shopping and unlocked the front door when I saw it. There, in front of my eyes, was a black thing. It wasn't real; it wasn't a human being. It was half shadow, half creature. It was moving at great speed down the hallway. I nearly collapsed.'

She could not remain alone in the house, yet had to be there for Quentin. She called Linda and had her come over. She vowed to say nothing about the apparition; she was convinced that her friend would not believe her. As it turned out, explanations were superfluous. The moment she opened the door, Linda recoiled in fright. She grasped Erin's arm and pulled her outside.

'Close that door quick!' she cried. She seemed near to hysteria.

'What is it? What's the matter?'

Linda could hardly speak coherently. She retreated down the path.

'Oh my God, Erin, *you* tell *me*. I just saw the most awful looking black thing on your stairs! What the hell is going on?'

In the stillness of a monastery in County Sligo, the venerable Father Ignatius McCarthy listened to Erin's story without interruption. She told him everything: about the car accident that had brought her into Ed O'Gribben's life, about his rapist of a father, the despicable mother who prostituted her own children; about Ed's incestuous siblings; about his gay lover, Father Lyons, and the paedophiliac crimes the pair engaged in. She told him of the paranormal events that had persecuted her in Dingle and followed her to Donegal. Lastly, she told him about the most frightening thing of all: the black entity that appeared to be no more substantial than a shadow.

For the first time in a long while, Erin experienced the relief that came of unburdening herself, of confiding her distress to this kindly stranger, in that silent, sanctified place, without fear of censure, or of not being taken at her word.

'I think that it's old Mrs O'Gribben, Father,' she said. 'She resented me from the beginning. And when she died . . . well, it was then that all those strange things started happening.'

'In the Dingle house, yes. But not now. I believe it's Father Lyons who's haunting you.'

'A priest?'

'Yes. But it wouldn't be the priest himself, you understand. It's whatever it was that got into him while he was alive. It still has him in its clutches, you see. And there's only one thing that will make it let go. Father Lyons needs your prayers and forgiveness, Erin. He won't leave until he gets them.'

It was the last thing she had expected. If she understood correctly, Father Ignatius was placing the burden of the manifestation on *her*. As though she had brought it all on herself. She felt anger well up inside her.

'Can you forgive him?' the priest asked.

'No, I can't. Not after all he did. To Quentin, and me.'

Father Ignatius patted her arm.

'Erin, forgiveness is a crucial part of healing. Forgiveness frees us from all those emotions Satan uses to keep us bound: hatred, unkindness, revenge, depression – all the unloving ways of being. Father Lyons did wrong; we both know that. But what he needs more than anything is the forgiveness of those he did most harm to. In this instance he needs *your* forgiveness.'

Erin found it difficult to return his steady, kindly gaze.

'I . . . I'll . . .' She was lost and did not know what to think or say.

'That's why he's come back, my dear. You must pray for his soul. Can you do that?'

'I'll do anything, Father.' Erin was weeping. 'I'll do anything you suggest – whatever it takes – to be free of this. Truly!'

'I'm glad.' Father Ignatius laid hands upon her head and prayed silently over her.

'I'll come tomorrow,' he promised, 'to offer a Mass and bless the house.'

It took Father Ignatius McCarthy more than three hours to perform his 'blessing' of Erin's home. It was a considerably more elaborate ritual than he had given her to believe, and differed greatly from that enacted by the other priest.

After offering Mass in Latin and English in the parlour, he went through the house, spending a considerable time praying in each room, and blessing it with holy water and incense. He requested that he be left alone in each of the rooms, and that all doors remained shut.

Erin has vivid memories of the sacrament. It evidently made a tremendous impression on her.

'It was an unusual Mass,' she recalls. 'After Father Ignatius had taken the communion host and sipped the wine, he raised his eyes heavenward and started praying in Latin – at least I think it was Latin. It sounded a bit strange at first, but as he went on I realized he was "talking to God" and that I was being given the privilege of witnessing something special.'

The sacrament being ended, the priest bade Erin and her son to remain where they were. He asked them to kneel for his blessing. He was going to anoint them, he said.

'It's oil, sweetheart,' Erin told Quentin. 'Father Ignatius is going to rub a little bit of oil on your forehead.'

'But I don't want to get dirty.'

The priest chuckled. 'It's not that kind of oil,' he told the child. 'It's sweet oil. It's like a sort of perfume.'

As is the case of holy water, holy oil – or chrism – a mixture of oil and balsam, is important to all Christian rites of exorcism.

Oil, when used by the faithful, is believed to negate the power of demons, their attacks, and the preternatural forces they invoke.

Father Ignatius moistened a thumb and went to Erin first. He paused, and frowned.

'I saw him looking past me,' she says. 'He was looking the same way Quentin did that day when I was helping him with his jumper. I had the distinct impression that Father Ignatius might be seeing something in the room behind me. But he never let on. I'm sure he didn't want to frighten Quentin. Or me, for that matter.'

It was growing dark when the last room in the house was purified to the satisfaction of the priest. If Erin expected a dramatic change to her home, she was disappointed. She could not help feeling that, far from helping, the Mass and the blessings had made matters worse. There was a eerie sense of foreboding about the place. Quentin must have felt it too; not in a long time had she seen him so morose.

Father Ignatius took her aside. He seemed to sense what she was feeling.

'You mustn't think that everything will be as right as rain now,' he said. 'These things take time. But be assured that from now on, those things that were afflicting you will lessen considerably. In time, they'll disappear altogether.'

'Remember what you said in the monastery, Father: that you thought it might be Father Lyons.'

'Yes, and I'm still of that opinion. That's why, when I get back to the monastery, I intend to storm heaven for the release of his soul.'

Erin would not know how many long hours of prayer lay behind that statement, and Father Ignatius, being a humble man, did not confide this to her.

'Don't forget now,' he said, as his taxi arrived, 'that prayer can work wonders. Pray for him, Erin. He needs your forgiveness and he needs the grace of God.'

'He was right about everything,' she recalls. 'When he left, there wasn't really what you'd call a great change in the atmosphere. But every day it would get better. I just knew everything would be all right. I had complete faith in Father Ignatius's power, and over the days he was proved right.

'The coldness, the foul smell, the crying, it all started to lessen. We had no more blackouts, no messing around with the electricity. Two weeks later we were totally free of all that, and our lives were back to normal.'

Father Ignatius McCarthy believes that Erin's case is a classic example of generational evil. He believes that, at some point in the family's past, an unholy thing entered the O'Gribben line, and persisted down the generations, tainting and corrupting all those born into that benighted house. It was Erin's great misfortune to unwittingly marry into such an ill-starred family.

The foul smell and the coldness coincided with the onset of her pregnancy. The house had not known a child's presence for many years, and the prospect of a child in the house again – in a place that had been the focus of so much incest in the past – was perhaps a cause for 'celebration' in the darkest realms imaginable. The old house had been the seat of repeated generational perversion. The fact that all the O'Gribben siblings of the present generation acquiesced in, and perpetuated, that perversion, meant that evil was allowed to flourish.

But, we wonder, is it not so that innocent little children have no choice in the matter?

Initially no, the priest concedes. But, by the age of seven – if not before – a child will know the difference between right and wrong. Furthermore, when a child is coerced by his abuser to keep silent about the abuse, or to deny it, he is being asked to lie, and the wickedness of the deed is thereby amplified. It is imperative that the child tells somebody about the abuse: his mother, a teacher, a neighbour, a grown-up whom he can trust.

'It would appear that in this unfortunate case, the mother – Martha – had chosen to accept the lie as well,' Father Ignatius says. 'I'm sure that in the beginning she was as appalled as any sane person could be, but then at some point she decided for the sake of security and family "unity" to keep quiet about it.'

'The Father of Lies!' he exclaims, uncharacteristically raising his voice. 'It is no accident how he came to be called such. The Devil seeks to oppose truth at every turn, and is no respecter of innocence. It is what he seeks endlessly to corrupt. Children are a prime target. The sexual abuse of children: can there be a more evil or effective way to poison humanity and destroy lives? The abused child grows up full of hate, not only for his abuser but for himself as well. In other words, he has allowed evil to enter him, and so perpetuates the whole dreadful cycle again. Ed O'Gribben is a good example.'

The priest's analysis of the O'Gribbens is hard to fault. But what of Erin? When she finally freed herself of that degenerate family, how is it that the evil pursued her and her son?

'Father Lyons died very suddenly,' the priest says. 'He'd no opportunity to repent and to mend his wicked ways. So he was still very much earthbound and attached to his earthly lusts. His soul could not be at rest, so he followed the little boy Quentin. That was all he knew. By persecuting the innocent he knew he could find some relief. Oh, he needed a great deal of prayer, a great deal.'

We are curious about the Mass, and especially if he saw anything when anointing Erin and her boy. He sidesteps the issue.

'Such things are dreadful,' he says. 'Whenever I hear of black shapes or shadows and suchlike invading a house, I'm on the alert at once, because it can only mean one thing: evil spirits are at work. I don't know what Erin or young Quentin saw before that day, but when such things make themselves visible it's a very bad sign. Let's say that, after offering the Mass, I had a clearer idea of the kind of danger Father Lyons was in.'

We wonder if the Kerry priest is at rest now.

'I expect he is,' Father Ignatius McCarthy says wistfully, then adds: 'Yes, we should always pray for the dead, especially when we believe that their immortal souls may be in danger. But even when we're convinced that a man has died in the state of grace, we should still remember him in our prayers. Every little helps.'

The bell for compline tolls and he gets up to go. There are important duties to attend to.

'Yes, every little helps,' he says again, 'and we should always pray for the dead.'

As this holy and humble man takes his leave, we understand that he is going to the chapel to do just that.

The Housewife and the Demon Dubois

N THE FACE OF IT, there is nothing magical about the ouija board. It has no powers, be they good or evil. It is simply a rectangular tablet of wood, much the same size as a Monopoly board. It has a long history, extending back to the ancient Romans, perhaps even predating Christ. Its present form emerged in the nineteenth century, and was patented by the American inventor and attorney, Elijah J Bond. Although many of the earlier boards were elaborate affairs that included angels, swastikas and signs of the zodiac, the modern variant is relatively simple. It is printed with the letters of the alphabet, the numbers 0 to 9, and the words YES, NO and GOODBYE.

The 'game' is played by two or more persons. Somebody will pose a question which the board attempts to answer. It does so with the aid of a *planchette*, literally a 'little plank'. Again, designs vary considerably, but generally speaking the *planchette* or pointer is a small triangular piece of wood or plastic that moves smoothly over the surface of the board. Often it has a 'window' of perspex, by which a letter or number is framed. Each of the players places a fingertip on the *planchette*. The board responds to a question, either by moving the pointer to YES or NO, or spelling out the answer by choosing a sequence of letters.

This is the first contentious aspect of ouija. Who – or what – is moving the *planchette*? Those who have used ouija relate with awe how the pointer moved of its own accord. Participants will swear to their fellow-players that they did nothing to influence the pointer's progress, and indeed most believe this to be the case. Ouija users often describe it as having 'a life of its own'.

Yet sceptics dismiss this. They speak of 'ideomotor' action: unconscious muscular activity by which minuscule movements are made without a person being aware that they are making them. Since it takes very little effort to set the *planchette* in motion, this theory might well be valid.

And yet, it is less important who or what moves the pointer than where the game leads, and the uses to which it is put. Some use the board to look into the future; others to make contact with the dead; still others as a means of experimentation in a spirit of fun. Ouija as board game – as innocent as a round of Pictionary or Trivial Pursuit. All might be well, were it not that dabbling with ouija seems to have had disastrous consequences for many users.

And one of Ireland's most prominent practitioners of the deliverance ministry suggests that all right-thinking people should shun it completely. He believes that ouija is a portal by which malignant forces can enter this world and cause great distress, even insanity. He recalls one of his most upsetting cases, that of a County Antrim woman whose life was turned on its head from the moment she dabbled with ouija. The 'game' was to cause her fifteen years of great distress and torment – one of the longest cases of demonic attack on record.

Julie's ordeal began on a cold and wet November afternoon in 1980, when her son Gordon came home from school in high excitement. The boy had learned of a new game. It required no board, or indeed any outlay at all. One needed only to divide up a sheet of paper and write the letters of the alphabet on the pieces, as well as numerals, and the words YES, NO and GOOD-BYE. Gordon had played it with his school pals.

They had put questions to the board, and it appeared to be able to foretell the future. It knew who would marry and when; what somebody would do on leaving school, what they would do

in later life, whom they would work for, if they would be successful in their career. It was uncanny.

His mother knew at once what he was referring to, though she
did not know ouija by that name. She had come across it from
time to time in rural Tyrone, where she grew up. The country people had called it the 'talking board'. They would play the game,
with or without an actual board, to while away a long winter's
evening. To the best of Julie's knowledge, it was simply harmless
fun. She followed her three children into the living-room, prepared the pieces of paper accordingly, and they settled down to
an evening's amusement.

The game began as solely that: an innocent diversion. Following Gordon's instructions, each of the four placed a finger atop
an upended tumbler. Somebody – Julie herself or one of the children – posed the first, formulaic, question.

'Is there anybody there?'

No one had expected the glass to respond, and so it came as a
surprise to Julie when it moved almost at once to the YES. There
was the customary reaction from the participants, each accusing
another of cheating, of sneakily moving the glass. But everyone
protested their innocence.

'Who are you?'

The second reply came as swiftly as the first, even though the
spelling out of the word took a little more time. The glass glided
about the table again.

S - E - A - M - A - N

Julie frowned. It was the last thing she had expected.

'You're doing that!' one of the younger children accused another. 'Mam, he's moving the glass.'

'Am not!'

'Children, behave.' She did not know what to make of the
strange message – if a message it was.

'What kind of seaman are you?' Gordon asked. He had the usual boy's fascination with the sea: the romance of it.

N - E - L - S - O - N

Gordon was perplexed. He was about to ask for clarification when, seemingly of its own volition, the glass progressed across the tabletop again. Five pairs of lips quietly vocalized each letter it paused at.

H - M - S   V - I - C - T - O - R - Y

And so began an eerie communication. Although the 'visitor' did not identify himself by name, he gave the family to understand that he had once been a lowly tar on board Admiral Nelson's celebrated warship. The glass sped rapidly over the dining-room table, spelling out the letters of each word communicated by the man who claimed to have lived and died centuries before. He related how he had fought in a number of sea-battles, and how he had perished at Trafalgar in 1805, when Nelson himself lost his life. And, throughout the telling, the mysterious seaman used an antique English, peppering his 'speech' with 'thee' and 'thou' and phrases such as 'It be said'.

The children were delighted. It was *Treasure Island* and Horatio Hornblower come to life.

'I remember when the ouija was telling us those things,' Julie says, 'a coal popped out onto the hearth, and we all jumped. And I thought at the time that I shouldn't be dabbling in such things. As a practising Christian I'd been brought up to believe that fortune-telling, like tarot cards and tea-leaf reading and the like, was wrong. But I didn't really believe it was dangerous.'

Nonetheless she packed away the 'game' and called it a night.

But next day it rained again, and the children – her younger son and daughter especially – persuaded their mother to repeat the game. With some reluctance, Julie cleared the dining-room table, Gordon helped distribute the pieces of paper, and they settled down to another session of fortune-telling.

Almost immediately, they made 'contact'.

J-E M-A-P-P-E-L-L-E D-U-B-O-I-S

This time it was no English seaman but a Frenchman, who went on to identify himself as Pierre. Pierre Dubois; it was the French equivalent of John Smith. An alias? No one could say. But the visitor almost immediately lapsed into simple English, full of misspellings. He had, he claimed, died at the time of the French Revolution. Without being questioned at all, the glass continued to move from letter to letter, spelling out what the newcomer wished to tell them about his life.

Julie and the children learned that he had been a blacksmith in a small town called Lessay in northern France; he communicated details of his family life, and 'spoke' of matters relating to his era. It was all very absorbing, but Julie still had her reservations. Then, without warning, the messages being transmitted via the glass began to address themselves to her alone.

'Julie,' the glass spelled out, 'I like stay here with you.'

She was shocked. Yet she plucked up the courage to ask why. The glass explained.

'I am tired wandring and need rest. . . . I was with relations in Suth Africa but not wanted there.'

Julie did not know what to make of it. And she remained sceptical, still believing that either Gordon or his young brother was moving the glass. 'Pierre' was to convince her otherwise. The glass began to spell out a most unusual message.

'Julie go in kitchen and shut window,' it read. 'Rain comes in.'

To her astonishment, she found this to be the case. The wind had blown open the kitchen window and rain was soaking part of the floor and worktop. She could not have known this; none of them could. From the dining-room it was impossible to hear or see what went on in the kitchen. . . .

Matters took on a more serious aspect at about 5 pm. Julie's husband John came home from work to find her and the children still engrossed in their game. He was a nurse attached to the ac- cident and emergency unit at the county hospital, and often did night duty. On this occasion he was working a double shift and wished to catch an hour's sleep before leaving again. He came into the dining-room, looked at the table and frowned.

'What's that you're doing?'

'Ouija, Dad,' Gordon piped up. 'It's great fun.'

'It's a load of ould nonsense,' John assured him with a wink.

'I'll get the tea,' Julie said. 'And change out of those things. You're soaking.'

But no sooner had he left the room than the glass – entirely of its own accord – began to spell out a message. It was for Julie.

'JOHN DOES NOT BELIEVE IN ME,' it read. 'BUT I WILL COME TO HIM IN NIGHT AS GHOST.'

Julie was terrified. 'Oh, please don't!' she cried. 'Go away.'

She gathered up the pieces of paper and flung them into the fire. They burst into flame at once, then browned and blackened. All, that is, except one, which fell, face down, on the hearth step. Julie bent down to pick it up. Without thinking, she turned it over – and immediately wished she had not. For it seemed that the ouija had given its response to her plea.

The paper read NO.

She was greatly shaken. 'No more of this, children. It's no fun any more. Time for homework.'

That night Julie was unable to sleep. Alone in bed, hearing the rain buffeting against the window, her thoughts kept straying to the silly 'game'. It remained for her a game; despite the enigmatic messages from Monsieur Dubois, despite his apparent ability to see through walls – and even to know her name – she was as yet unconvinced of the seriousness of ouija.

Her husband returned from the hospital in the early hours. He kissed her cheek and enquired after the children.

'I hope you stopped playing that silly game,' he said. 'That ouija nonsense. You'll be giving the kids nightmares with that spirit stuff.'

She was still a little nervous. She reflected that the children were far less afraid of the 'spirit stuff' than she was. She had looked in on them earlier and all were sleeping soundly. She tried to make light of what the mysterious Frenchman had told her.

'You're the one who should be scared, John,' she said with a grin. 'The ouija said it was going to come to you tonight as a ghost.'

Her husband chuckled, turned over on his side and was soon asleep.

Not so Julie. Her ordeal was about to begin.

She drifted into an uneasy sleep, but not for long. Half an hour later she was wide awake again. Something was wrong; a change was coming over the bedroom. Julie describes her experiencing 'a sense of dread'. She sat up, fully alert, straining her ears for the slightest untoward sound, but all was silent except for the little, trusted noises of the night: the ticking clock by the bedside, her husband's light snoring, the steady rain, a car hissing past on the road.

But she noticed something odd: an unnatural coldness was stealing over the room. The heating had been on for a good five hours, and had only just switched itself off. How could it be so cold? She shivered, ducked back under the covers and tugged them more snugly about her.

It did not help; the cold kept increasing.

She pulled the covers over her head, chiding herself for being silly, and willing herself into sleep. But the terrible dread kept gnawing at her. She tried to think pleasant thoughts, tried to ignore her thudding heart, and tried to pray. Her attempts brought little comfort; the fear continued to build. She sensed that something frightful was about to happen. She held her breath and waited, not knowing what to expect, but in the conviction that the ouija was making good its threat.

Before too long, she heard a sound: the unmistakable creak of the doorknob. The springbolt was sliding back with little clicks. She froze.

Very slowly, the door began to open.

They had no pets. Nor could it be one of the children; they never came into their parents' room without permission; even the youngest was too big for that.

Julie still had the covers over her head. An inner voice was urging her to remain so, not to look in the direction of the door.

Her fear quickened further as she heard the tread of heavy, booted feet approaching the bed. She wanted to call out to John but some alien force was willing her to silence. She felt helpless in the face of that power.

The bedclothes were no defence against what happened next. To her horror, she felt a man's body pressing down on hers. It was cold and heavy, stifling her, almost suffocating her. And still she could not cry out. She had the sensation of a face against her own, could feel the roughness of unshaven cheeks, could hear the rasp of laboured breathing. Yet she saw nothing. Later Julie would describe how loathsome and overpowering the stench was; she likened it to the odour of decay given off by a dead creature. And she could identify another smell, commingling with it: that of burning coal or soot.

Then began the assault.

'It molested me sexually,' she says frankly. 'You wouldn't believe how long it took for me to actually come out and say that to anyone . . . not even my husband. I was so ashamed.'

She tried to rouse her husband, but her arms as well as the rest of her body were frozen into immobility. Nor could she speak. Frantic thoughts were churning about in her head. When she tried to pray, the words kept slipping from her as if they were in some alien language. She had never been so frightened in her life.

She is unsure about how long she lay there, pinioned to the bed. She believes that she passed out, to regain consciousness hours later as dawn was breaking. By then, the coldness had lifted. The stench in the room was now only just perceptible. She experienced what she describes as a sensation of 'lightness', and knew at once that the unholy visitor had gone.

Only gradually did the paralysis leave her. Feeling returned first to her fingers, then her hands, then to the rest of her body. She was in a cold sweat, and utterly terrified. When John woke next to her she remembers him commenting on an odd smell in the room – 'like a campfire', he said – and concluding that someone outside must have been burning rubbish, or perhaps had 'lit their chimney'. She recalls feigning sleep, afraid that if she spoke, he might notice something that would betray what she had been through.

She heard him go downstairs to make breakfast. Next thing she knew he was waking her with a cup of tea. She managed to tell him that she was feeling unwell and needed to sleep more. He left the tea on the bedside locker.

'That's all right, love,' he said. 'I'll see to the kids and leave them to school.'

Half an hour later Julie heard them leave. She remained in bed, feeling wretched. She had ample time to consider what it was that had come to her in the night. When examined in daylight, the visit appeared as unreal as a bad dream. Perhaps that's what it was, she thought: a bad dream. She got out of bed, feeling a little better.

'I really did believe it had all been a nightmare,' she says. 'The more I thought about it, the more logical it seemed. But God, when I went to the bathroom and looked in the mirror, I nearly died of fright.'

The glass reflected all too clearly the terrible truth. On the left side of Julie's face – the side that had been in contact with the unshaven visitant – was an angry red rash. Horrified beyond words, she backed away from the mirror and fell against the bathtub. Nightmares were not supposed to intrude upon one's waking hours, and certainly not in such an utterly ghastly way.

If the County Antrim housewife thought then, in that autumn of 1980, that the experience was an isolated incident – one that would teach her a salutary lesson about the dangers of ouija – she was very much mistaken. Julie Neville was to endure many long years of the company of the creature who called himself Dubois. He would return again and again. There was no fixed pattern; his visits seemed random. Sometimes he would haunt her every night for a week; sometimes weeks – and even months – might separate his visits. But, like some infernal bad penny, he never failed to turn up.

Julie's tormentor was conforming to the nature and behaviour of the incubus – literally 'one who lies upon' – a male demon said to sexually assault women in their beds. Although the entity is generally believed to visit its victim in nightmares, there have been reports of women experiencing the assaults while in the waking state. The succubus is the female equivalent, and appears in the account contained in the chapter 'The Good Presbyterian and the Succubus'.

The entity would intrude most often while Julie was alone in her bed; but he came also while her husband slept soundly beside her. All her attempts to banish Dubois through prayer would have no lasting effect. Whenever she thought she had got rid of him, he would return with a vengeance. He gave her to understand that he was not prepared to go quietly, and, were an attempt to be made to cast him out, then Julie would have to come with him.

But that was later.

The night following the first assault, as ill luck would have it, Julie had to sleep alone; John was again at the hospital. In desperation she had pleaded with him to cancel, to get another to cover for him. She was not feeling well, she said. Anxious. He told her not to worry; Gordon was there to protect her. Besides, he had used up all his free time. He would see her the next day.

She got the children off to bed early and retired to the living-room. She intended staying up as late as possible, in order to postpone the dreaded hour. Her Methodist upbringing had impressed upon her the importance of regular Bible study and she turned to the Good Book now.

'The Lord is my shepherd; there is nothing I shall want.' She whispered to herself the ancient words of praise, willing them to bestow upon her the peace they had seldom failed to deliver in the past. 'He leadeth me in the paths of righteousness for His name's sake. Yea, though—' She stopped.

Behind her, the door was opening.

Julie gripped the Bible more tightly. She thought it might be one of the children, unable to sleep. At the same time, she wondered why she had heard no footsteps on the stair. She stood up and turned to face the doorway. She did not know what she might see.

The light in the hall was on, but there was no one there. She strove to remain calm. It opened by itself, she reasoned; the door handle was always faulty anyway. With this thought uppermost, she went and shut it, returned to the sofa and continued reading.

'Yea, though I walk through the valley of the shadow of death, I will fear no evil; for you are with—'

It happened once more.

This time she was more irritated than frightened. She strode across the room to shut the door again. But, as she did so, as her fingers gripped the handle and turned it . . . she felt the handle being grasped from the *other* side. It was turning back all by itself. The door could not be shut; a countering force was pushing it open again.

'I fear no evil; for you are with me . . . *God, please!*' Julie cried out. The opposing force was winning; she could not shut the door. Her strength was failing.

'For you are with me, *please, dear God, please!*'

The Bible fell from her hand. The door flew open, its impetus sending her reeling across the floor and sprawling into an armchair. She struggled to her feet again.

The horrid stench and the coldness were back. 'It' was in the room. The thought terrified her. 'It' could attack her anywhere. Where could she run to? It was two in the morning; the children were asleep; she could not leave the house. Nor could she go outside to await the daylight; it was unthinkable. Julie felt crushed. She climbed the stairs again to her bedroom, Bible in hand. With great deliberation, she placed it on her bedside locker.

It cannot have been easy for Julie to draw back the covers, return to bed, and face the darkness. Yet she did, and she lay there, praying and sobbing and waiting . . . simply waiting.

'I had the mad idea that if he saw me crying, he'd take pity on me and leave me alone,' she recalls. 'How innocent I was! I know now that these things feed on your fear. The longer it went on, the more fearful I became, and the worse it got.'

Through her quiet weeping Julie heard what she was dreading. The door began to ease slowly open.

One might wonder why she did not run screaming from the room at that moment, but Julie states that, with the opening of the door, a peculiar numbness crept over her, rendering movement impossible. She describes the feeling as perhaps similar to being conscious under anaesthetic; her mind was alert but her body seemed paralyzed. The entity appeared to have the power to immobilize her from a distance.

Again she was aware of the vile odour suffusing the room. She heard the dull footfalls crossing the carpet. Moments later, the crushing weight was upon her; the stubbled cheek bore down on hers. She thought she would go insane. Her ordeal began anew, and the hours dragged past. At some stage, through terror-induced exhaustion, she blacked out.

She awoke in a worse state than the previous morning. She was shattered, could barely speak. She made other arrangements for the children and went to see the family doctor. Although his practice was two streets from her home, Julie arrived there on the verge of collapse. She recalls that she had to stop twice on the way, and lean against a wall for support.

As it was, the GP confessed bafflement. He could find nothing physically wrong with her, though he was dismayed by her appearance; her two nights of terror and insomnia showed. She seemed to be teetering on the verge of a nervous breakdown.

She told him as much as she dared. To her surprise and relief, the doctor did not dismiss her story out of hand. On the contrary: he asked if she had ever had a brush with the paranormal. He wondered aloud if perhaps she might be 'acting as a medium'. She had been doing nothing of the sort – nor had she any wish to – she told him in no uncertain terms. In the end he prescribed a course of diazepam and suggested that she keep up her prayers. There was, as yet, no talk of exorcism.

Julie returned home that day, invigorated by the doctor's support and sympathy. She commenced the course of antidepressants at once. She had hoped that they would help. In fact, things grew worse.

'My life and my home were never the same after that day,' she says. 'I felt uncomfortable, especially when I was alone. I began singing French songs and the French national anthem, even though I had never learned French. Every night I'd sit up as late as possible because I was so terrified of what was going to happen. Even when I tried sleeping in another room, it would still come for me. I hinted to a few friends, like I was hearing things in the house. I asked if they believed in ghosts, that sort of thing. But I couldn't come right out and tell them . . . I just *could not* bring myself to tell anybody, not even John, about the sexual assaults, about what was really happening to me. It was a living hell.'

The months passed and the hauntings continued. Having her husband beside her at night helped somewhat. But John was no defence against the evil that lurked in the darkness of the bedroom.

'Through time I was forced to accept my suffering. There was nothing else I could do. The more I prayed, the more I was tormented. If he didn't come for me before I fell asleep, I'd wake up to find him pressing down on top of me. He was determined that I had no peace, no peace whatsoever.'

She was startled into wakefulness one night, as if from a 'falling' dream. Dubois had changed tack.

'It felt as if an invisible fist was pounding my pillow,' she says. 'I can find no better way to describe it. The pounding was so fierce that my head was bouncing off the pillow. It went on for a whole minute, maybe two. Then it stopped altogether. I was asking myself if I hadn't dreamt the whole thing. So I tried to get back to sleep again; I was really tired. But whatever it was that was hitting the pillow obviously didn't want me to sleep, because the next thing I knew the bedclothes were whisked off me – in one fell swoop – and dropped at the foot of the bed.'

It was the start of a new series of attacks. As time went by, the pounding on the pillow and the removal of the covers became such routine occurrences that they failed to unnerve her; she would simply leave the bed half-asleep and rearrange the covers.

Pierre Dubois had taken up residence in the Neville home. More odd things began to happen: occurrences that could not be explained away by logic or science. Lights would flicker for no reason; water taps would turn themselves on, then off. There were minor anomalies in her bedroom: little changes that only she would notice. She would sometimes find the items on her dressing-table mysteriously rearranged. On several occasions she discovered her perfume hidden in a corner of the wardrobe. One night she drew the curtains, went to the bathroom, and returned to find them pulled open again. The children began to complain of hearing mice in the night, but Julie was certain there were no mice in the house.

Often when she had friends and neighbours round, they could very clearly hear floorboards creaking upstairs, as though somebody was walking about. The children heard the creaking too but, as is often the case with children, they got used to it, and to the other noises and unexplained presences.

Julie urged them not to speak of those things at school or elsewhere. It was bad enough that she was subjected to the disturbances and torment; the last thing she wanted was to attract undue attention to her family and herself. People do not, as a rule, react compassionately to reports of preternatural infestation; many tend to suspect that the victim has somehow, whether by word or deed, 'brought it on herself'.

It reached the point where Julie could no longer be alone in the house during the day. The uninvited 'lodger' was no respecter of the daylight hours; he could appear at any time.

'I was faced with a choice,' she says. 'I could stay in the house and go out of my mind, or get out as often as I could.'

She decided to go to work again, and found employment as a shop assistant. It helped.

But working by day served only to postpone the nocturnal ordeal; Dubois would be there on her return. In the evening, as soon as she turned the key in the hall-door, she felt that someone or something had been waiting for her. There was the pervasive smell of burning coal, and a heaviness in the air.

Monsieur Dubois was watching her.

The years passed. The entity continued to keep its night-time appointments with Julie. It was a battle she fought practically alone. She kept it from her husband; she kept it from her children.

It is interesting to observe how quickly the abnormal can become a commonplace in a person's life when paranormal activity takes hold. It seems that, as was the case with Julie, and in the absence of rational explanations or solutions, the beleaguered person is forced to accept this unorthodox situation, and somehow learns to live with it.

'I know how strange that might seem to a lot of people,' she says. 'But, you see, I was prepared to put up with it because there seemed to be nothing else I *could* do. In the course of time I saw a pattern to it. Whenever I prayed really hard to be rid of Dubois, things would get worse and he'd attack me even more – try to suffocate me, or worse. Those times I didn't pray, I found that he'd be just a presence in the house. I'd hear him walking around upstairs, or sense him standing in the corner of the bedroom or on the landing.'

Julie was coming to a better understanding of the entity's motives, what Dubois was trying to do to her. He was attacking her very faith.

'I know now what his plan was. That I'd give up my religion and go over to him. It took me a while to see this, even though all the clues were there. For long periods I stopped going to Sunday worship, and saying prayers at all, simply to get some peace. Now I know that that's how demonic oppression works. By getting me to give up on God, the demon was priming me for something far more horrific, but I couldn't have known that at the time.'

Julie's 'more horrific' development occurred at the beginning of 1992. The manner of the haunting shifted dramatically. The experience left her with the conviction that Pierre Dubois was intent on much more than molesting her at night. He wished to possess her – body and soul.

A single incident was enough to convince her of this. One night she awoke to the familiar pattern of oppression: the paralyzing weight, the obnoxious smell, the stubbled cheek. But this time there was an additional torment. A hand was tightening about her throat; she could barely breathe. Dubois was attempting to throttle her. Her battle with the entity had become a fight for survival.

Unable to move her limbs, she sought in desperation for sacred words that might thwart the demon. At last she remembered the prayer a Catholic friend had instructed her to say if she ever felt threatened.

The words came to her, but the pressure on her throat was so great that she could hardly give voice to them.

'In . . . the name . . . of . . . of Jesus . . . *Christ!*' The pressure lessened. 'Get out of my life!'

Sure enough, the exhortation proved to be very effective. Julie felt the fingers relinquish their stranglehold. She was free.

She gave thanks to God, convinced as she was that her speaking the name of Christ had saved her. At the same time, she knew from bitter experience that Dubois would not take her victory lightly. Sooner or later he would seek vengeance.

He did so within the hour – just when she thought the coast was clear, and was drifting into sleep again.

This time there were no footsteps, but a low 'zooming noise', as Julie puts it; one that grew as it approached the bed. She remembers sitting up to investigate, only to be pushed back down again by a hand pressing against her chest. She was attacked again, not throttled as before, but by increased pressure of the crushing weight upon her body. So great was the pressure that she was certain that the entity was trying to crush the life out of her.

The housewife had never been willing to fully face the true nature of the creature that called itself Pierre Dubois. A part of her had been willing to accept the lie it fed her: the story of the Frenchman and his concocted history, the ruse by which a malevolent force had inveigled its way into her home. Now she felt certain that 'Dubois' had never walked the earth as a human being, never been a blacksmith, never drawn breath. He – *it* – was a demon. And now it wanted her dead, so that it could drag her off to whatever dark region it inhabited.

She summoned the strength to resist as best she could, willing her arms to move and to push the vile thing away from her.

'I'd never really feared death, but I did then,' Julie says. 'The terror of that, the fear, is impossible to put into words. I was fighting not only for my life but my soul as well. I was convinced that if I died I'd be brought face to face with that thing that had tormented me for so many years. I'd be lost for ever.'

She pleaded with her Maker.

'Dear Lord, don't let me die,' she implored. 'I don't want to see its face. Please, Lord, please!' Anything was preferable to that. Julie uttered one final, desperate, entreaty.

'In the name of *Jesus Christ*,' she cried out once more, as loudly as she could, '*get out of my life!*'

Again, the weight lifted from her, and again she braced herself for the counter-attack.

Strangely enough, it did not come. She switched on the bedside lamp and sat up, gasping for breath.

'I dearly wish I had not put that light on,' she says. 'But by then it was too late.'

A shadow was rearing up at the foot of the bed. Julie describes it as 'a blob, like a smoking black cloud, not the shape of a person;

just a thing, but a terrible thing. The absolute evil that came from it was overwhelming. I was so gripped with terror, I could not move and I knew that if it came towards me I'd be swallowed up . . . destroyed, and that would be the end of me.

'Imagine what it feels like to know that you're going to be killed and the person torturing you is deliberately making you suffer beforehand. That's how it was. I felt a level of fear that is beyond words. I implored the Lord to keep it away from me and, thank God, it stayed where it was. Then I heard the voice.'

For the first time ever, her tormentor actually *spoke* to her. There was no French accent but plain English, as though the entity realized that the game was up; as though it knew that it no longer could hide behind the deception that it was the spirit of Pierre Dubois, once a living human being.

The male voice was hoarse, stertorous, angry almost.

'Be quiet!' it commanded. 'Go to sleep.'

Julie did exactly that. She was instantly asleep – chilling testimony to the control the demon had over her. When she awoke the next morning, however, it was with the possibility, and the hope, that the end of her long ordeal might well be in sight. She felt ready to finally speak of her torment to someone else.

She threw caution to the winds. She was past caring that the demon would exact vengeance if it thought it were threatened. She confided in the most devout believer of the family: her sister. Margaret advised her to see a minister at once. She persuaded her that an exorcism, carried out in the home, was her only recourse. Before Julie left, Margaret gave her a framed picture of Jesus with the inscription: CHRIST IS THE HEAD OF THIS HOUSE, THE UNSEEN GUEST AT EVERY MEAL, THE SILENT LISTENER TO EVERY CONVERSATION. Julie hung it in her bedroom.

Having shared her burden with her sister, she felt some relief. She still could not confide in her husband but hoped that soon her troubles would be at an end. Margaret was eager to help her to find a suitable clergyman. There were bound to be many, she said, who were proficient in the deliverance ministry.

'I was very much mistaken,' Julie says. 'I went first to my own minister. He told me he'd never done an exorcism, but he gave me the name of another man. I went to him, only to be told the same thing. I must have gone to five or six, and none of them felt able to help me. I really think when they heard what I'd come through, they were too afraid to even visit my home. Honestly, I was really beginning to despair.'

During her search for a suitable exorcist, the siege of her home continued. The incursions could assume a variety of forms.

'There was one night in particular,' Julie recalls. 'I was on my own in bed again, and some sort of loud noise woke me up. I was only half-awake, wondering what the noise was. I don't know why but I thought it might have been a dog barking. I waited for it to bark again. But we had no dog; nor did the neighbours on either side. I told myself that I'd imagined it, closed my eyes and tried to get back to sleep. Then I heard the sound again: the one that woke me up.'

She knew at once that it was no dog, or indeed any earthly creature. Julie remembers it still with a bone-chilling clarity, and dearly wishes that she could forget it; forget both the sound and the malignancy that pervaded the bedroom when it had died away.

'It was a man's laugh,' she explains, 'a horrible, mocking, evil laugh. It filled the room, but it was inside my head at the same time. I remember putting my hands over my ears to try and block it out, but that didn't stop it. I couldn't get out of the bed, I was just powerless to escape it.'

In the dim light from the street she saw, on the far wall, the picture of Christ given to her by her sister. It was hard to make out the features, but Julie had contemplated it so often while at prayer that she could call it unerringly to mind.

'I started to pray out loud to the image of Jesus,' she says. 'But Dubois was not amused.'

The entity vented its fury in yet another demonstration of its power. As Julie concentrated on the face of Jesus, unseen hands gripped the picture, lifted it from the wall, and smashed it to pieces on the floor.

We have seen that, throughout the many years of her ordeal, Julie Neville had somehow managed to keep her children in the dark with regard to the demon Dubois. They were aware of *something* of course – the noises, and the taps turning themselves on and off were hard to ignore – but the two boys and their sister were never privy to what went on in their mother's room when she was alone.

'I could put up with the torture so long as it didn't go near the children,' she says. 'I knew deep down that I should never have allowed Gordon to play with the ouija in the first place. And as a mother I had to take responsibility for my son's mistake. I was paying the price, but I promised myself that if it ever *did* attack one of them, I'd have to take action at once.'

Eventually, what she feared most came to pass. In the summer of 1994, John and Julie went on holiday with the younger children, leaving Gordon in charge of things.

He was looking forward to the freedom of the house and having his friends round. He was ill prepared for the phenomena he was to experience.

Gordon, now in his thirties, recalls that harrowing time.

'The first night wasn't so bad. I did feel kind of uneasy. I remember it being very cold, especially on the landing and in my bedroom, and turning up the heating. But I thought it was just me, being on my own in the empty house for the first time. On the second night I made the big mistake of sleeping in my parents' bedroom. I thought it would be more comfortable. Well, "sleeping" actually isn't the right word, because I didn't get any sleep.'

It started – as such phenomena often do – with an apparent accident, a fairly trivial occurrence as far as Gordon was concerned. A little wooden cross fell to the floor.

It had hung on the far wall, in the place left vacant by the picture of Christ, the one Dubois had destroyed. Gordon had not known of its existence. He would, in any case, have considered it to be no more than an item of idolatry; he was not a believer.

His mother had compensated for its loss with the cross, found when clearing out the attic. Gordon had his back to it when it fell. It made only the dullest of *thucks* as it struck the carpet. He turned, bemused, but by no means alarmed. Perhaps he should have been.

'The strange thing was,' he says, 'that when I went to hang it back up again, I discovered that it couldn't have just fallen unaided, because the nail that held it was still in the wall and the loop of cord on the cross wasn't broken.'

Gordon got into bed.

'The cross shook me up a bit,' he says. 'But I told myself I was just being silly, and after a while I dozed off.'

Not for long, though.

'I woke up because I heard this creaking sound coming from the wall on the left. My mother had a wardrobe on that side of the room: a big, heavy thing stuffed with her clothes and shoes and things. And there would have been a gap of about four feet between it and the bed. Anyway, I sat up to see what was going on and I just couldn't believe my eyes.'

The heavy wardrobe appeared to be growing in size, its dark bulk rising towards the ceiling. Gordon, still drowsy with sleep, blinked to focus his eyes. Bafflingly, the wardrobe continued to grow. It was filling his vision. It was making noises too; they sounded for all the world like a great beast groaning in pain. And all at once he knew the truth. The wardrobe was not growing. It was toppling slowly forward, its triangular pediment seemingly set on a collision course with Gordon, *as if somebody was pushing from behind*. The groaning changed to a deep bass sigh as the wardrobe's feet gave way beneath the weight.

Gordon sprang from the bed. The wardrobe crashed down.

'I tell you, I never moved so fast in my life,' he says with a shiver. 'That thing was so heavy I thought it had crushed the bed itself. Later on, when I discovered what my mother had been going through for so long, I really freaked, because I realized that Dubois didn't like the fact that I had taken over her bed and was actually trying to kill me.'

Gordon spent the rest of the week at a friend's house.

When Julie learned of her son's experience, she knew that she could no longer keep her secret from the family. If the demon could attack Gordon, then why not his brother and sister? She was greatly afraid for them. She called the family together and revealed all, for the sake of the children omitting only the most disturbing details. Dubois had occasioned enough sleepless nights in the Neville household.

John Neville was shocked and horrified; throughout the long years of his wife's ordeal he had remained blissfully unaware of the demonic presence in his very bedroom. To be sure, he had suspected that all was not as it should have been, but had attributed Julie's troubles to depression. He was determined that she suffer no longer. He joined her in the search for a churchman who could put an end to her misery.

One man's name kept coming to the fore: that of Charles Cartwright, the rector of the church of St Timothy in the coastal town of Newcastle. Those whom the couple spoke to were loud in their praise of this man's qualities. Their search seemed to have borne fruit. It was February 1995.

Finding the exorcist had proved easy; getting hold of him

was another matter. Julie believes that shadowy forces were at work to thwart her, that Dubois was determined that the exorcist would not cross his path.

'I tried the rector's number every day for a week,' she says, 'but the phone just kept ringing unanswered. I checked with the operator, and I did have the correct number. But each time, it would ring out. The rector told me later that his phone hadn't been ringing at all at the times I said. He told me that that was a common feature in his experience. The evil spirit knowing it's about to be cast out will do everything to stop it happening.'

Reverend Charles Cartwright proved to be a gentle, soft-spoken man who received Julie with great compassion and understanding, putting her immediately at her ease. He arranged to visit her home the following evening – and perform a deliverance. There would be no preamble, no more time-wasting; she had suffered enough and for far too long.

'I thought I'd feel great relief when I heard that,' she says, 'but instead I remember this feeling of absolute dread coming over me.'

The rector appeared to read her thoughts. 'Don't worry,' he said, 'your troubles will soon be over. Have faith. But yes, it most likely *will* step up its activities now that plans are afoot to cast it out.'

Those words proved chillingly correct. On returning home, Julie was assailed by a terrible atmosphere in the house. The foul odour that had become synonymous with Dubois' presence was overpowering. The demon was indeed mustering its forces for the coming battle.

She threw open all the windows and started to clean the house, but the unpleasant smell persisted. Nevertheless, fortified by the rector's words, she determined that she would not be driven out of her home in broad daylight. When she had finished dusting, however, the stench was so overpowering that it made her sick. She rushed outside and retched. It took courage to return indoors. The last chore was the hoovering.

But Dubois held a card or two in reserve, and was about to play one. Julie suddenly recalled the old dictum, *Cleanliness is next to godliness*, and all at once she thought to divine its deeper meaning. Dubois was about to show her its opposite. Before she could finish, the note of the vacuum cleaner changed eerily.

'It began to groan and squeal,' she recalls, 'like a trapped animal. It was horrible. I had no choice but to turn it off. When the kids came home from school, I phoned John at the hospital to tell him we'd all be staying with Margaret that night. No way was I going to risk it.'

At 8 pm the following evening, Reverend Charles Cartwright arrived at the Neville home, accompanied by two assistants. He remembers the expulsion of the demon that called itself Pierre Dubois as a trying affair.

'Having lived in Julie's house and oppressed her for so long, it felt it had the right to stay put. Always difficult,' he says now, looking back.

We are having tea in the front room of his Newcastle home. The jovial, seventy-four-year-old exorcist is the antithesis of the doleful demon-hunter that Hollywood would have us believe is the norm. His spirited demeanour and optimism belie years of having fought and routed the darkest of foes.

'When these things manifest themselves,' he continues, 'they should be stamped out as soon as possible. The longer a person waits, the more entrenched the malignancy, and then the harder it is to shift.'

The rector describes his encounter, beginning from the moment he arrived at the Neville house in Ballymena. As soon as he entered, the oppressive presence was almost palpable.

'It was worse than I thought,' he says. 'There was a very peculiar atmosphere in the house. I suppose I would describe it as "hostile". The smell of burning and the coldness were very strong, especially on the stairs and in Julie's bedroom. But one's faith never wavers in a situation like that. The power of the Lord is always present.'

Julie, her husband and Gordon gathered in the living-room for the ceremony. Brief introductions were made. It could begin.

Charles Cartwright donned his surplice and laid out on a table the sacred objects for the celebration of the Eucharist: a simple cross on a stand, the communion paten, a chalice, two candles in silver holders and a bottle of holy water.

'I hear the private confession of those who live in the house,' the rector explains, 'before the service begins. This is a very important part of the ritual. If anyone refuses – and most especially the person who is being oppressed – it generally means that they have something to hide, and in all likelihood the exorcism will not be successful. In my experience, a severely demonized person will find the act of repentance very difficult, if not intolerable, and from their behaviour you very quickly come to realize you're dealing with the exorcism of an individual, as opposed to a home.'

'Thankfully, that was not the case with Julie,' he continues. 'She had been oppressed by that demon and suffered it so long that she was more than eager to be rid of it. She willingly rejected all associations with ouija and the occult, and recommitted her life to the Lord.'

Once Julie had formally, and in the presence of witnesses, rededicated herself to Jesus, Reverend Charles was ready for the service of the Eucharist.

The group arranged themselves on a row of chairs facing a makeshift altar. The assistants sat on either side of Julie, with John and Gordon flanking them. The rector extended his hands over the Holy Book, and read from Luke's Gospel.

'The seventy returned again with joy, saying, "Lord, even the demons are subject to us in your name." And he said to them, "I saw Satan fall like lightning from heaven. Behold, I have given you authority to trample on serpents and scorpions, and over all the power of the enemy; and nothing shall hurt you."'

The rector joined his hands and bowed his head in silent prayer. The participants did likewise.

It had been raining steadily for most of that winter afternoon. Now the wind was up. It could be heard whistling and sighing at the window. Julie was reminded of a similar winter's evening all those years ago; an evening when a much happier but gullible young woman had placed her finger on a glass and allowed something unclean to intrude upon her life. She shivered at the memory, and at what might lie ahead. Would the demon Dubois put up a fight, make her suffer further? Or would this kind man of God be able to drive the horror from her life for good?

Charles Cartwright blessed the bread and wine, and distributed them amongst the participants.

The Eucharist is an intrinsic part of an exorcism, the rector explains. Every Eucharist is a proclamation of the death and resurrection of Jesus. It therefore celebrates His absolute, complete and total victory over Satan.

He returned to the altar and, extending his hands over the Holy Book, gazed heavenward.

'Strengthened and refreshed by the Body and Blood of Christ, we are now ready to exercise the authority and power of Jesus Christ against whatever evil is disturbing this place.'

The wind blew more fiercely at the window. It seemed to shriek and howl like a demented animal. Julie was reminded of the groaning sounds she heard coming from the vacuum cleaner the day before.

'But, strangely enough, when I heard it I wasn't afraid,' she recalls. 'I knew that God was in the room and I felt totally safe.'

'We rejoice in your great love,' the rector's voice rang out with confidence, 'and in the victory of your son Jesus Christ over sin, death and hell. We pray you send angels to gather to this place any spirits that may have been active here.'

Overhead the light bulb flickered, then dimmed. John kept his head bowed, too afraid to look up. Gordon, on seeing his father's response, likewise buried his face in his hands. Of the three, Julie was the one who remained calm. She sat with her hands folded in her lap, gazing serenely at the cross upon the altar.

'Spirit, I address you now in the name and with the authority of Jesus Christ,' Reverend Charles continued undeterred. 'I have power to bind you and power to release you. I—'

The light went out. The room was in darkness, save for the candles on the altar.

'I command you to go immediately to the place that Jesus has—'

Slowly, the door was opening. Gordon and John looked wildly about the room. On seeing that the others did not share their consternation, they bowed their heads again, a little embarrassed.

Reverend Charles waited. One of the assistants went and shut the door.

'I command you to go immediately to the place that Jesus has appointed for you!'

The wind stepped up its howling. The window blew open. Strangely enough, the candles did not die. Again, the assistant rose; he secured the sash.

'You will go and you will not return to this place again for ever. The angels appointed by God will take you to your own place and there you will remain.'

The exorcist paused and bowed his head again. As he did so, the wailing at the window began to subside. The presence was departing. He spread his hands and gazed upward.

'Father, we thank you that this spirit is now leaving and going to where you want it to be.'

The light in the room flickered into life again. John and Gordon looked up with relief. They seemed no longer afraid.

'We ask you to cleanse this house from all defilement, that it may become, for those who dwell here, a house of peace.'

The rector sprinkled holy water at different points in the room. His voice was gentle, no longer that of the scourge of demons.

'Send your angels to guard this house and protect those who dwell here. Unite them in love and draw them to yourself so that they may rejoice in you as their Saviour and Lord for ever.'

Even before Reverend Charles Cartwright had ceased praying, the atmosphere in the room was changing. An air of dread and danger was giving way to peace.

The service ended with the Lord's Prayer and prayers of thanksgiving. Afterwards, the rector requested that the others remain kneeling while he and Julie went from room to room, and he blessed the house.

Holy water is important to every exorcism. It is symbolic of baptism and the three benefits Jesus promises through its use: forgiveness of sins, defence against the wickedness of Satan, and the gift of divine protection.

'There was a strange thing when the Reverend was blessing the kitchen,' Julie recalls. 'We discovered that the window above the sink was open. I was really uneasy when I saw it because I knew for certain I'd locked it. It was the same window that blew open all those years ago when me and the children were messing with the ouija, and Dubois told me to go and close it.'

So what was the rector's reaction?

Julie smiles. 'When I saw it I nearly jumped out of my skin, but he didn't even flinch. He just smiled and went and closed it again, and said something that really made me laugh: "Well, that's the end of *him*, Julie. Pierre Dubois has left the building."'

At a little after ten that evening, the exorcist and his assistants took their leave. All were conscious of a prolonged battle having ended, an evil firmly routed.

It was over.

The demon – the entity that complained of being tired of wandering, and was in need of rest; the entity that had been to South Africa and was not wanted there; that had come to a town in County Antrim, and for fifteen years held to ransom the life of a vulnerable, God-fearing woman – that terrible entity had finally departed.

One wonders where it afterwards went, if it had indeed obeyed the command of the exorcist and returned to its 'own place'. Or if, once loose again, it felt free to roam. If perhaps, at some later date, another poor unsuspecting individual, whether by chance or design, placed a *planchette* on a ouija board – or a finger on an upturned glass – and in so doing gave refuge to the demon that called itself Dubois.

The Temptation
of Father Fintan

FINTAN DONNELLY'S TRIALS began even before he took Holy Orders. It was June 1976 and he was twenty-three. He had joined a number of young men, all of whom had received a calling to the priesthood, all of whom were in the final days of their transitional diaconate. There were ten in his group. That year a total of seventy-three ordinations of Roman Catholic priests took place in the island of Ireland.

This is in strong contrast with recent years. In 1965, a decade before Father Fintan's ordination, 282 young men became diocesan priests, and the religious orders received a further 377. This was a watershed; throughout the later decades of the twentieth century, vocations continued to plummet. Various theories are offered to account for this: the Church scandals of the time, in particular the seam of clerical paedophilia that came to light. Others point to a deepening secularization of Irish society. Whatever the reason, the present situation shows little sign of improvement. At the time of this book's going to press, St Patrick's College in Maynooth, the sole surviving seminary, had produced only eight ordinations.

Fintan and his fellow-seminarians were sent on a week-long retreat to the Rosminian monastery in Glencomeragh, County Tipperary. It was a tranquil place, with fine gardens and secluded walks, perfect for a young man to be alone with his thoughts – alone save for God, whom he would shortly vow to serve. He was among the chosen who conformed to the Church's requirements that they 'have integral faith, are moved by the right intention, have the requisite knowledge, possess a good reputation, and are endowed with integral morals and proven virtues and the other physical and psychic qualities in keeping with the order to be received.'

The retreat was presided over by one of the Rosminian Fathers, a man who had spent much of his time abroad in the capacity of missionary. In light of what Fintan Donnelly was to experience in that otherwise idyllic place, it was appropriate that he could confide in this much-travelled priest who had seen many wonders and encountered a multitude of strange beliefs.

It was Wednesday, and Fintan was to be ordained that coming Sunday. He was elated; the sacrament would be the culmination of perhaps twenty years of anticipation; his boyhood dream was about to become a reality. That night he was unable to sleep, and at about three in the morning decided to steal into the chapel to gather his thoughts. He would not have far to go; the monastic community of Glencomeragh occupied an old mansion left to the order by a member of the landed gentry. The chapel had once been the ballroom and had retained the tall French windows through which the guests of old would have exited, to catch their breath on the lawns during the nights of the summer dances.

It lay a short distance from the dormitory, down one flight of stairs. Fintan Donnelly left his bed while the others were sleeping, and minutes later was seated in a pew close to the little altar. The chapel was hushed and lit only by a handful of night-lights glowing redly in their glass holders. Beyond the tall windows, the mountains of Tipperary were visible in the quickening pre-dawn light. Nearer at hand the trees that enclosed the grounds were dark and brooding, as if in expectation.

No sooner was Fintan lost in the serene atmosphere of the place, however, than he heard the soft click of the door being opened. He smiled to himself, imagining that another young would-be priest was experiencing his own excitement at the approaching ordination. He remained with his eyes fixed on the

THE TEMPTATION OF FATHER FINTAN

image of the crucified Christ behind the altar, and did not turn round. He heard footsteps approach; the visitor stopped and slipped into the pew immediately behind his. It briefly crossed Fintan's mind that it was odd, what with an all-but-empty chapel, that the newcomer should choose to occupy that particular pew.

He is not certain as to when he noticed the change coming over him, but thinks that some minutes had passed. It started as a coldness creeping into his heels. The oratory had been cool upon his entering it, but by no means cold. There was nothing that could explain the iciness that he felt engulfing his feet. It moved up his calves, then to his knees, until he felt a chill all the way to his head. It was at this point that the voice spoke.

Fintan did not experience the words as emanating from an external source; they seemed to come from inside his own skull. Nor was the voice threatening in any way. It was a perfectly ordinary voice, not raised, but calm and gentle. It spoke to him.

'What are you playing at?'

He found himself answering the voice. Looking back on that night, he recollects no panic on his part, no shock that a disembodied voice should begin speaking to him.

'What do you mean?' he enquired of the presence.

'You're praying.'

'Yes, of course I'm praying.'

'But there isn't any God,' the voice said. 'Don't you know that God doesn't exist? What are you praying to? You're praying to a wall.'

'I don't believe that,' Fintan said, vexed that his prayers were being interrupted. 'I believe there is a God.'

'But you're praying to that metal box.' The seminarian knew that the voice was alluding to the tabernacle. 'There's nothing in that. Nothing, nada, nihil. De nihilo nihil, in nihilum nil posse reverti. That's your God for you, Fintan. A great big nothing. You've been conned.'

There was a pause. The cold seemed to be increasing.

'DO YOU REMEMBER THE TWENTY-EIGHTH OF JUNE IN NINE-TEEN SEVENTY-THREE?' the voice asked presently.

'No.'

'DO YOU NOT REMEMBER WHAT YOU DID THAT NIGHT? DO YOU NOT REMEMBER THAT YOU COMMITTED AN INDECENT ACT, A MORTAL SIN YOU MIGHT SAY?'

'What do you mean?'

But he recalled all too well. He recalled that he had had a very brief sexual encounter on the night in question. It had been relatively harmless, little more than a fumble in the dark, yet it was enough to send the young, would-be priest hurrying to the confessional at six o'clock the following morning.

Now the voice, the presence, led Fintan Donnelly through each and every detail of the encounter. He listened glumly and meekly, ears burning.

'ALL THIS IS GOING TO BE DISCOVERED BEFORE SUNDAY,' the voice told him. 'YOU WON'T BE ORDAINED AND YOU'RE GOING TO BE DISGRACED. SO MY ADVICE TO YOU NOW IS TO GET OUT WHILE THE GOING IS GOOD, AND THIS WILL NEVER COME OUT ABOUT YOU. *MELIUS EST PRAEVENIRE QUAM PRAEVENIRI.*'

Fintan was in a cold sweat by then, whether through fear of being found out or fear of the 'presence' – for by then he was in no doubt at all what he was dealing with, and the nature of the voice.

In his six years in the seminary he had never once heard the Devil being mentioned by name. On reflection, thirty years later, he considers this a very curious omission on the part of the theologians who had informed his religious education.

'There are ten references to the Devil, or Satan, in the Catholic Catechism,' Father Fintan notes. 'But we never talked about him. It was as if he belonged to the Dark Ages.'

He cites one particular Catechism passage. It cautions that

evil is not an abstraction, but refers to a person, Satan, the Evil One, the angel who opposes God. The Devil (*dia-bolos*) is the one who 'throws himself across' God's plan and His work of salvation accomplished in Christ.

Once Fintan Donnelly had drawn the conclusion that the voice was that of Satan, he knew in his heart what he must do: pray. He would kneel down in the pew and pray. But he found that he could not. The cold had stiffened his joints, incapacitating him. He could barely even move his hands. Panic gripped him; yet he told himself that prayer could be said anywhere, in any position, whether kneeling or seated. Remaining upright in the pew, he began to recite the Lord's Prayer.

'It was amazing the effect it had,' Father Donnelly recalls. 'I must have said those words a million times. I mean, I'd been reciting the Our Father since I was a boy, for as long as I can remember. But I'd been saying it by rote, like a sort of Christian mantra. I'd never grasped the fullness of its meaning. I did then. When I reached the entreaty, "deliver us from evil", I said it with more conviction than I'd ever felt in my life.'

With the intoning of the first prayer, Fintan could sense the presence beginning to relinquish its hold over him. He continued, saying another Our Father, concentrating even more on the import of the words.

'I could feel the cold ebbing away from my muscles and joints,' he says. 'By the time I'd begun my third prayer, I sensed the presence was weaker. But it was still there.'

Slowly, very slowly, he turned in his seat.

'I don't know what I was expecting to see. I was shaking. But there was nothing, no one. I had the chapel to myself.'

He stumbled from the pew, his stiff legs threatening to buckle under him. Without pausing to genuflect, he fled down the aisle, the circulation returning to his limbs more strongly with every frantic step. On exiting, Fintan did not return the way he had come, but hurried to an outer door of the monastery. He flung it open and rushed out into the dawn, gulping great mouthfuls of air as he went.

The lawns, the trees, the mountains beyond, were all in place, as serene and beautiful as they ever were. The only change that had taken place was that within himself.

Father Fintan Donnelly had learned two important lessons on that Wednesday morning, four days before he was to become a priest and go forth to do Christ's work. One: he had discovered that the House of God offers no deterrent to evil; that the Devil may come and go at will, and no consecrated walls will stop him; that he is no respecter of altars and tabernacles. This startling revelation had a profound effect on the young man, as it would on most Christians. Works of fiction, books and films, have created and nurtured the false beliefs that religious symbols of themselves have the power to ward off evil, that churches are no-go areas for the demonic, that evil will shrivel up and vanish when confronted by the image of Christ crucified, that holy water will burn the flesh of the possessed. They are all superstitions; artefacts have no such powers. However, when those artefacts are used in conjunction with prayer and faith, they become powerful weapons in the battle against evil. So saith the exorcist. This was the second lesson that Father Fintan learned early that morning.

He was to call upon the power of prayer soon again – much sooner than he expected. It came about when he responded to an urgent summons from a convent in County Kilkenny. One of the nuns, Sister Jude, a family friend of the Donnellys, had a strange story to tell. It concerned a little rural parish, and Fintan learned that all was not well with the parish priest. The nun was vague on the details; she did not wish to be drawn.

'It's not the sort of thing you can talk about over the phone,' she said.

'Well, what *can* you tell me?'

'Only that we feel that Father Colum shouldn't be by himself at this time, Fintan. He needs another priest with him.'

'Are there no priests in the area?'

'There are of course. But what's needed is somebody who can move in for a week or two, and do his services for him.' She paused, and he knew she was covering the mouthpiece, consulting with another. 'You'd be doing us all a great turn,' she said presently.

'Give me a clue,' Fintan said. 'What's wrong with the parish priest?'

He learned that the priest, Colum O'Hehir, a man in his early fifties, was an alcoholic. It was, Sister Jude told him, 'a terrible situation'. If he wished, he was welcome to stay in the convent and go to visit the priest each morning. Father Fintan, unaware as yet of the seriousness of the situation, elected to stay in the presbytery. He had a month or two free that summer, therefore it was not too much of an inconvenience. The nun thanked him profusely and he made arrangements to travel that very day.

His train was delayed; there was a further delay in getting a taxi in town, and consequently Father Fintan arrived at the parish church a little before midnight.

The first thing that struck him on alighting from the taxi was the odd setting of the house. There was a cemetery abutting the church; and the presbytery was, to all intents and purposes, within the cemetery, both church and house being surrounded by graves. To arrive there after nightfall was an eerie experience.

Sister Jude had given him instructions on where to find the key to the front door, and in the darkness he fumbled for it. At that moment, he heard the sounds of a quarrel from somewhere deep within the house. Two men were arguing, although it was impossible to make out the words. There were two very distinct voices, one of deeper pitch than the other; they were accompanied by loud noises – bangings and crashings, as of objects being hurled about. Father Fintan found the key and let himself in. The noises and sounds of quarrelling stopped at once, to be replaced by dead silence.

The interior was in complete darkness and it was some time before he found the light switch. When he turned on the lights he stared about him in disbelief. Sister Jude had given him to understand that the house might be in disarray, because Father Colum had no housekeeper.

Yet the house that Father Fintan stepped into had the appearance of one that had lain abandoned for twenty years. There were the strong odours of must and mould. The floor of the big kitchen was littered with broken crockery. Rubbish was strewn everywhere; flies buzzed about rotten food.

There was no one on the ground floor and no sign of the parish priest. Father Fintan decided to investigate the top storey. As he made his way up the stairs he heard the voices starting up again, and by the time he reached the landing they were loud; loud enough to enable him to distinguish words. He was bemused to hear a language that was still fresh in his mind from his seminary days. He had never thought to hear it much outside the celebration of the sacraments. The one voice seemed to be declaiming a text, and the other – a harsher, supercilious-sounding one – was bent on interrupting.

'*Si autem in luce ambulemus sicut et ipse est in luce societatem habemus ad invicem—*'

'*Societas? Caeci caecos ducentes!*'

'*—et sanguis Iesu Filii eius mundat nos ab omni peccato. . . .*'

'*Sacerdos, vos es stultus!*'

'*Deus lux est et tenebrae—*'

'*Lux?* Ego *sum lux! Meus nomen opes lux!*'

Again he heard bangs and crashes as if a struggle was taking place in one of the bedrooms. He grew very concerned, thinking that a burglary – or worse – might be in progress, and considered calling the Guards. Instead he went to the bedroom door.

To his astonishment he discovered that the doorknob was icy to the touch; it was as though the door let out onto a cold yard instead of into a bedroom warmed throughout the day by a late-summer sun.

He entered the room. It was dimly lit and bitterly cold. A double bed had been pushed up in front of the hearth. The room was bare except for two occasional tables and a chest of drawers in front of the only window.

Atop the chest of drawers sat a middle-aged man.

He was dressed in pyjama bottoms and a dressing gown. He was emaciated, seeming half-starved. He was shaking visibly and appeared to be in a daze. Sister Jude had cautioned Fintan about Father Colum's drinking and he had expected to see signs of it. But, although there were two whiskey bottles on a table and one of those bottles was empty, Father Colum did not appear inebriated. He looked frightened, hunted, a man who had given up all hope, a man bordering on despair.

'I'm Fintan,' said Donnelly gently, trying to reassure him. 'Sister Jude sent me.'

The parish priest simply stared and said nothing, waving away questions with weary gestures. He allowed himself to be helped back to bed. Father Fintan tidied up the room as best he could and went downstairs again. Sister Jude had been around earlier in the day and had left milk, ham and cheese, and fresh bread. He made some tea and sandwiches and brought them up to Father Colum.

'Thank you very much, Fintan,' he said. 'I haven't eaten in days, you know.'

He ate greedily, wolfing the sandwiches down as if to confirm his great hunger. Father Fintan went and made some more.

'I'll be staying on for a bit,' he said. 'I can take care of you until you're on your feet again.'

'You're very good,' the parish priest said. 'You can have the room next door. It's comfortable enough and you'll find fresh linen in the hot press.'

Father Fintan waited while the older man finished his supper. He asked if he needed anything else, was told 'no', bade Father Colum a good night and went downstairs again. He tidied up the kitchen and prepared for bed.

But the room next to the priest's was far from comfortable. It was cold, damp and had the air of disuse. The wallpaper looked to be decades old; there was a rickety table with a bowl and water jug, and a narrow bed in one corner. For all the comfort it promised, it might have been a nineteenth-century prison cell. There were no curtains on the window. Father Fintan looked out onto his new surroundings. It was not a cheering sight: the light from the bedroom shone on a collection of headstones and overgrown paths between the graves. He thought about Sister Jude's offer of accommodation in the convent, and considered telephoning for a taxi to take him back to town. But the hour was late, and he had vowed to help the parish priest. He could not desert him now.

He went out to the airing cupboard; it proved bare except for two or three old, grey blankets. Like the house itself, they smelled of decay. But there was nothing else.

'It was only when I was returning to the room,' Father Fintan tells us, 'that I noticed it. There was this ugly red stain running down the wall next to the window. I thought at first that perhaps it was due to a leak from copper in the roof, but when I examined it closely it looked more like a bloodstain. There was a pattern to it . . . a spatter-like pattern, I suppose, as if something had been dashed against the wall. That really unnerved me, because it gave me the idea that maybe something terrible had happened in that room. I sprinkled some holy water and said a prayer.'

He made up the bed with the old blankets, and in the absence of a pillowcase, wrapped one of his shirts about the single, lumpy pillow. He fetched his crucifix from his overnight bag, switched off the light, and held the crucifix firmly in his right hand as he lay down to get some sleep.

But, just as he felt himself drifting off, voices began to emanate from the adjacent room. They were low at first, but he thought he could discern the parish priest's voice. The volume grew, and once again he was hearing a quarrel, as if two men were trading insults. It sounded, too, as though items of heavy furniture were being pushed about. Fintan knew full well that he had left the priest alone in the room. The door had remained shut. Besides, if another individual had entered the room in his absence, he would surely have been aware of it. He could find no rational explanation for the second voice.

'I was really nervous now,' he says, 'scared, and I thought nothing would faze me when I was that age, but I plucked up courage and went out into the corridor very quietly. The noise was awful . . . the raised voices again. They were shouting in Latin, I think, from what I could gather anyway, but now the speech was so rapid it was hard to tell. I remember standing there between the Devil and the deep blue sea, as they say, wondering if I should brave it and go in. But as I was reaching for the door handle, the quarrelling stopped, and there was this really eerie silence. I had the awful feeling that whatever was in there could actually *see* me, was daring me to come in, and I just knew I couldn't – mentally as well as physically – because when I put a hand on the doorknob, it nearly stuck to it. It was as cold as a chunk of ice.'

The young curate slept fitfully that night, lying as he did between the musty blankets, praying often and with the crucifix held to his chest. In the morning he looked in on the other priest and found him sitting up in bed, appearing wasted, as though suffering from exhaustion. In daylight he seemed almost skeletal, like a man who had engaged in a protracted hunger strike. He looked up in alarm as Fintan entered.

'Who are you?'

'I'm Fintan Donnelly. Don't you remember me? I arrived last night.'

'I don't.'

Father Fintan cast an eye about the room. He noted that items of furniture were no longer in the places he remembered seeing them. It looked as if somebody had tried to drag a heavy chest of drawers to the door, to bar it. To keep something out, Fintan thought – or to keep something in? He could no longer contain his curiosity.

'Father, what's going on?' he demanded.

'Nothing.'

'I'm sorry, but that's not good enough. What was all that about last night? All that banging and shouting.'

'You wouldn't want to know,' Father Colum said abstractedly. 'No, you wouldn't want to know.'

'I'd like to help, Father. Is there anything I can do?'

'You're very kind, son, but it's all right. It's my fight.'

'But who are you fighting?'

The elder priest said nothing, but pointed to a framed picture of modern Italy's most famous stigmatic.

'Padre Pio,' he said at last. 'He fought him all his life.'

A shiver ran through Father Fintan. He knew immediately what was meant and feared what he might hear next. He swiftly changed the subject.

'I'll make us some breakfast,' he said and left the room.

As the priest prepared the meal, he pondered the life of the extraordinary holy man known as Padre Pio.

The Capuchin friar, born in 1887 in San Giovanni Rotondo, is not only known for suffering the full stigmata – the five wounds of Christ – for fifty years, but on account of his innumerable battles with Satan. He described those assaults in many letters to his 'Spiritual Father', Dom Agostino. In one dated 13 February 1913, he wrote:

> Now twenty-two days have passed since Jesus allowed the devils to vent their anger on me. My Father, my whole body is bruised from the beatings that I have received to the present time by our enemies. Several times, they have even torn off my shirt so that they could strike my exposed flesh.

It is alleged that the Devil would often take the form of savage animals in attempts to intimidate and frighten the holy man. The friar first saw him in 1905, not long after he had joined the abbey of Sant'Elia a Pianisi as a seminarian. He heard a commotion from a neighbouring cell, and entered to find there a monstrous black dog, with what he took to be sulphurous smoke issuing from its mouth. The brute spoke. 'It's him! It's him!' it growled, before disappearing. (Interestingly, in later years Father Fintan would have a brief encounter with just such an animal.)

Satan is said to have tormented Pio throughout his life, assuming a variety of guises. He appeared as a troupe of naked dancing girls to test his chastity. On many occasions he took the form of Pio's Spiritual Father; at other times a guardian angel, St Francis, Pope Pius x. He even masqueraded as Jesus and the Virgin Mother. Over time, like Teresa of Ávila, the padre learned to tell the difference. The genuine sacred visions would inspire in him a sense of love and humility, and leave in their going a great sense of peace. The false visions, on the other hand, would initially arouse in him exhilaration and joy, to be swiftly followed by depression and a sense of loss when they had vanished.

All this and more did Father Fintan contemplate that day and in the days that followed. He set about cleaning the house from top to bottom, in the conviction that a purge would help. He was convinced that there was something unclean there, as if the base thing that had taken possession of Father Colum had extended its influence to the surroundings as well. Fintan prayed harder than he had ever done, and said at least two Masses a day, most dedicated to Michael the Archangel, by tradition the Devil's greatest adversary. He took to lighting candles as well, and sprinkling holy water in each room.

Father Colum remained steadfastly in his bedroom for three days, seemingly afraid to venture out into the rest of the house for fear of what he might find there. During the second night of Fintan's stay, a similar commotion was plainly audible, but this time it lasted for no longer than a half-hour. The following night Fintan heard it for only a few minutes. Whatever it was, it seemed to be retreating before the young curate's prayers and Eucharists.

On the fourth day, he helped Father Colum to shave and tidy himself up. By this time he had won the parish priest's trust, and could persuade him to leave the room and come downstairs. Fintan had set up an altar in the front room complete with lit candles. He had Father Colum sit with him, a stole about his shoulders. It seemed to calm him. They prayed together.

Fintan Donnelly remained in the house for ten days in all. In the course of the first few days, Father Colum continued drinking, but managed to cut down on his intake. He grew progressively more tranquil, and the nightly commotions were of shorter duration. Eventually they ceased entirely.

He never confided to the young priest the exact nature of the disturbances, and Father Fintan thought it wiser not to pursue the matter. His prayers were being answered and that was all that counted.

He left the house a better – and cleaner – place, and returned to his own parish. A year later he met Sister Jude again and en-quired about Father Colum O'Hehir. He learned that the priest had stopped drinking and joined Alcoholics Anonymous. He had also joined the prayer group in Sister Jude's convent and was at-tending two or three times a week.

'Drink is an awful curse,' the nun said sadly. 'No wonder they call it the "demon drink".'

Father Fintan reflected that she could not know how close she had come to the truth about Father Colum's predicament.

His final meeting with the troubled priest was some time later. It was during a conference held at the RDS, Dublin, organized by the Charismatic Movement. He barely recognized Father Colum. He had put on weight and seemed in rude good health. He was as calm and contented as any man could be.

But Fintan had to know the truth, if only to satisfy his own youthful curiosity.

'What was all that about?' he asked. 'All that shouting. Was it the drink?'

'It was the drink, I suppose, Fintan. But there was more to it than that. I'm sure you guessed as much. I'll put it this way: Old Nick had me by the scruff of the neck. But Old Nick came before the drink. I was drinking to stop the pain of what he was doing to me.'

'How long had this been going on?'

'Years. And it might have gone on a lot longer if you hadn't come along.'

'It wasn't me, Father,' Fintan told him with commendable self-effacement and humility. 'It was all due to the power of the Eucharist.'

Fintan Donnelly was under no illusion that his struggle with the Devil had ended with the priest in rural Kilkenny. He had actual-ly spoken to the Adversary in a retreat house chapel, and learned how persuasive he could be. Fintan thought back to his seminary days and his lessons in theology. He is a little critical of certain aspects of those studies. He feels that it was not sufficiently emphasized that the priesthood is the first line of defence against evil. Older now, and wiser to the ways of evil, he understands why the priest will be unusually vulnerable to attack.

'Old Nick won't waste his time going for the sheep,' he says with a rueful smile. 'He'll go for the shepherd instead. By weakening the shepherd he can get at the flock.'

Father Fintan was to receive first-hand experience of this when, a few years later, he took up a post as junior curate to two senior priests in an inner-city parish in Dublin. At first he suspected nothing out of the ordinary when the two began to speak and act strangely; he put it down to some sort of initiation procedure in which he was the neophyte. He imagined that, being the 'new boy' and unaccustomed to the rough and tumble of the big city, he was being played with, that he was being 'greened'.

For what he encountered was very much at odds with his training and his brief experience of the priestly life. He was astonished to learn with what contempt one of the senior men held the parishioners, the elderly and infirm in particular.

Fintan is convinced that Father Kevin, the priest in question, was suffering from some sort of demonic oppression, if not possession itself. Certainly he was eccentric in many ways. He cut an odd figure, too; he was a man who elicited stares wherever he went. He had unhappy, strange eyes that forever held a doleful look, as if they were windows onto a deeply troubled soul.

'Right from the word go I was on my guard,' Father Fintan tells us. 'There was just something not quite right about Father Kevin. And I'm not saying he was crazy or anything like that. Far from it. No, I believe it went deeper than that. I really dreaded being in his company. I was afraid of him, afraid of what he might do at any given moment. And don't ask me to explain that further, because I can't. I went to enormous lengths to avoid him.'

This statement is interesting in light of what we have learned in the course of our investigations. We asked a number of exorcists if they would recognize a person touched by evil. The consensus was that, in many cases, such resident evil is indeed discernible. Some reported feelings of 'discomfort' and 'confusion'. One priest commented that there were occasions when he had felt 'quite unwell' in the presence of a demoniac.

This is not so surprising, Father Donnelly explains, when one considers that, in such individuals, most if not all of the transcendent qualities – those which attest to our humanness – have become inverted. Love has turned to hatred, compassion to cruelty, purity to obscenity, truth to lies. Such a state of being will often evoke a sense of revulsion or disgust in a devout person because, consciously or unconsciously, they recognize the characteristics of the 'unclean'.

Fintan Donnelly arrived in the parish full of enthusiasm, wishing to do as much good as possible for the poverty-stricken people of the area. On his first day, Father Kevin brought him to a window that overlooked a dingy block of flats. The young curate was expecting to hear some words of encouragement, perhaps something about the problems he was likely to face when tending to his new flock. Perhaps a pep talk. He was therefore unprepared for the older priest's words.

'I want to tell you something, son,' he said. 'The people here are as thick as bottled pigshite. There is nothing you can do for them. So what I would advise you is go about your duties, bide your time until you get a better parish.'

Father Fintan was aghast, hardly believing the evidence of his ears. Yet he was to grow to expect such sentiments from Father Kevin, and in the weeks to come he was to hear much worse.

'Naturally, it had a very negative effect on me,' he says. 'I found myself struggling with the unreality of the whole thing. I mean, what was this man doing in the priesthood? I'd always believed it was God who called young men to His service; that it was the ministry that chose the man and not the other way round. Now I began to have grave doubts. This really was an eye-opener.'

Having made some discreet enquiries, he learned that Father Kevin had never wanted to become a priest. His late father, a school principal, had been a very disturbed individual. In time – but rather belatedly for the young Kevin – he was diagnosed a schizophrenic. In his school and in his home his word was law and none dared to disobey him. When he decided that Kevin should enter the priesthood, it was futile to argue with him. It would not have been the first time that a young Irishman had taken holy orders against his will, and it led to great resentment on Kevin's part. Once ordained, he set out to 'make the best' of the life that had been forced upon him. By the time Fintan Donnelly encountered him, he was paying no more than lip-service to his office. It seemed to his colleagues that he took an almost fiendish delight in making fun of the Church and its institutions, even the very sacraments. He would boast that when the liturgy changed from Latin in 1964, he had never bothered to buy a copy of the new breviary in English. He appeared to be a priest in name only, going through the motions as it were. Fintan Donnelly never once saw him pray in private.

He was not alone in his concerns about Father Kevin's spirituality – or, rather, lack thereof. Once a month, the parish received a visit from a Franciscan priest, an exceptionally pious man. He would come to give a retreat, to which priests and parishioners alike were invited. On one such occasion Fintan Donnelly found the Franciscan alone in the church. He was seated near the altar, breviary in his lap but eyes tightly shut. He was trembling.

'My boy,' he said with feeling, 'the Devil is in your presbytery.'

Father Fintan accompanied him outside and they strolled together in the grounds. Eventually the visiting priest had calmed down sufficiently to explain his outburst. He had been having dinner with Father Kevin and could hardly believe that a priest's conversation could be so coarse.

'Every other word was that four-letter word,' he said. 'You know the one I mean.'

'The "f" word,' Father Fintan offered.

'That's the one. And he was telling me the most revolting jokes I'd ever heard in my life. Every one of those jokes concerned women's genitalia and pornographic subject matter I'd rather not speak of, if you don't mind.'

It was obvious to Fintan that the Franciscan was deeply disturbed in spirit. He was not the only religious whom Father Kevin affected in this way. The priests of the parish took turns saying Mass for a convent of nuns in the vicinity. Fintan Donnelly learned from them that they feared Father Kevin whenever he came to celebrate the Eucharist. They were, they said, 'afraid of his eyes' and what they saw there.

'There's something terribly wrong with that man,' one of them said when she and Father Fintan were alone. 'If you ask me, he's not right at all.'

'You mean he's mental.'

'No, not mental, Father. I mean there's something ungodly about him. Something evil.'

It was the first time that Father Fintan had heard a nun speak so frankly about a priest, and her words gave him serious pause for thought. The episode in the oratory prior to his ordination, coupled with his sojourn in the priest's house in County Kilkenny, had alerted him to the reality of the preternatural. Yet he had not considered the possibility that the Devil might seek to control a person, and certainly not a priest of God. Now he found himself having to confront that possibility. He had to confront the likelihood that Father Kevin was possessed.

* * *

An instance of demonic possession is one of the most formidable challenges that a priest can encounter. It lies so outside the scope of his normal pastoral duties that it may appear only once in the course of his entire career. When it does manifest itself, it cannot be taken seriously enough. Some theologians contend that complete demonic possession is impossible; they argue that we are all creatures of God and therefore the Devil can never claim ownership of a human being. When we speak of 'possession', then, they say, we are really speaking of demonic *influence*.

Understandably, most churchmen are reluctant to even discuss the matter of possession, let alone set in train the mechanisms and procedures which will lead to the banishment of the demon.

Fintan Donnelly found himself in a very awkward position. He felt that he ought to inform the church authorities that Father Kevin needed help; at the same time, he was only the curate, and knew it would be his word against that of his parish priest. He therefore made careful enquiries with the bishop's staff, testing the water. Oddly enough, the consensus seemed to be that Father Kevin was a hard-working priest who forever had the spiritual well-being of his parishioners at heart.

'You'll be up against the bishop,' someone said. 'It's you they'll boot out, not Kevin. My advice? Leave it be. Do your work, keep your nose clean, and keep an eye out for a new parish.'

But the situation in the presbytery was, if anything, worsening by the day. Father Kevin had always been fond of the drink; now he was bingeing at an alarming rate.

'I don't know how I got through that awful time,' Fintan says. 'I soon learned that Father Kevin, like Father Colum before him, was a raging alcoholic. Now don't get me wrong; I've nothing against drink; I take a drink myself. But at least in the Kilkenny case I could cope with Father Colum's illness; it wasn't a permanent thing. But here I was, having to share a house with this man – in effect my boss – and with no choice but to put up with it.'

'You hear it called the "demon drink" and there's a lot in that,' he goes on. 'But to my mind Father Colum was a good man. He was naive almost; I could see that. And Father Kevin was the total opposite. There was a slyness about him. He was bad enough sober, but when he hit the bottle, living in the same house as him was an absolute nightmare.'

Fintan is referring to the parish priest's ability to almost know what he was thinking. To the best of his knowledge, he had not given Father Kevin any indication that he was considering getting help for him. But Father Kevin, in some mysterious way, seemed to know what was afoot, and began turning his baleful attentions on the young curate. He would get very drunk in the evening, come upstairs and stand outside Fintan's room, cursing and swearing and kicking at the door.

One night it was particularly bad and Fintan was dreadfully afraid. He decided to leave his bed and sprinkle holy water. For protection, he explains.

'I was reminded of that first night I stayed in Father Colum's house in Kilkenny. It was dreadful. I felt that if I opened the bedroom door something terrible would happen. His language was awful: really obscene, stuff you wouldn't believe anybody could use, and especially not a man of the cloth.'

He waited in the darkness, listening. At last the drunken rage died down; he heard feet drag themselves away, and presently the sound of Father Kevin's door being shut.

Fintan left his bed, took a bottle of holy water, went outside and sprinkled it both in the corridor and on Father Kevin's door. He returned to his room. He saw that it was 1.29 am. He fetched his trusty crucifix, held it against his chest, and drifted off into a troubled sleep.

Once a month, Fintan Donnelly would return to the parental home in his native Limerick, there to spend a long weekend. A few days following the episode with the holy water, he took the train from Dublin and was welcomed by his family. His mother, as always, made him tea on his arrival, and they both sat down together. He saw that she was upset by something.

'You seem a bit nervous, Ma,' he said. 'Is there something the matter?'

'Gosh, son, how can I put this? I had a very strange experience the other night. It would have been Thursday. About half one in the morning. It was terrible altogether.'

Fintan looked at her. Her hands were trembling and the teacup was rattling on her saucer.

'I was lying in bed and Maeve was beside me.' Fintan knew that it was not unusual for his youngest sister to climb into her mother's bed. The girl had been born mentally handicapped, an affliction that gave her an exaggerated fear of the dark. 'She jumped up suddenly and started shouting the most awful things.'

Father Fintan managed to coax the truth from his mother. Apparently eight-year-old Maeve had indulged in an orgy of swearing, using the foulest language that her mother had ever heard. Some of the words were entirely new to Mrs Donnelly. Normally, the child was placid and innocent, and was never known to utter a single uncouth or inappropriate word.

He was transfixed. He was remembering Father Kevin's own orgy of swearing on the same night.

'But Fintan, that wasn't the worst of it,' his mother said. 'When I got Maeve settled down . . . God, Fintan, I don't know how to tell you this.' She was plainly embarrassed.

'I'm a priest now, Ma,' he said, taking her hand. 'I hear things in confession. It's hard to shock me.'

'All right so. Well, I felt this thing on top of me. A man's body – I knew that much. The weight, and the smell of it, was awful. God, son, I could hear him breathing!'

Fintan was listening with a mounting sense of dread.

'What kind of smell would this have been, Ma?'

'Terrible altogether. Like sewage; just awful. I tried holding my breath but I couldn't. It was like it was everywhere. And the weight on top of me was desperate, crushing the life out of me.'

'Go on.'

'I started to pray then,' she said. 'It was all I could do. After a bit, it went away, thank God.'

That evening, Fintan gathered his mother and siblings together in the front room of the house. He said a Mass and proceeded to sprinkle holy water throughout the house, paying special attention to the room where his mother slept. When leaving for Dublin that Monday, he urged her to get in touch at once if anything untoward should occur, no matter how trivial she thought it might be. She promised to do so. In the event, nothing did. Whatever it was that had visited the Donnelly home that night never returned.

Father Fintan arrived back in the Dublin parish to receive some unexpected news. He was being moved elsewhere. To this day he does not truly know why; the reasons given him were vague. It is impossible to say whether his relocation had a bearing on Father Kevin. It is an odd fact, however, that he had no more trouble from that quarter. Father Kevin continued his drinking and his unpriestly ways, but did not bother the young curate again.

Father Fintan Donnelly is fifty-four now. He has been a priest for thirty years and has served in different parishes throughout Ireland. He had hoped that those early brushes with Satan would be the sum total of his experience of the preternatural. But it was not to be. His most recent encounter occurred in the year 2000 – and in a most unexpected setting.

The temptation in Glencomeragh had shown him that consecrated buildings were no safeguard against the encroachment of evil; he should therefore not have been too surprised when evil presented itself to him at one of the Catholic Church's most important shrines: that of Lourdes, in Bigorre, France, the site at which Our Lady is said to have appeared on many occasions, the first being to a young country girl named Bernadette.

Father Fintan had led a group of 120 pilgrims to the shrine. The visit had been a resounding success, for the priest as much as his flock; in the afternoon of the third day all were filled with a high degree of religious devotion and fervour. Father Fintan suggested an all-night vigil in the Grotto, the place where the Mother of God chose to manifest herself. It would start with a Mass in one of the churches at 11 pm, to which all were invited. Everyone in the group responded wholeheartedly. The Mass being ended, the people filed out in procession to the Grotto. Once there, in the huge cavern that was the setting for so many apparitions, the pilgrims settled down to pray. They were not alone; several hundred others of many nationalities were doing likewise.

Eventually, though, as the night wore on, the Grotto emptied, until at roughly 2.30 in the morning, Father Fintan and his group were all who remained. Somebody suggested that they pause in their vigil to have some refreshment, and the priest readily agreed. The pilgrims would move out of the sacred area and cross to a tea-room on the other side of the river. The priest assured them that he would join them presently. He wished to have five or ten minutes to himself.

'It's not often you can be alone in the Grotto at Lourdes,' he says. 'Normally the place is full of people. I couldn't pass up the chance of saying a few private prayers there. I reckoned I'd never have the chance again.'

As the great candles burned in the recesses in the rock below and about the statue to Our Lady, and nothing was heard save the clicking of distant cicadas, the priest opened his breviary and applied himself to his devotions. He was thus engrossed when, a minute later, he felt a strong hand grip his shoulder.

'Well, not a hand, exactly,' Father Fintan expands, 'more like a hand missing two or even three fingers, a set of pincers almost. These prong-like fingers were digging into my shoulder. I wasn't too worried, because Lourdes has its fair share of mentally disturbed individuals wandering around. They have a tendency to "latch onto" clergymen – often in the literal sense – in the fevered hope that by being close to men of God they might get cured. So I didn't pay much attention to this thing gripping my shoulder because, naturally, I thought that this was just another unfortunate desperate for a miracle.'

The grip was tightening. He was in pain; the strong fingers were buried in the muscle of his shoulder, causing his eyes to water. Father Fintan decided to 'grin and bear it', not wishing to upset somebody who might have been *in extremis* at that moment because of mental suffering.

'But suddenly my breviary flew out of my hands. It must have jumped about thirty feet. It hit the rock wall of the Grotto. The next thing I knew, I was pushed to the ground by the invisible hand. It felt like somebody's weight was being forced down on top of me. I couldn't move.'

From somewhere in the Grotto came a voice the priest recognized: that of one of his parishioners who had helped to organize the pilgrimage.

'Somebody get an ambulance!' the man was shouting. 'Father Fintan is after having a heart attack.'

'The group were coming back,' he says. 'It was very strange because more time must have passed than I was conscious of. I seemed to be in a kind of trance. I was aware of people approaching from the entrance. I couldn't move my head, say anything to them.'

But the mysterious occurrences in the Grotto were not over. Before Father Fintan's startled eyes, a young nun detached herself from the party. She was a missionary sister, one of the most pious individuals of the group. Without warning, she ripped off her veil and rushed towards the statue of Our Lady.

'It's all a farce!' she cried out. 'This is all a hoax. There's no God here!'

In the next instant Father Fintan heard a scream go up from the pilgrims. It was a cry of horror that issued from many throats. He understood none of it. But then people were bending over him, the pressure on his back was easing. Hands were helping him to his feet.

'Are you all right, Father?'

'I'm fine now,' he assured them. 'What was that screaming all about?'

'It was a dog.'

'A dog?'

'A big black dog, Father. A huge brute. It came rushing out from behind the altar there. I never saw the like of it. Like a mad thing it was, eyes all red, and it slavering at the mouth.'

Father Fintan was reminded of Padre Pio's first encounter with Satan. The 'monstrous dog' that appeared in his cell one night and spoke. He thought also of Hilary, the fourteenth-century saint, who is reputed to have driven a demon from a camel. The beast's 'eyes were bloodshot, his mouth filled with foam, his rolling tongue swollen, above every other source of terror was his loud and hideous roar.'

'You do not alarm me, devil,' Hilary had said bravely, 'huge though your present body is. Whether in a fox or a camel you are just the same.' On hearing the saint's words, the demon departed, and the animal reverted to its old, placid, self.

Father Fintan recovered by and by, and order was restored in the Grotto at Lourdes. Later that same day, when he had reassured his distressed group of pilgrims, he paid a visit to another priest, a man he had met a day or two earlier, a 'veteran' of many annual visits to the shrine. There he learned a sobering truth.

'There have been eighteen apparitions in all here, since the first one in eighteen fifty-eight,' the older priest told him. 'That's to say: eighteen holy apparitions. But here's the point, Fintan: there were also eighteen unholy ones. Yours brings the total up to nineteen.'

The Father Fintan Donnelly who returned to Ireland was a more thoughtful man than the one who had left for Lourdes. On the flight back, a question kept ringing in his head:

Is nothing sacred?

In truth, he was beginning to suspect that for the Devil nothing or nobody is ever sacred. His ordeal in the Grotto had reinforced a belief of his, founded many years earlier: that the persons most prone to attack from the preternatural are the servants of Christ. He understood, too, that it is a never-ending struggle – or, to put it in his own words: 'The struggle will end with the end of the world. Until such time, evil will continually attempt to win us over. It's up to us to see that that doesn't happen. It's our choice. This is where free will comes into play.'

Today, Father Fintan has his own parish in a prosperous southern town, with two priests to share the parochial duties. The serenity of the sitting-room in his presbytery, whose walls are hung with original works of art by modern Irish painters, seems worlds removed from the turbulence he experienced when a young priest. We wonder if he still thinks about Father Kevin.

'Of course I do!' he says brusquely, almost as if our question is an assault on his faith. 'Hardly a day goes by when I don't think about him. I include him in my prayers and Masses. God knows he needs them.

'He's a sick man now. Cancer, they tell me. I saw him not too long ago, in fact. In a supermarket. He looked terrible. He saw me but I don't think he recognized me.' Father Fintan appears troubled. 'I wanted to speak to him but I didn't. There was something holding me back. Only later, when we'd gone our separate ways again, did I know it for what it was. It was fear. I was still afraid of him.'

A question, unvoiced, hangs in the air. Father Fintan answers it unasked.

'No, I don't think he's changed his ways. More's the pity. But I never lose hope.'

He is thoughtful. He gets up from his armchair, goes to the window, turns and spreads his hands.

'He has to repent. Father Kevin made a choice and he has to unmake it. When he confesses his sin and shows repentance, then the Lord will forgive him. God will always forgive the sinner. But first the sinner has to choose God; he has to prove himself again. He has to undo all the harm he's done. Only then will he obtain forgiveness. That's the way of it.'

We talk at some length about hell and the rest of the Catholic Church's teachings on the afterlife. Father Fintan believes unswervingly in the existence of hell. How could he not, when three times in his ministry he has had a brush with the ruler of that 'place'?

Such confrontations tend to dispel all doubt.

The Unquiet Spirit of Child Sarah

THE LITTLE GIFT SHOP was about halfway along a parade of shops, sandwiched between a fashion boutique and an up-market off-licence. Stephanie Rooney, a petite twenty-four-year-old, had not noticed it before; that said, her trips to Derry rarely brought her to that part of town. She was curious. She was also fired by the acquisitive passion of the new home-maker, never letting pass an opportunity to add to her growing collection of bric-à-brac. She pushed open the door. She was half-expecting the jangle of an old-fashioned shop bell – it was that kind of place – and was delighted instead by the melodious tinkling of what could only have been Tibetan wind-chimes.

The shop's interior was heavy with cinnamon, vanilla, apple, lavender, and a myriad of other luscious scents. Stephanie hardly noticed them at first because there was so much to please the eye. There were statuettes whittled from dark wood, each with the likeness of an African deity; there were elaborate carvings from southeast Asia, showing elephants intertwined with luxuriant foliage; she marvelled at crystals, hefted small Chinese spheres that seemed to hum with esoteric music.

Then the jute sacks caught her eye.

They were ten in number and each was no bigger than a carrier bag. Each was unfurled to reveal its contents of tiny wooden marbles, smaller than ping-pong balls. As Stephanie drew closer to the sacks, she realized that the scents which had so delighted her did not emanate from potpourri, as she first thought, but from those curious little wooden balls.

'They're a popular line,' the assistant told her. 'Especially the strawberry. I have them all over the place at home.'

Stephanie picked one up and held it under her nostrils.

'They're divine,' she said.

'Buy ten, get two free,' the girl told her. 'I forgot to put the sign up this morning.'

'In that case I'll take a dozen of the strawberry,' said Stephanie, counting them into a tiny wicker basket provided for that purpose. She brought them to the counter.

'Hmm, you've got thirteen here,' the assistant said with a smile.

'Oh, right. Sorry.'

'Och, don't worry about it. Sure we won't quibble over one extra. You can have it for luck. Isn't that what they say: thirteen, lucky for some?'

'Thanks very much,' said Stephanie. She fished in her handbag for some small change. 'Yes, we can all use a bit of luck, can't we?'

She was still musing on luck and its many and varied interpretations as she re-emerged from the little gift shop. For Stephanie considered herself a very lucky woman at that time, on Tuesday, 16 September 2003. The sun shone brightly on the Maiden City, and the carefree post-office assistant was enjoying an afternoon off work. She was happy. Just six months married and already living in a brand new house (or 'des. res.' as her mother called it) on the outskirts of town, she felt that life could not get much better.

Her priorities had shifted since she and Declan had moved into 8 Cedar Close, Dungiven. There was a time when much of her income went on clothes, make-up and evenings out; now all her spare cash went towards making her new home as cosy and attractive as possible. She thought a bowl of the scented balls would look pretty on the hearth and create a lovely perfumed atmosphere in the living-room. It was, after all, the room where she and her husband spent much of their leisure time.

She found a porcelain bowl, a half-forgotten wedding present from a young niece, dusted it off, and arranged the scented balls. She placed them on the living-room hearth, stood back, shut her eyes and revelled in their fragrance. Their magic, she thought, was working already.

Declan noticed the wonderful scent as soon as he came home. He thought his wife was baking a strawberry tart or making a dessert of some kind, until she explained about her little purchase and brought him into the front room. He nodded his approval.

'Hmm, that's odd,' said Stephanie, puzzled. Three of the scented balls were lying loose on the hearth. 'I put them all in the bowl. I know I did.'

She shook her head, scooped up the stray balls and held them out for Declan to savour.

'Smells good enough to eat,' he said. 'Now, what's for supper? I'm starving, so I am.'

But how, Stephanie was asking herself, did the scented balls get out of the bowl? They had no children, no pets. She thought of mice, and shuddered. But logic told her that one did not as a rule find mice in new houses. In the country, perhaps, but not here in town. Bemused, she replaced the balls and followed Declan into the kitchen.

'I'm still wondering about the wooden balls,' she said later. 'How could they leave the bowl all by themselves? How could they do that?'

Declan stamped twice with his heel on the kitchen floor. Like that in the living-room, it was of pine, beautifully polished; it was brand new, unblemished, without a scratch.

'Y'know, them wooden floors have a spring in them before they get bedded down,' he said. 'Probably you walked out of the room in a hurry and the vibration upset the bowl. It's a shallow bowl; light too.'

Stephanie was thoughtful. She wanted to go to the living-room at once and test his theory, but something dissuaded her. What if he was wrong? What if the wooden balls had somehow left the bowl all by themselves? She did not wish to consider this possibility, and all that it might imply. She had to see to supper and was looking forward to settling down in front of the television later on. They were showing one of her favourite Johnny Depp films on UTV. That would certainly take her mind off things.

Several days passed and Stephanie thought no more about the scented balls. Her best friend Michele was celebrating her twenty-fifth birthday that coming Saturday, and they were invited. The Rooneys remember that birthday party with absolute clarity, perhaps because the carefree atmosphere and the good time they had that evening contrasted so sharply with what awaited them on their return home.

It was 2.15 am when they arrived back at Cedar Close. Declan went upstairs at once, leaving Stephanie to switch off the standard lamp in the living-room. They tended to leave the downstairs lights burning for security reasons, even though burglaries were rare in the neighbourhood; it was one of the reasons they had chosen it.

Stephanie was pulled up short. The French carriage clock in its gilt case occupied the central position as usual, flanked left and right by a Belleek china harp. But the photographs – the three framed photographs, one of Stephanie and Declan, two of family members – had been turned to face the wall.

'Declan!' she cried, backing towards the door.

He came down the stairs quickly but with some annoyance, his toothbrush still in his hand.

'What's the matter?'

Stephanie was pointing at the mantelpiece. He saw that her hand was trembling. He stared in disbelief at the picture frames. There really was no logical explanation. Declan knew that all windows had been firmly secured and doors locked before they left the house. How could the framed pictures have turned themselves round? He was prepared to believe that their footsteps across the new wooden floor might have jolted some of the scented balls free of the porcelain bowl, but this was a phenomenon of a different order.

'Look, we'll talk about it in the morning,' he said gently, trying to reassure Stephanie. 'There's always a rational explanation for these things. Always.'

With that he shut the living-room door, took the added precaution of locking it, and they retired to bed.

They were tired. Declan fell asleep almost at once but Stephanie lay awake for a time. She tried to quell her disquiet by re-running scenes from the birthday party, smiling again at Michele's awkwardness when she introduced the new man in her life. It helped. Stephanie felt herself drifting off. But without warning something jolted her wide awake again.

She sat up. She was sure that she had heard a loud thud from downstairs. It had come from the living-room; it lay directly below the bedroom. She shook Declan awake.

'Listen!' she whispered urgently. 'I heard something downstairs.'

'What?' He sat up, drowsy. 'I locked all the—'

'Shush!' Stephanie was trembling. 'The living-room.'

They sat in the darkness without speaking. They heard nothing more.

'Look, you only imagined it,' whispered Declan wearily.

'Maybe.'

But, just as they were about to settle down again, it sounded: the unmistakable thud of an object falling from a height.

'Oh, my God!' gasped Stephanie. She switched on the bedside lamp. Declan sprang out of bed.

'Where are you going?'

'Where d'you think?' Declan tried to keep the fear out of his voice. He could see how frightened his wife was becoming. For her sake he simply had to remain calm and seemingly in control.

'You can't go down there! What if . . . ?'

'—what if it's a burglar? If it's a burglar I'll deal with him.'

He reached into the walk-in closet. He had been putting up shelves and knew instinctively where to find his tools. He picked up a hammer.

'I'm coming with you,' said Stephanie. Despite her fears, she could not allow him to venture downstairs alone. She switched on the lights. All was quiet; they heard nothing but their own rapid breathing.

Gingerly Declan turned the key to the living-room door. In one deft movement he flung it wide; Stephanie threw the light switch. They stood in the doorway, staring in astonishment. The carriage clock and the china harps lay on the hearth rug. On the mantelpiece, the three framed photographs, which Stephanie had righted not an hour before, were again reversed.

A locked room. There was no sign of forced entry, no sign at all that anybody had been and gone – only the items arranged so bizarrely. The fright the couple experienced in those moments can only be guessed at. Fifteen minutes later they were dressed and in the car. They would go to Declan's mother's house. Remaining in Cedar Close that night was unthinkable.

The following day, Sunday, following a fitful night's sleep, the couple returned to their home. It was around noon. Everything was as they had left it, and for the remainder of the day they experienced no further disturbance. Encouraged by this – after all, it might well have been an isolated incident – they stayed the night. On Monday morning each left for work as usual.

But Declan's new-found optimism was shattered that evening on his return home. He usually arrived about six; on this occasion he was much earlier. He turned the key in the front door and let himself in.

The living-room seemed in order: the framed photographs were in their customary places on the mantelpiece, as was the carriage clock. On closer inspection, however, Declan noticed something amiss. He checked his watch. It was half past four, but the clock read a quarter past three. Odd, he thought. The clock was new and always accurate. Of course, it was entirely possible that the battery had run down.

But the clock was very audibly ticking, and not missing a beat, as far as he could tell. The battery could not be at fault. Puzzled, he set the time and went to check on the other clocks in the house. To his astonishment, he found that each one read a quarter past three – and all, like the carriage clock, were still ticking. With a mounting sense of unease, he reset them all and returned to the living-room.

The carriage clock had reverted to three fifteen.

Now Declan was filled with disquiet. Of one thing he was certain: he would say nothing about the clocks to Stephanie. If she noticed them, so be it. His own watch told him that he had an hour to kill before collecting her from work.

An hour. He was thinking of time again, and thinking of time caused him to look at his watch – and the clocks. He was going mad; he could not stay in the house. He still had time for a drink. He felt he could use one.

They got back to Cedar Close a little after six. Declan need not have worried. All the clocks were showing the correct time again. Thank God for that, he thought: with any luck that would be the end of the latest mystery. He kept quiet about the clocks.

All returned to normal – or so it seemed. Later that same

evening, however, it was the turn of the scented wooden balls again. Declan recalls that he was lulled into a false sense of security; the house seemed more peaceful than ever. The street was silent; no sounds intruded from outside. After supper they settled down to watch some television before going to bed. Stephanie dimmed the lights in the living-room and they sprawled, as they always did, on the big sofa.

But no sooner had Declan poured himself a lager than they heard a loud, sharp report on the floor directly behind them, followed by the sound a rolling marble makes. It was one of the wooden balls from the hearth.

Stephanie was startled, though still not persuaded that something unnatural was taking place in her home. Looking back now, she admits she was in denial.

'I thought right away that Declan was messing around. I don't know; he has a sense of humour, likes a laugh. I thought: it would be easy for him to put one of the wooden balls in his pocket; then, while we were watching telly, he could throw it over his shoulder. The room was dark and I wouldn't see him doing it.'

But one look at her husband's face was enough; he was as frightened as she was. An unknown agency had tossed the ball.

'We're getting out of here,' Declan announced.

They left immediately and again spent the night at the home of Declan's mother. They were not to know it then, but this pattern of staying overnight with relatives would soon become routine. Whenever they returned to Cedar Close, something would happen to drive them out again.

'The house', Stephanie says, 'was telling us something. At first we thought it wanted to get rid of us. In fact it was drawing attention to itself. It was saying: "Look what *I* can do."'

Much of the paranormal activity was centred on the wooden balls. They would execute manoeuvres that left the Rooneys perplexed.

At times there seemed to be no design or purpose; they seemed to be acting at random. At other times they had, according to Stephanie, 'a mind of their own'.

They would spring out of the ceramic bowl of their own volition, form patterns, hide in different parts of the house, then reappear later in the middle of the living-room floor. Often a single ball would go missing. Often one would roll after Declan as he walked down the hall to the kitchen. It would stop abruptly, then reverse back up to the hall-door – and launch itself into a potted palm that stood there. Sometimes the scent of their perfume would become overpoweringly strong.

Declan turned to his father for advice. Mr Rooney seemed to know the answer.

'Do you know what I think, son? And your mother agrees. I think it's only a poltergeist.'

Only a poltergeist. It might be useful at this point to examine briefly what is meant by poltergeist activity. There is a consensus among modern investigators of psychical phenomena that such paranormal manifestations are not in fact spirits, but evidence of 'psychokinetic' energy at work. It is generally believed that this energy resides in the person who is undergoing the haunting.

The trouble with the psychokinetic (or PK) theory is that the phenomenon has never been scientifically proven. There is, to be sure, a vast body of research, most conducted since the 1930s. This is not to say that the human body contains no energy. It does, and experiments show that our bodies can generate enough static electricity to power a light bulb. What is more, if the body is subjected to a high charge of electricity, this is sufficient to cause the same light bulb to glow when held a centimetre or two away from the body.

But this falls far short of the phenomenal amount of energy one would require to propel that same bulb through the air without the use of one's hands. Nor does the theory explain how larger objects can fly about a room or transport themselves from place to place. An energy source is needed in each case, and the first law of thermodynamics states, in brief, that the universe contains a constant amount of energy; in order to move an object, energy must be converted from one form to another. Although the human body can store about eighty watts even when in repose, the brain itself uses on average only twenty watts. Anyone who has tried to read by the light of a 25w bulb will appreciate that this is a minute amount of energy. The notion that a human brain can move objects, unaided by the rest of the body, seems absurd.

Frequently, investigators of poltergeist activity will allude to the onset of puberty in one of the principals. We are asked to believe that a hormonal change in the body of a boy or girl will somehow release sufficient energy to send pictures toppling from walls or electrical appliances running berserk. It seems so implausible. Puberty is no more than that period in a child's development when the body begins to produce hormones: testosterone in boys, oestrogen in girls.

Generally speaking, puberty affects the body. The child's demeanour is also affected, causing moodiness, as any parent with moping and listless pubertal children will confirm. But there is no truly dramatic upset to the young person, and certainly not enough to send objects hurtling about the home.

To speak of poltergeist activity in such terms, then, seems to be yet another ploy to explain the inexplicable. The truth is that no one knows what it is, what causes it and the nature of the forces at work behind it. It is also true that such activity does not confine itself to the places where there are pubertal children. In the case of the Rooney house there were none.

'We ought to try and catch your poltergeist in the act,' the elder Rooney said.

To this end, father and son devised a means of 'observing' the phenomena at work. They would leave a tape-recorder switched on overnight. It would be voice-activated, so any sound louder than the ambient noises in the living-room – the ticking of the clock, the hum of the water-heating system – would trigger the recording mechanism. There was the added possibility that, were a prankster at work, his footfalls and other tell-tale sounds would be recorded as well.

The experiment was a success. Every morning, when the tape was rewound, the *clack-clack-clack* of the wooden balls bouncing on the wooden floor was clearly audible. But that was all; if a human agent were at work, there was no record of such activity on the tape. Far from bringing reassurance to the Rooneys, the recordings only increased their anxiety. Something *very* strange was going on.

In time, things began to happen upstairs as well as down. The Rooneys would hear the bedroom doors being opened and shut again; bathroom taps would turn themselves on. More than once, they discovered drawers pulled out and their contents disturbed. It was as if someone was searching for something.

The couple were distraught. Their work was suffering, and they were reluctant to come home in the evening. The house in Cedar Close, the dream home they had sunk all their savings in, was becoming a liability. What could they do? They asked themselves whom they could turn to.

'When this sort of thing happens to you,' Declan says, 'the last thing you want to do is let on to the neighbours. If you do, then word gets out that your house is haunted, and nobody wants to come near it. We were going out of our minds, but we had to keep it all to ourselves.'

It was hard to know whom to turn to for help. A physician can cure disease through surgery or medication; a psychiatrist may soothe mental anguish through therapy and pharmaceuticals. But who can attend to that which appears to be not of this world, that which lies beyond our understanding? The Rooneys faced a choice: they could enlist the help of parapsychologists – what Declan deprecatingly called 'ghostbusters' – or they could turn to religion. Stephanie's mother urged them to seek help from their parish priest.

The young couple, though brought up in the Catholic faith, were not especially devout. Like so many of their contemporaries, they did not take religion very seriously; they would pray only when occasion demanded it. They took no active part in parish affairs, and were therefore on little more than nodding terms with their parish priest, Father Duncan O'Malley.

The good Father, a jovial man in his fifties, suggested that a lack of faith could cause 'these things'. He prayed with the couple in their front room, before blessing the house both inside and out. Declan and Stephanie were pleased that he had treated their problem as a serious matter. He left them a prayer to Michael the Archangel and counselled that they say it every morning and last thing at night.

It is perhaps important to mention how this prayer (reproduced both in full and in abbreviated form in APPENDIX TWO) came into being. It was written by Pope Leo XIII soon after he experienced a very traumatic vision. On 13 October 1884, he collapsed unconscious while attending a meeting of his Curia. The comatose pontiff was shown a vision of hell, and of the Archangel Michael overcoming Satan and his legions.

'Saint Michael the Archangel,' Father O'Malley declared grandly, 'our greatest champion in the face of the Enemy. Write it out, learn it and place a copy in every room in the house.'

Stephanie was examining the text of the prayer with a mixture of gratitude and unease. 'You don't think, Father, that it's . . .' She blushed, unable to say the dreaded word. 'That it's *him*? I mean—'

'The Divil himself? Aye, who else would it be?' the priest thundered, frightening the pair even further. 'The Divil, Oul' Nick,

176

Satan himself. He slithers about like a snake in the grass, waiting for his chance to strike!'

'Prayer and devotion,' he urged again, getting up to take his leave. Then, considering perhaps that he had been over-zealous, he swiftly changed the subject.

'I see ye play the Scrabble,' he said eyeing the cardboard box under the television set.

'Haven't played it for a while, Father,' said Declan, trying to keep calm. He wondered whether Father O'Malley realized how much he was frightening them – Stephanie in particular.

'God, d'you think he was serious about . . . you know?' she asked nervously, when the priest had left. She was gathering up the teacups in the living-room.

'Och, no. I wouldn't think so, Steph. Nobody believes the Devil is real these days.'

'Oh, my God!'

Declan heard a cup shattering on the pine floor. He turned from the window, to find Stephanie staring at the hearth. It was once again the unfathomable. There on the step, neatly lined up at equidistant intervals, were three sets of Scrabble letters.

RUN   HIT   HIDE

Intriguingly, the Scrabble box itself appeared undisturbed.

Who and where to turn to now? Declan's first impulse was to appeal to Father O'Malley. Stephanie was in two minds.

'Look,' she said, 'if we tell him about the Scrabble, he'll be very disappointed that his blessing didn't work.'

'Well, I didn't want to say it to his face because I know he meant well, but all this holy water and blessings and crucifixes and things belong in the Dark Ages. I mean it's—'

'That's hardly the attitude, Declan! Maybe if you had a bit more faith, the blessing would have worked.'

'Oh, right, so *I'm* to blame now, am I?'

'No, I'm not saying that . . . Oh God, I don't know *what* I'm saying. There's bound to be more priests around who can deal with these things. But where do you begin?'

Two days later the answer presented itself. Stephanie was visiting an old acquaintance she had not seen in several months, and confided in her. The friend showed her a newspaper article she had been saving.

'Maybe *he* can help,' she said.

Stephanie scanned it. The writer, she learned, was an Anglican minister from Newcastle, County Down, with considerable experience in the deliverance ministry. Over the years he had brought his unusual skills to bear on troubled situations, some involving individuals afflicted by unwelcome entities, others involving places beset by poltergeist activity.

'Can I keep this?'

'Please do, dear,' the friend said. 'I'm sure you'll find him in the phone book.'

Reverend Charles Cartwright is well used to the ringing of the telephone. His services have been in demand for many years, but more so in the last decade. He is not surprised by this increase and contends that 'the turning away from God by the masses in western society has made natural man vulnerable to attacks by spiritual forces.'

He is careful to keep an open mind whenever a fresh instance of paranormal manifestation is presented to him. He is not a man who sees demons everywhere. He will question relentlessly and not jump to conclusions. A deeply spiritual and caring man, the emotional welfare of the individual is his main priority.

As Declan Rooney related his catalogue of strange events taking place in the house in Dungiven, the rector's first thought was: 'child's play'. The activities – the scented balls being bounced around the floor, the Scrabble letters arranging themselves into words – all struck him as being the pranks of a mischievous 'spirit' child.

At the same time he believes that it is wise to nip such activity in the bud. He is keenly aware that, left to itself, such activity – child's play or not – can quickly get out of hand. He arranged to visit the Rooney home without delay.

Shortly before nightfall the following evening, Reverend Charles and his wife Alison drew up at 8 Cedar Close. They were surprised to find a large number of people – family, near and distant – gathered for the occasion. That fact alone put the rector on his guard. In his long experience, the afflicted did not, as a rule, 'shout from the rooftops' about their paranormal encounters, nor did they, in the initial stages, invite whole gatherings to witness events.

His puzzlement grew when he had spoken at length to Declan and Stephanie.

'I began to wonder if they hadn't got their priorities a little bit skewed,' he says. 'They seemed to want to talk about the shenanigans of the scented balls, and precious little else. But, for me, those were only minor phenomena. The Rooneys were glossing over the real issue: the phenomenon that set this case apart from most of the other cases I'd been called in to help with down the years. I was more interested in that sinister aspect: the reversed photographs.'

Nevertheless, he listened to a tape recording of the balls being tossed about the room, and was shown photographs of them arranged in various patterns. He concluded that such 'evidence' could easily have been faked, but for the time being kept his suspicions and doubts to himself.

For all that, Charles Cartwright was prepared to accept that the phenomena were genuine, and so acted accordingly. He celebrated what he recalls was 'a beautiful Eucharist', and one throughout which 'the Lord was verily and powerfully present'.

The rector left the house in Cedar Close, satisfied with a mission well accomplished. Indeed, in the weeks that followed, he learned through regular contact with Declan that his home was peaceful once more.

The Rooneys got on with their lives and endeavoured to put the troublesome episodes behind them. As the weeks passed without incident, and weeks turned to months, they felt tremendously grateful for the peace which the rector had restored to their home. But they were heedful, too, of what Father O'Malley had said at the time of his visit, and they took his advice about praying regularly. They recited the prayer to Michael the Archangel every night. Stephanie copied it out several times, as the priest instructed, and placed a copy in each room of the house.

A full nine months went by, and all was normal. Then a change occurred: one which, in Declan's words, 'ratcheted things up a notch'.

Josie and Noel Brady live at 10 Cedar Close, the house adjoining the Rooneys'. Josie, a no-nonsense woman in her late thirties, had been aware of 'problems' with the couple next door, but she prided herself on not getting caught up in the gossip that seemed such a part of community life. Unlike her other neighbours, she was new to the area, and therefore did not feel it was any of her business to interfere in the lives of others. She had heard the rumours about number eight, but chose not to believe in 'all that malarkey'. Ghosts and banshees, in Josie's book, were merely superstitious nonsense circulated by those who had nothing better to do and who wanted to draw attention to themselves. She found Declan and Stephanie a pleasant young couple, but rarely saw them, except at the weekends or when they had time off work.

On Wednesday, 5 May 2004, she was upstairs in one of the

children's rooms, collecting laundry, when she heard something unusual. She remembers checking the time on her daughter's Barbie clock. It was 12.30 pm.

'As I was making the bed I heard an almighty hammering on the party wall,' she recalls. 'In fact it was so sudden and fierce, it made me jump.'

Josie immediately thought that Declan was doing a spot of DIY. But she was sure she had heard the couple leave around 7.30 as usual. She went at once to the window. She was correct, their car was gone. Never mind, she thought, perhaps they had employed someone to do repairs in their absence. Without giving it further thought, she heaped the laundry into the basket and went downstairs.

Several days passed and Josie forgot all about the disturbance. Until a similar incident occurred.

She was upstairs again when she heard the rapid thumping on the wall. She looked at the clock and froze. It was 12.30 – the same time as before. But now the noises seemed more urgent, and were somehow more deliberate and purposeful. There was something eerie about the pattern of sound, as it travelled to various points on the wall, each time repeating a succession of what she could only describe as 'hammer blows'. Josie was becoming uneasy. She hurried from the room, slamming the door shut behind her.

Once downstairs she berated herself for being so silly. There was only one thing to do: knock on the door of number eight and find out who was causing the commotion.

It was a still, mild day and Cedar Close appeared to be otherwise deserted when she pushed open the gate to the Rooney house. She had an odd sense of foreboding. The feeling was made all the more powerful when, just as she was about to ring the doorbell, a magpie swept down as if from nowhere and landed on the doorstep. Josie jumped back, her hand to her heart. In her fright she trampled on some geraniums. The bird took flight.

An old-wives' tale common to many parts of Ireland suggests that it is unlucky to espy a lone magpie. In order to dispel the misfortune, one is encouraged to wave or to salute the bird. This Josie knew; the vestigial echoes of superstition from a rural childhood would never quite disappear. She made the prescribed gesture in the wake of the fleeing bird.

The sense of dread had not left her. She rang the doorbell. There was no response; she heard no sounds from inside the house. She rapped on the stained-glass door panel and waited for a few moments more. Still no response. Josie was undeterred; she went round to the patio doors at the rear and tried again. Still there was no answer. She stood perplexed; perhaps the handyman was a shy person who did not like to be disturbed. As she was turning to go, however, something in the kitchen caught her eye.

The kitchen was similar to her own. The patio doors allowed a great deal of light to bathe the area, revealing a sizable area of floor space to someone looking in. Josie also had sight of the hallway and staircase. But her attention was on the kitchen floor, and something quite remarkable.

Shielding her eyes against the glare of daylight, and peering more closely, she tried to come to terms with the inexplicable. Plumb in the middle of the pine floor was a lighted candle in a small brass holder, and next to it an open book. Its bulk, and the red silk ribbon lying askew across the pages, told Josie it was a Bible.

But the house at number eight was not done with surprises. She discerned movement on the staircase. What she took to be a bright orange 'ball of light' was swiftly descending.

'It certainly wasn't the reflection of the sun,' Josie says, 'because there was no sun to speak of that day. It moved with such speed anyway. I got really scared because I thought I was going to see it at the glass. I never ran so fast in all my life.'

Back in the safety of her own home, she recovered by and by, and went to put the kettle on. She thought a cup of tea might settle her nerves. But the calm did not last long. From upstairs came the unmistakable hammering on the party wall again.

Josie Brady grabbed her coat and car-keys and left the house in haste.

A few hours later, Declan and Stephanie pulled into their driveway. The first thing they noticed was the unlatched garden gate.

'Bloody postman,' complained Stephanie. 'I know who it is too. Lar Stewart. He's on a New Deal scheme and he doesn't much care what he does.'

'I know how he feels,' said Declan, locking the car. 'I remember when I was unemployed they made me do that nonsense as well. Slave labour if you ask me. They put me to picking mushrooms for an oul' frigger outside Claudy. God, he was a tight oul'—'

'Yes, Declan.' Stephanie was in no mood to listen to a story she had heard countless times before. 'Just look at our geraniums. That's Convery's bloody dog – or Stewart's big feet. I'll tell you something: I'm going to read him the riot act tomorrow.'

'Er, it wasn't the postman,' he said. 'Look: no letters.'

'Who was it then?'

'The ghost?'

'Please, Declan! Not even in jest, okay?' And she went upstairs to change.

From the time their troubles began, the couple had made a habit of locking all the doors before leaving for work. At the same moment that Stephanie was putting her key in the bedroom door, Declan was unlocking the door to the kitchen.

Upstairs and down there was evidence of fresh mischief.

Stephanie was staring at the drawers of her dressing table. All had been pulled open and their contents rifled. The bedroom window was tightly shut, exactly as she had left it. There could therefore be no doubt: their otherworldly visitor had returned.

Downstairs, Declan was struggling to come to terms with the burning candle and the Bible.

Curiously, in those moments, each decided that they would not alarm the other by telling of what they had seen.

With trembling hands, Stephanie rearranged her effects and quietly closed each drawer. Meanwhile, Declan had picked up the Bible. It was open at Proverbs. He slammed it shut, afraid to read what might be written there, and stowed it away in a kitchen cupboard. He blew out the candle. If he threw it into the bin in the yard, he reasoned, Stephanie would never know.

He was sliding back the patio door when a thought struck him. Perhaps this was someone's idea of a practical joke. After all, he was sure that the whole neighbourhood, and beyond, knew about their 'problems' by that stage. But he was remembering something else.

Declan was in the habit of popping into his local on his way home most Fridays. The regulars had got to know him. He was friendly with them all, with the exception of one individual: Scottie Byrne. No one seemed to like Scottie. He worked in a shoe repair shop in town, but he also cut keys. The word was that he could not be trusted. With his knowledge of locks, who knew what he might be capable of?

He had met Byrne the previous Friday, as he was leaving the pub. Scottie was a little drunk.

'Hey, Rooney,' he said with a smirk, 'did that ghost of yours ever come back?'

Thinking back on it now, and still puzzling over the strange tableau on the floor of his kitchen, Declan was asking himself if the unsavoury Byrne might not have something to do with it.

He returned indoors and tucked the candle-holder away in the back of a drawer. He hoped his wife would not notice it. He would clean up later. He needed time to think matters through.

He made coffee and carried the tray into the living-room.

'What's that smell?' Stephanie asked, coming downstairs.

'Smell?' Declan had not reckoned on the smell. He wished he had sprayed some air freshener.

'A burning smell. Like candle wax.'

'I think it's coming from outside,' he said. 'I opened the back door to put something in the bin and it got in. Somebody burning rubbish or something. So how was your day?' he added, quickly changing the subject.

Much later that same evening, Josie Brady was telling her husband about *her* strange day.

'It's not like you to go snooping around neighbours' houses,' he said.

'But it was awful! You'd have done the same, Noel. There's something not right about all of this. We should do something.'

'What do you suggest we do?'

'Well, you could talk to them. Say there might be burglars in the neighbourhood.'

Noel checked with the Rooneys, and came away satisfied that Josie had indeed been imagining things. No, the Rooneys had not employed a handyman. Furthermore, they assured him that the house was locked between 7.30 am and 5.30 pm and that they held the only keys. Noel, in his wisdom, said nothing about what his wife *thought* she saw: the orange light on the staircase, and the Bible and candle. He would have felt a bit stupid relating such things. Even if Josie were mistaken – and he believed that she was – he had no wish to upset the young couple further.

The Rooneys closed the door on Mr Brady's retreating back and looked at each other in dismay.

'My God, Declan, it's coming back!'

Stephanie was devastated, close to tears. In her confusion and anger she did not know what she dreaded more: the return of the manifestations or the whole street knowing about them – and suspecting it was somehow the Rooneys' own fault, that they had done something to invite this thing into their home. If Father O'Malley could think it, then why not others?

Declan tried to console. 'Look, maybe that woman was hearing things. You just don't know with people.'

He thought again of Scottie Byrne and his brief encounter with him the previous week. What if Byrne was behind it? Byrne was laughing. Was he laughing at his own sick joke? Declan did not doubt that Byrne could gain access to his house via the rear entrance; the man was forever bragging that he could pick a lock faster than any burglar, and leave no trace. What if he was responsible for that trick with the candle? Why not run upstairs and hammer on the wall for a laugh as well? Annoy the neighbours. Annoying others seemed to be his stock-in-trade. It was a daft idea, but Declan thought Byrne was a little bit daft.

He decided to share his suspicions with Stephanie. She was not convinced.

'That wouldn't explain the drawers in my dressing table.'

'Oh? What about them?'

'You might as well know,' she said with resignation. 'They were all pulled open when we came in. Just like before!'

'Well, there you are then, what was to stop him, after hammering on the wall, messing with the drawers on his way out?'

'I suppose he could have,' Stephanie slowly conceded. 'But why would he do a thing like that? We've never done him any harm. It just doesn't seem logical. For heaven's sake, I've never even spoken to the man.'

'I know. But even so, there are some very strange people in this world. Characters who get a kick out of seeing others upset. I've never liked Byrne. Wouldn't trust him as far as I could throw him.'

This much did Declan say to Stephanie. He was being less than honest, though. He did not believe that Scottie Byrne was the culprit. Nor was he prepared to face the possibility that there were paranormal forces at work. Wooden balls bouncing about the room were one thing; lighted candles and open Bibles in the kitchen were something else again. Ghosts and poltergeists, in Declan's book, did not do such things; people did. He was considering a number of possibilities. He was asking himself if he or Stephanie had made an enemy of someone without being aware of it. He was asking himself if somebody was trying to frighten them into leaving the house in Cedar Close. For what purpose? Was there perhaps something buried on the site? Stolen money? Something more sinister?

Declan was determined to solve the mystery. He would unmask the intruder. Before going to bed that night, he put his new plan into action. Over the pine floorboards in the kitchen, he sprinkled a fine covering of salt. If somebody entered the kitchen, they would leave their footprints in the salt, and prove that intervention of the human rather than the ghostly kind was at work. He made sure to lock the patio doors, and took the added precaution of locking the kitchen door as well.

While Declan was engaged downstairs, Stephanie was kneeling at her bedside, praying fervently to Michael the Archangel for protection. At the same time, she was hoping that her husband's supposition was correct, that all this was somebody's idea of a joke. If that were so, she vowed that the creep would pay the price. Nobody was going to drive her from her own home.

But something woke her in early morning, in the pre-dawn.

Stephanie sensed that a voice – a child's voice – had spoken to her, though she heard nothing further. She lay very still, hoping to hear the voice again. Strange to say, considering her fears of the night before, she did not feel frightened. She heard Declan breathing lightly in his sleep and had no wish to rouse him. Perhaps she had simply been dreaming. She lay awake, wondering about the child's voice. Though her eyes were shut, she was aware of the first light of day beginning to seep in at the window.

Idly she began to think about children, and how fine it would be to have a child of her own. She and Declan had discussed it from time to time. The plan was that in a couple of years' time, when they had enough money saved, they would start a family. Like so many young women, Stephanie hoped that her first child would be a girl.

She was picturing a delightful little girl in a frilly pink dress and auburn pigtails: a little girl not unlike the toddler she had once been. She saw her clearly in her mind's eye. The child was running to meet her, laughing and reaching out to be hugged.

What happened next was extraordinary.

Stephanie felt what could only be a small hand squeeze her upper arm. She was wide awake immediately. She sat up in bed, and switched on the bedside lamp, even though it was dawn by then. Her heart pounding, she peered at her bare arm, expecting to see a mark there. There was nothing.

She was convinced nonetheless of a presence in the room. She sensed that the little girl was still there, gazing at her and her sleeping husband. Gone was Stephanie's fear; tenderness for the child had replaced it. She sensed a need.

'Who are you, sweetheart?' she managed to whisper. 'What do you want?'

Stephanie waited with a hand on her heart. There was no response but still she sensed the presence nearby. Declan stirred in his sleep.

The atmosphere in the room was subtly changing. Stephanie, for reasons she could not understand, was drawn to the rattan chair beside the bed. Something was telling her that the 'spirit child' was seated there.

'What do you want, sweetheart?' she asked again. 'What's your name?'

This time, a response came.

'Sa—rah.' It was the voice of a little girl, a half-whisper of a voice that filled Stephanie with sadness and poignancy.

'I want to help you, Sarah,' she said, near to tears. 'What can I do?'

She waited, and waited. But no answer was forthcoming.

Minutes later Declan was awakened by his wife's loud sobbing. He understood none of it. Eventually, as he helped her down the stairs, he learned what it was that had upset her so much.

He unlocked the door to the kitchen.

'Coffee,' he said, since there was not much else he could say. 'I'll put the kettle on.'

By this time, it was fully morning. When Declan pushed open the door, the sun was bathing the kitchen in bright sunshine.

Stephanie said nothing. She remained in the doorway, staring with open mouth at the floor. Declan's plan had worked – perhaps too well. But there were no footprints in the salt he had scattered.

'God!' Stephanie had found her voice at last. 'Oh, God.'

Scrawled in the salt, in a childish hand, was a single word.

SARAH

Declan experienced a terrible sense of dread. But anger quickly took its place. He had had enough.

'Who the hell *are* you?' he yelled. 'Why are you doing this?'

The following day, the couple moved out of their house again, and went to stay with in-laws.

When Charles Cartwright encounters a particularly difficult case, as the Rooney case was proving to be, he calls on the help of a close friend of many years' standing. Florence Miller possesses what is known as the 'gift of discernment', and, being a deeply religious and devout lady, uses it freely to help others.

Florence accompanied the rector and his wife on their second visit to the Rooney home. As they journeyed there, the trio prayed for a successful outcome. Charles Cartwright was disappointed – and a touch surprised – that his first attempt had not borne fruit. It had seemed to be a fairly low-key haunting, the sort of paranormal scenario he frequently encounters. As Florence prayed, she began to receive a vision. She saw an old fireplace. She did not know what it meant, but knew the design was from another era, perhaps the late nineteenth century. She hoped that its significance would become clearer on their arrival at the house.

Reverend Charles was dismayed to see how distressed the couple were. Stephanie appeared to have lost weight; she and her husband looked tired and drawn. Present also at the house were Declan's parents. In fact, it was his mother who had persuaded him to engage the rector again; she, more than anybody else, was convinced that something unholy had entered her son's home.

The group settled down in the living-room and, over tea, the visitors listened as Declan and Stephanie told of the catalogue of manifestations that had plagued their home.

Florence is a quiet woman who prefers to take a back seat at such times. She tends to listen, awaiting signs and indications of extraphysical presences. She held her counsel as the Rooneys spoke of the new developments. She was waiting for what she terms a 'signal': a communication, whether auditory or visual, from the 'other side'. It helps her to establish who – or what – is creating the disturbance. As yet, nothing had come to her. She allowed the couple to finish their account, then posed a single question.

'Is there an old fireplace in this house?'

The Rooneys assured her that there was not. In fact only one room had an open fire: the room they were seated in. The fireplace in the living-room was – as one would expect – of contemporary design.

Reverend Charles Cartwright, for his part, was most intrigued by the name traced in the salt.

'What do you think it means?' he asked the Rooneys.

Declan confessed bafflement. He knew nobody named Sarah, he said; not unless they could include a girl by that name he had dated when a teenager. The rector pressed him further. Declan trawled his memories.

Florence, in the meantime, was noticing a change coming over the room. It was a sensation she had experienced on numerous occasions; she describes it as a kind of 'tightening apprehension', akin to what one might feel when a thunderstorm is brewing. She could hear Declan's voice receding, as if someone was turning down the volume on a radio. She waited for what she calls 'the happening'.

All at once it came. At another mention of the name 'Sarah', a pebble flew through the air and landed at their feet on the hearth-rug. It had entered from the open doorway.

The pebble had obviously come from the driveway. But how, with the hall-door shut, had it managed to materialize inside the house, alone and unaided?

'Somebody's playing games,' Charles Cartwright announced.

It was the first time he had witnessed an incident of this nature in the Rooney home. Like everyone else, he was puzzled, but the occurrence reinforced his initial theory that a child was play-acting, teasing the house's occupants. He prepared to celebrate a second Eucharist. Since the pebble had been thrown into the living-room, he judged that it would be the appropriate focus for the sacrament.

As on the first occasion, the Eucharist progressed without incident. Nothing untoward occurred to disturb the liturgy; no more pebbles were flung. After the service the rector went from room to room, cleansing the house in the name of the Lord.

As a rule, Florence never discloses anything of her experiences to the victims directly, fearing that they may hear things that would undoubtedly cause further distress. Only afterwards does she discuss her observations with the rector, and together they look for connections that may prove helpful.

On the return journey to Newcastle, Florence shared what she had experienced. She had had two psychic encounters.

The first occurred as the rector's car approached the Rooney home. She had the distinct impression that the area – the entire estate – was filled with what she called 'territorial spirits'. She claims that she could see them everywhere. Yet the interesting part of her vision concerned the Rooney house itself. Of all the houses in Cedar Close, it alone was being protected by a 'ring of angels'. She saw them circling above the roof of the property.

Her second vision occurred while the Rooneys were speaking to the rector and the pebble had landed on the hearth-rug. Florence had looked, as everyone had, to the open doorway. But no one else could sense what she sensed. She had the compelling impression that they were in the presence of a spirit child: a little girl.

Reverend Charles had suspected it in the first instance; now they felt certain that the 'playful' activity was the work of the mysterious spirit child. He was glad, and for good reason. Florence's vision had helped in establishing that there was no evil at work in 8 Cedar Close. A full exorcism would not be necessary. The best course was to pray for the child, that her spirit might find rest.

He counselled the Rooneys to do likewise.

Declan could rule out Scottie Byrne or a mischievous neighbour. In the days to come he was almost sorry he had entertained either possibility. When he thought about it, it appeared increasingly unlikely that human agents were behind the disturbances. Declan was in two minds about this. Like everyone who comes face to face with the inexplicable, his need to rationalize became paramount. If he were being asked to believe in ghosts – if there was a little girl named Sarah, who was somehow connected with an antique fireplace – he wished to know *why* she was troubling his home. He wanted it all to make some kind of sense.

He started to make inquiries. For a long time, they appeared to lead nowhere. But on 10 October 2004, five months after Charles Cartwright's second visit, and a full fourteen months after the Rooneys' problems began, Declan made a breakthrough. He had been hunting down facts that might have a bearing on the case, and had examined countless documents in local and national archives. In the historical department at Queen's University Belfast, he turned up something of great significance. In the nineteenth century, two children went missing close by what would become Cedar Close, in the area known as Ballylouth. The little girls, nine-year-old Mary Magee and Sarah Logan, aged ten, were never found.

So there she was: Sarah, the mysterious child Florence had seen, the child wearing the soiled dress. Declan experienced a tremendous sense of relief on unearthing this information. The pieces of the puzzle that had haunted him and his wife for so long were finally coming together. He hurried home in high excitement and related the good news to Stephanie.

They knew the identity of their ghost. They could pray for her now.

Stephanie went to Father O'Malley and arranged for a Mass to be said for the little girls. She anticipated that the priest could have no objection; this proved to be the case. She felt it was prudent, too, to say nothing about the intervention of a priest of another faith.

On Father O'Malley's recommendation, the Rooneys began a

nightly recitation of the rosary for the repose of Sarah's soul. Nor did they ever neglect the prayer for the protection of Michael the Archangel. Since the onset of their troubles, it had become a routine part of their lives. They knew it by heart and no longer needed to refer to the written version. Nevertheless, Stephanie was reluctant to remove those copies of the prayer she had placed in every room.

Over the previous months their house, understandably, had become a repository of sacred objects. The Rooneys and their relatives had come to the conviction that such objects were talismans against the unknown. The crucifix was now a permanent fixture on the living-room wall. A holy picture or novena hung in every room.

One thing remained to be investigated: Declan still had not satisfied his natural curiosity with regard to the fireplace that Florence had seen in her vision.

'It must mean something,' he said to Stephanie.

'I wish you'd leave it alone. What's the point in stirring it up again?'

'I think it's important that we know, Steph. Why would Florence Miller see a fireplace?'

Declan had a hunch that the answer lay on his property. He sought out the contractor who had built the development. But Mr Heaney seemed reluctant to discuss the matter. Yes, there had been a terrace of old houses. So what? No, he did not know who the 'previous owners' were. Did Rooney think he was chairman of the archaeological society or what? He had bought the land to build houses on, not for the purposes of digging up the past.

Declan asked around. Somebody must know something, he reasoned. And somebody did. In exchange for a pint or two, Kevin McTeague, one of Heaney's former employees, divulged some interesting information. He claimed that the Cedar Close development was built on the site of a fairy fort.

This gave Declan more pause for thought. He knew a little about fairy forts. There are perhaps 40,000 all told in Ireland. Most are knolls or dunes, either naturally or artificially constructed. The fact that the provenance and purpose of these mounds were unclear to the country folk gave rise to the belief, in less enlightened times, that they were the homes of the 'little people', or fairies. The superstition persists that if anyone disturbs such a site, great misfortune will befall him.

'That area beside your house is where it was,' McTeague told him. 'Heaney had it levelled, but made sure he didn't build on it. He wasn't taking any chances.'

'Oh, that's just great! Now I'm hearing this when it's too late. It would have been nice to know this before we bought the place.'

'Depends on whether you believe in all that fairy stuff,' said McTeague. 'But I remember when we were working there, it took ages for us to get the bloody job finished. Everybody took sick, one after the other. Then deliveries would be delayed; calls that Heaney made went astray. He lost a lot of money on the project. We were happy to see the back of Cedar Close, I can tell you. When I heard about your troubles, I wasn't surprised at all.'

Declan was not in the least superstitious; he did not believe in ghosts. Yet events over the past year had caused him to look closely at his scepticism. If the spirit-child theory was correct, and it had the appearance of being so, then why not the fairy story?

But what to do with such information? They could hardly sell up, not after barely two years. Besides, even if they could sell the house, it would probably fetch a much-reduced price – given the talk in the neighbourhood. McTeague had demonstrated to him that even casual acquaintances knew about the phenomena. No, Declan decided, selling up was out of the question.

If Charles Cartwright were to be believed, then the problem of the spirit child could be solved through prayer and faith. But the fairy fort? Nothing could be done about it, short of having

Heaney bulldoze the site – an unlikely, and absurd, scenario. Declan's only consolation lay in the fact that he had not been responsible for disturbing it in the first place. Perhaps McTeague's story was true: insofar that Heaney and his workforce were culpable.

Declan shared his concerns with Stephanie.

'Look,' she said, 'so far, for a whole six months, we've had no trouble – touch wood. So long as we keep praying for that little Sarah, things will be okay. God knows what happened to the poor wee thing.'

'I know. But what if it all starts up again? All that spirit stuff.'

'It won't!' she snapped. 'I wish you'd have a bit more faith instead of listening to oul' pub talk. I don't believe that fairy fort nonsense. Fairies are what alcoholics see when they've got the DTs, so I'm not surprised Kevin McTeague believes in them. He's never out of the bloody pub.'

And that seemed to end the discussion. They said their prayers and retired.

It may have been coincidence. Stephanie is not so sure. Her own feeling is that Declan's inquiries had somehow opened a door on some secret or other, and in so doing had left both of them vulnerable to aggression from 'the other side'. Whatever the cause or motivation, that night Declan was physically attacked. Of that there was no doubt. He awoke the next morning to find that scratch marks had mysteriously appeared on his torso.

A rubicon had been crossed; war was declared. From that night on, events took a turn for the worse.

Physical injury to a person by a paranormal agency is rare. According to psychical researchers, when physical interaction is present in a haunting it generally takes the form of touching, squeezing, or the sensation of an oppressive weight, none of which, in the main, leaves marks on the individual. The aggression to which Declan was subjected signalled a very worrying development. These were no longer the antics of a 'play-acting spirit child'. The rules of engagement had changed radically.

Over the coming days, and following on from the physical attack, the Rooneys would come face to face with something they had dreaded from the outset. The entity would demonstrate, by targeting the sacred objects, that it was anti-religious. When this occurs in cases of paranormal activity, when consecrated, protective objects come under attack, one must face the possibility that evil forces are at work.

The couple vacated their home yet again. Each day, they would look in after work – and each day would be confronted with incontrovertible evidence of evil intent. Over the course of a week, all the religious objects in their home were targeted.

It started with the crucifix above the fireplace. They discovered it lying on the hearth, where it had evidently been hurled with some force. What is more, the Fatima rosary that adorned it had been pulled apart and its beads scattered.

On at least two occasions, they fled the house crying out in shock and physical pain. Incredibly, the holy water in the font by the hall-door was so hot that it burnt their fingers. They had made a habit of crossing themselves on leaving the house. Something was trying to prevent them from continuing the practice.

Lourdes water, which Stephanie kept on her bedside locker, inexplicably turned to ice. More holy water was emptied onto the kitchen floor, and the bottle that contained it was flung under the table. A novena prayer to St Jude was removed from its frame, torn into tiny pieces and strewn about the bedroom floor.

But perhaps the most startlingly malign incident – and one which confirmed for the Rooneys that demonic influences were at work – involved the prayers to Michael the Archangel, those which Stephanie had placed in five separate rooms.

She discovered the words HIDE HERE NOW scrawled as if by a child's hand on the reverse of each prayer. She thought of the

Scrabble letters: they had spelled out RUN HIT HIDE.

'"Hide",' Declan mused. 'Maybe the two wee girls are playing hide and go seek together.'

'And maybe I'm going out of my f***ing mind, Declan,' said a distraught Stephanie.

He looked at her with concern. She never used that kind of language; not unless she were *truly* upset. Yet he could not let go of the idea that the phantom children were playing games again. It was better to believe *that* than to question the nature of an entity that seemed to take delight in, by turns, boiling and freezing sanctified water.

The new cycle of manifestations increased in frequency and grotesqueness. The prayer leaflets would become the focus of something even more sinister and alarming. Mysterious symbols appeared one day on the walls of the living-room, kitchen and hallway.

One, drawn at head height – about five and a half feet from the floor – resembled a staring eye. The symbols did not appear to have been applied with a writing implement, such as chalk or felt-tip marker, but seemed smudged, as if a finger had been dipped in a dark pigment of some kind. Declan thought at once of runes or hieroglyphs, but the drawings were like nothing he had ever seen before, whether in books, magazines or TV documentaries.

A curious odour pervaded the house, as of charred paper. The couple noted that it was stronger on the staircase. They hurried upstairs and inspected the bedrooms. Every copy of the prayer to Michael the Archangel was burnt. They concluded that the ash had been used to daub the graffiti on the walls downstairs.

It was time to seek help again.

Reverend Charles Cartwright is understandably disappointed, but never dispirited, when he learns that his efforts at cleansing places or individuals have not been entirely successful.

'We don't know why one exorcism works immediately and another takes longer,' he says. 'But I believe that it's all a matter of faith. The unshakable faith of the deliverance minister must be matched by the unwavering faith of the afflicted.'

Strictly speaking, in the Christian ministry there is no formalized ritual for exorcising places. Nor is there a biblical reference to the purification of dwelling-houses. The deliverance minister is therefore free to act at his own discretion. Rome's chief exorcist, Dom Gabriele Amorth, describes how he and his fellow-priest Candido Amantini go about this task.

> The Rituale [Romanum] includes some ten prayers beseeching the Lord to protect places from evil influences. They include the blessing of houses, schools and other buildings. We intone several of these prayers. Then we read the first part of the First Exorcism of persons, adapting it accordingly. Next we exorcise each room, in much the same way we would bless a house. We follow with another circuit of the rooms, this time dispensing incense. We end with more prayers. After the exorcism, it is very efficacious to celebrate a Mass in the house.

'Very often the blessing of a house and a service of the Eucharist will be enough,' Reverend Charles adds, 'but there are those cases that demand more robust measures. The infestation of the Rooney household was one such case.'

When the rector visited the house for the third time – again accompanied by Alison and Florence – he was struck by the threatening atmosphere. It was almost tangible even as they entered.

'Evil invariably comes with a coldness,' he says. 'Science has never been able to explain why this is so. I was not aware of it on the first two occasions but I had the impression – and Florence confirmed it – that the child spirit had been replaced, or to be more accurate, "used", by sinister forces to gain access to the house.'

He celebrated another Eucharist in the presence of the Rooney family. More prayers were said; the rooms were blessed a third time. As before, the rector and his party left Dungiven in the belief that whatever it was that had laid siege to the house had departed, never to return.

'We felt liberated then,' says Stephanie. 'We felt that a door was shut.'

It was a door that had been opened by the restless spirit of a little lost girl named Sarah, and used as a portal for evil to enter and disrupt the lives of an innocent young couple.

We wonder about the scented wooden balls that started it all. Where did they end up?

'Oh, we burnt them a long time ago,' Stephanie says. 'No more of that for us. We see them from time to time in the shops, and most people would say they look pretty and smell nice. But Declan and me, whenever we see them, well, a shiver runs through us. And who can blame us for that?'

MR GANT AND THE
NEIGHBOUR FROM HELL

MALACHI GANT AND Charlie Sherrin had never quite been friends, yet had an understanding. Charlie is a neighbour, who shares a quiet road in a quiet town in the northwest of the country.

Malachi is retired now, and has been for a good ten years. He was always a hard worker, and in the course of four decades or more had built up a very successful hardware business with a presence in three midland towns. When he sold the shops and retired, he had enough left over to realize a lifelong ambition: to see as much of the world as he could within a timespan of two years. His wife Blainead – 'Blenny' to all who know her – was delighted by the prospect. She had rarely ventured far from her native Sligo.

First, they flew to America. Malachi's younger brother lived in Boston. They stayed with the family for a month, before renting an RV and setting out in the direction of San Francisco, taking in no fewer than sixteen states in their leisurely progress across the continent. They devoted four more months to exploring California and Arizona, before travelling on down to México and South America. A year later they found themselves in Florida, booking a cruise to Egypt.

It was 1996; it would be some years before the attack on the Twin Towers induced Americans to stay at home, and in particular to avoid the Middle East. The passenger list was full when, at the beginning of October, the liner set sail out of Fort Lauderdale. Two weeks later, the Gants' party arrived in Alexandria, wended their way slowly down the Nile to Cairo, and at last to Luxor. It would be the finale of their Egyptian sojourn, before they moved on to a resort by the Red Sea.

The cruise company had laid on a special treat for that evening. As dusk settled over the Nile, the Gants and the other guests were escorted by uniformed guides down the long Avenue of Sphinxes connecting Karnak and the temple of the old gods. There they were, scores of them: ram-headed, floodlit and magnificent, crouching stark against a background of palms and a sky the colour of cobalt. Costumed light bearers had been stationed at intervals, each holding aloft a flambeau. It was kitsch but it was breathtaking. It was calculated to set the mood for the remainder of the evening.

Apéritifs were served in the colonnaded temple. Thereupon the guests entered the magnificent open-air dining area, and were seated at tables laid with white and gold linen. Candlelight bathed the scene, and the floodlit, ancient columns formed a stunning backdrop on three sides. The air was laden with rich spices and the aromas of the East. Waiters in traditional costume glided from one table to another, serving a four-course dinner as music emanated from a classical quartet.

'This is the life, eh?' someone said. 'Sure beats an all-you-can-eat shrimp supper down at Al's Seafood Diner.'

His friends chuckled. The food was excellent, the company convivial. The wines, too, were fine and copious.

Halfway through the meal, however, just as the musicians had ended one piece and were about to embark on another, the tranquil atmosphere of the evening was shattered. A terrifying scream rent the air, sending a chill through the assembled diners.

'It was like a wounded animal, not human at all,' Malachi recalls, 'and it frightened the life out of everybody, because everybody stopped eating at once. You could've heard a pin drop, as they say.'

All eyes were fixed on a solitary man at one of the tables. He seemed oblivious to what he had just done, and sat staring into the middle distance, at something it appeared only he could see. Moments later he got to his feet, letting the chair fall back with a clatter. Malachi recognized him; he had spoken to him earlier: the usual friendly chit-chat. His name was Walter Ehrlich and he seemed an amiable sort. He had been to Egypt on a previous occasion, he said, many years before. His wife had been with him then but she died in 1978. This year he had come alone.

Perhaps that brief conversation had endeared Malachi to Ehrlich, because he now appeared to single him out. Slowly but deliberately he approached the Gants' table, a glass of wine in his hand. The other guests could only stare; some were frightened, others uneasy. Their hosts seemed unsure of what to do.

'Where did you say you were from?' Ehrlich asked, fixing Malachi with a look of mild aggression.

'Ireland.'

'Catholic, right?' He drank out his wine glass and replenished it at once from a decanter. In a loud voice he said: 'All you Irish are Catholics, that right?'

Somebody tut-tutted. Mr Ehrlich was introducing a very sour note into what should have been a perfect evening.

He pointed directly at Malachi and lowered his face to meet the Irishman's eyes. For a fleeting moment, Malachi could not believe what he was seeing. Even now, years later, his voice quavers as he recalls the incident.

'God Almighty, I'll never forget that face,' he says. 'Blenny saw it too and she was very upset.'

The face before him was no longer that of Walter Ehrlich. The features had transmogrified into something thoroughly freakish: a mask of utter malevolence. The lips were pulled back in a terrible grimace. And the eyes: they were no longer the eyes of a human, but hooded, like those of a cold-blooded creature predating mankind.

'Let's go, Malachi,' Blenny urged. 'Let's get out of here.'

He felt her hand on his wrist. She was trembling. But he was already recoiling from that awful face. He felt that he could not get far enough away from it.

Walter Ehrlich was not through with him just yet, though. As quickly as the dreadful, reptilian aspect had taken hold of his features, so did it seem to leave. The face returned to normal. Walter straightened and stepped back from the table.

'F*** *you*!' he roared. He looked fiercely about him, and Malachi will never forget the shocked expressions of the other diners. 'F*** you all! *We* f*** you all, and to hell with the lot of you. There's no God here. Your God is dead!'

To everyone's astonishment, the troubled guest emitted a loud squeal, ran in the direction of the pillars to one side of the temple and vanished into the darkness beyond.

All present – dinner guests, organizers, waiters, musicians – were appalled.

'Alcohol,' muttered the Egyptian maître d', shaking his head, his Islamic sensibilities repelled by the display. 'To drink so much, not good.'

'I don't think so,' said a white-haired man, turning to Malachi. 'No, I don't think it's alcohol. There are demons at work there.'

'You're joking.'

'No joke,' the American said. He was frowning. Blenny had exchanged pleasantries with the man's wife during the cruise. She had learned that he was a pastor of some kind, retired for many years. 'That's demonic. I've seen it before, lots of times. When a man starts using that kind of language – and referring to himself in the plural – it's pretty clear that there are demons at work.'

The dinner was upset, but not ruined. The quartet struck up again, playing a lively set. A waiter righted the fallen chair and removed what remained of Walter's meal. Malachi Gant was intrigued; he wished to learn more from the retired pastor. He was disappointed; the American was reluctant to discuss such matters. He murmured something about 'leaving well enough alone', and went on to ply a neighbour with golf stories.

Next morning, Malachi and Blenny found the 'demoniac' at a poolside table. Walter looked pale, red-eyed and nervous, and was – even at that early hour – nursing a cocktail of some description. He studiously ignored Malachi, and for that matter everybody else in the party. The Gants never saw him again. According to the tour guide, Mr Ehrlich had cut short his cruise and caught a plane back to Atlanta, his home-town.

Malachi and Blenny returned to Ireland in 1998. They had visited four continents. They had seen more sights than some will see in a lifetime. They brought back with them so many wonderful memories, but Malachi is keen to stress that not all their memories were pleasant ones. Blenny and he had seen the world in all its facets, and some were unsettling, even gravely disturbing. He cites the Luxor incident involving Walter Ehrlich as being the most disturbing of all.

Today, at seventy-four, and having endured four torturous years of demonic oppression, Malachi is forced to admit that the event in Egypt haunts him still. In hindsight he sees it, not as an isolated, random occurrence, but as part of a whole: the sinister beginning of his troubles.

'What if I hadn't gone on that cruise?' he asks despairingly. 'It was as if that "face" followed me all the way home. I've never been the same since.'

Malachi is a nervous individual. This seems at first out of character because he is an imposing man: well over six feet tall, broad in the shoulder, with a grip like a blacksmith's. He towers over Blenny, who, having brought coffee and biscuits, leaves Malachi to his story.

'She knows something of what I'm going through,' he says, 'but

I keep the more frightening bits to myself. I can't have her getting upset.'

His hands are shaking as he stirs his coffee. He seems genuinely frightened of something. We are here on the referral of a priest who has told us only a little about the case. It may well be that he wished us to hear the details from the 'sufferer's' own lips, that we could arrive at a more objective analysis. Malachi seems hesitant about sharing his experience. He reminds us from time to time that he is speaking of it 'only because Father Ignatius asked me to'.

His story centres on his neighbour Charlie Sherrin. He is a widower, some thirty years Malachi's junior, who lives down the road with his two teenaged daughters.

Malachi has known the Sherrin family all his life. He went to school with Charlie's father; he watched the sons and daughters grow up and one by one leave the parental home. Charlie was the eldest; he remained. He is good with his hands, Malachi tells us; he practically rebuilt single-handedly the house he inherited, doubling its floor area, and in so doing, quadrupling its market value.

When Malachi had his hardware business, the Sherrins were among his regular customers. He remembers how Charlie's father would come to him for everything from a nail to a bench grinder.

'Dan was a creature of habit,' he says. 'If he bought from you once, he was a customer for life. He did a lot of nixers for people in the town here, mostly in the evenings and at weekends. I'd hire big things out to him: generators, sanders, rotavators, that kind of thing. Charlie got a lot of that from the father. Terrible good with his hands. Never idle.'

On retirement, Malachi disposed of the business but kept some stock. He extended his garage to accommodate it all. He is an altruistic individual and well liked in the area, not least because of his habit of lending power tools and the like to friends and neighbours. When his daughter married, he helped her to buy her first home, and even lent a hand with the decorating. His son-in-law got on well with Charlie Sherrin. They drank together, moved with the same crowd.

All that ended five years ago, however, on a summer's night when Charlie showed his dark side. The incident is an open secret on the road – yet nobody mentions it, not even Blenny.

'We don't talk about it,' Malachi says. 'We never discuss it. As far as she's concerned, it's over and done with. That's how she likes to keep it.'

So what did happen on a balmy June night in 2001? What was it that transformed Malachi Gant from a healthy and vigorous man into a nervous wreck? The answer must lie a few hundred yards farther along the road, behind the well-kept hedges of the Sherrin family home. But Charlie is saying nothing. It is also futile to question the other neighbours, including Malachi's son-in-law, who was one of the eyewitnesses to what occurred. What is left is circumstantial evidence – which is nonetheless compelling – and Malachi's own harrowing account.

Charlie Sherrin called round at about ten that evening. It was dusk and still warm. He was returning a hedge-trimmer which Malachi had kindly lent him. They strolled back together from the shed. Malachi suggested a glass of whiskey. He had 'the remains of a bottle' in the house and, as he himself was not much of a drinker, did not want it 'going to waste'. Charlie readily agreed.

'But no sooner had we made ourselves comfortable in the parlour than he started,' Malachi says. 'Complaining about everybody and anybody, so he was: the children, his in-laws. But that's the way he was: always finding fault. I think he must have had a run-in with everybody he met that day. Maybe the weather had got to him. It was a very hot day, and I remember he was still in his shorts when he came round with the trimmer.'

Malachi was not surprised to find Sherrin in such a state. He hoped that the whiskey would calm him.

'He carried so much hatred in him,' he tells us. 'Or maybe it was bitterness; I don't know. He was forever running people down and he had such a vicious temper.'

The temper is something that Malachi returns to time and time again. He recalls Charlie's behaviour towards his children as they were growing up.

'They were great kids. But he'd often fire stones at them in a temper. Big stones. I'd see him at it and think: if one of those stones was to hit that little girl it'd do serious injury.'

He goes on, painting as he does a picture of a strangely unpleasant and volatile man.

'He'd lose it completely. I remember one time I was helping him mix some cement for the floor of a conservatory he was building. Something went wrong with the mixer – I don't know what, but the cement was coming out all lumpy. Now anyone else would have switched the thing off and had a look at it. Not Charlie. He starts kicking the thing and cursing. The language was terrible, very obscene. He ended up destroying the mixer, so he had to pay for it in the end. That's the sort he is: he just goes into a blind rage and doesn't know *what* he's doing any more. I pity the daughters; always have.'

For years, Malachi has been concerned for their welfare. Nor was it only their father's violent temper they had to fear; it seemed to Malachi that Charlie's relationship with the children was always a little suspect.

'He never got on with one of his daughters,' Malachi confides. 'The oldest one. I don't know what was going on there. It could be anything. He'd talk about things in front of the girls that wouldn't be nice among adults. He'd always have language that wasn't good, or yarns and dirty stories, always of a sexual nature.

Given what he did to me, I would say that it wasn't only physical abuse those children suffered at his hands. He could be terrible obscene. I don't know how many times I saw him even going to the toilet in front of his daughters.'

Malachi sees our confusion. He explains.

'I'd be in his back garden. In the summer, like, maybe he'd have a barbecue.' He shakes his head sadly. 'He wasn't *all* bad, you know. But he'd be after drinking I don't know how many cans of lager and be wanting to go to the toilet. So in front of the girls he'd open his pants and let go against the hedge or something. It was a strange thing to do, but Charlie saw no harm in it.' Malachi pauses, reflecting. 'Or maybe he did know it was wrong, and did it out of divilment. He was like that. The children were afraid of him. They were always very quiet, never a cheep out of them.'

He continues his account of the June evening. Charlie Sherrin had appeared to be his customary complaining self; but there was nothing out of the ordinary that Malachi could see. They had drunk a glass of whiskey and he had poured another, finishing the bottle. He turned to fetch the water jug. Then something happened that made his blood run cold. All at once, he was right back in Egypt, hearing once again the ear-splitting howl of the demoniac, Walter Ehrlich.

Charlie Sherrin was squealing like a pig.

The pig has had a hard time of it throughout history. In at least two major religions, the animal is looked upon as an 'unclean' creature, whose flesh is denied to the faithful. There is no satisfactory reason for this, despite repeated attempts by Jewish and Islamic scholars to copper-fasten the proscription on the basis of biological or nutritional science. Yet pigs crop up often in cases of demonic disturbance.

In addition, devils and satyrs were traditionally depicted with cloven, pig-like, hoofs. No doubt the oft-quoted biblical story of the Gadarene swine did much to associate the pig with the demonic in the Christian consciousness. The fact remains, however, that pig sounds are identified with several of the most notorious episodes of diabolic infestation. They were reported in one of the most shocking: that of the Smurl family in Pennsylvania, a haunting that lasted many years. At the height of the disturbances, porcine noises were heard coming from within the walls of the family's home.

Malachi froze on hearing the blood-curdling squeal. But, before he could react, he felt a tremendous blow to the back of his skull. Only later did he conclude that Charlie Sherrin had struck him with the empty whiskey bottle. He passed out.

When he recovered consciousness, he was lying outside on his front lawn. Evidently Sherrin had dragged him there.

'He proceeded to kick me; he kicked me very badly,' Malachi recalls.

In fact, the attack was so vicious that the victim required six days of hospitalization. Malachi, dazed and bewildered, lay screaming on the grass as the neighbour assaulted him most brutally. He was dimly conscious of Blenny emerging from the house, of his neighbours Jim and Margaret running down the garden path that separated their property from his own. He remembers all three attempting to pull Sherrin off him. It proved impossible. He seemed to have the strength of ten men. Malachi heard Blenny scream as she was flung across the grass. Margaret and Jim suffered a similar fate.

But Malachi's nightmare was only beginning. His hands are shaking as he relives that terrible night and relates what next occurred.

'Sherrin pulled the clothes off me,' he says. 'I couldn't believe what was happening. It was like it was happening to somebody else. He tried to have sex with me – there's no other word for it. He was trying to have sex with me. I was semi-conscious and I couldn't move. The weight of him was indescribable. It was like as if I had the weight of a big plough-horse lying on top of me.'

Then the unbelievable – and truly terrifying – took place. As Malachi lay on his front lawn, in great pain and with his clothing in disarray, he was aware of something extraordinary happening to the ground itself, within a radius of three feet of him. It was slowly splitting open.

'When Sherrin was on top of me he kept trying to force my face into the ground, but I managed to keep my head up so that my chin got buried instead. That way I was just about able to breathe. With my head in that position and my body paralyzed, the only part of me I could move were my eyes, or so I thought. I could see this big curved gash opening up in front of me and I knew something dreadful was about to appear. I tried to squeeze my eyes shut, but I couldn't . . . I just couldn't.'

The vision that Malachi was forced to witness was indeed more dreadful than anything he could have imagined. Five objects began to rise slowly out of the earth. They formed a rough semicircle about him and the man who was trying to sodomize him. Maddened by pain though he was, Malachi was in no doubt as to what the objects were. They were human heads.

'They were terrible looking. It was the grotesque face that I'd seen in Egypt, multiplied five times – only worse. These faces were disfigured: all sores, terrible teeth and mouths, and they were all biting, like biting towards me. It was like a vision from hell, worse than anything you could ever dream about, and the stench coming from them was terrible. They just rose up out of the ground, staring at me, trying to attack me – but they couldn't because they had no bodies that I could see. Just the heads. I'll never forget them. I thought I was going to die at that moment. I was calling out to my wife and Jim and Margaret. The heads were shrieking. It was as if they were waiting for Sherrin to kill me. Like I was some sort of offering that he was making to them.'

It is an astonishing account of a near-apocalyptic vision, the agony of a severely traumatized man. But, leaving aside for a moment the most bizarre aspect – the nightmarish heads – the account is scarcely credible. On a calm summer's evening a neighbour suddenly goes berserk; without provocation he attacks a man who has always been kind to him; he drags him out in front of his house, strips him, and tries to rape him in the presence of his wife and next-door neighbours. It defies belief.

Malachi remembers that, for a moment, the great weight pressing down upon him relaxed. He found his voice.

'Jesus help me!' he cried out. 'Jesus help me!'

At the sound of his entreaties Charlie Sherrin abruptly left off his attack. The ghoulish heads, their mouths still opening and shutting obscenely, began to retract into the earth. Malachi felt the weight on his body ease a little further. But his ordeal was not yet at an end. Suddenly, the hair on his scalp was being yanked upward with great violence. Before he knew what was happening, his abuser was crouched down in front of him; their faces were almost touching.

But the face that confronted Malachi was no longer that of his attacker. He was looking into features that resembled those of the hideous heads. He began to scream uncontrollably. Sherrin thrust his victim's face into the earth to muffle his screams, and turned to address the onlookers.

'We're not finished yet!' he crowed. 'We're going to make an example of Malachi.' In an eerily calm voice, he told them in obscene detail what he intended to do.

Malachi was reminded of another frightening parallel with that of the Egypt incident: the use of the word 'we'. He remembered the pastor's words: 'When a man starts using that kind of language, and referring to himself in the plural, it's plain that there are demons at work.'

The pastor had good grounds for saying this. The Gospels of Luke and Mark record how Christ came upon a possessed man who evidently lived in a cemetery. On being asked his identity he replied, 'My name is Legion.' Luke explains the curious name: 'He said Legion because many devils were entered into him.'

Sherrin returned his attention to his victim and attempted to enact that which he had just described. Malachi is shaking more than ever as he recalls the attack. He avoids detail. Mercifully, it seems to have been over quickly. At last, his terrible work done, Sherrin left without a word. When the coast was clear, Blenny and the others rushed to Malachi's side and helped him into the house.

'They got me in the door,' he says. 'I couldn't get up the stairs and lay there very badly broke up. Blenny got the doctor for me. He took me into hospital.'

Malachi told the doctors and nursing staff that he had fallen down. No one believed him; his injuries were not consistent with a fall. It was evident that he had been attacked. They asked him if he knew the identity of his attacker. He lied. They asked him again. Somebody wanted to alert the Gardaí but Malachi stubbornly refused to involve the law. Even in his suffering – and the appalling sense of shame and outrage the assault had engendered – he still had consideration for Sherrin's daughters, and had no wish to cause them hardship.

As Malachi lay recovering in hospital, his mind was a riot of thoughts, all frantically trying to explain his neighbour's atrocious and thoroughly unprovoked conduct. He could find no explanation. It did occur to him, however, that it might not have been the first time that Charlie had assaulted a man in this way. The more he thought about it, the more little memories of Sherrin began to stir. He was remembering certain words and actions, and hints left by the children and others. . . .

Yet Malachi is an unusually forgiving and understanding man. When, three days following the attack, Charlie came to visit him in the hospital, he received him without rancour. Charlie, for his part, denied any recollection of the incident. He looked with dismay at Malachi's bruises, some healed, many not. Malachi insists that he almost saw compassion in that look; compassion mixed with remorse.

'I don't remember a thing,' Sherrin said.

'Well, *I* do!' Malachi told him. 'Why did you do it, Charlie?'

'I honestly can't remember a thing,' he insisted. And with that he jumped up from his chair and hurriedly left the ward. That was the last time Malachi spoke to him. Five uneasy years have now passed.

'My trouble didn't stop there,' Malachi Gant says. 'The heads gave me an awful turn and I couldn't forget them; they kept returning to haunt me.'

It is undoubtedly the motif of the grisly heads that transforms the case of a man being attacked by a deranged neighbour into something altogether more sinister. One's initial response to such outlandish accounts must be to query the state of mind of the narrator at the time. Certainly Malachi, by his own admission, was in no fit state to think clearly. He had been knocked senseless by a blow to the head, dragged from his home and kicked mercilessly, in the head as well as the rest of his body. He was dazed. In such a state of disorientation it is easy to imagine things. Yet a vision of ghastly heads, such as Malachi claims to have seen, seems to belong more properly in the realms of drug-induced hallucination than a vision brought on by pain. Not even the horrors reported by those experiencing delirium tremens come close to this description. It has more in common with the terrible visions recounted by the saints and mystics of antiquity.

In short, the heads are the false note in the story. The vision is easily discounted – and would have been, had Malachi's story ended there. It did not. Some weeks after the attack, when he had recovered from his injuries, he had another ordeal. Fearful though it was, it was infinitely more benign than the first.

Father Ignatius McCarthy's monastery is in the next county; over the years Malachi was a frequent visitor. He would give his services freely to the monks when they needed odd jobs done or – as was often the case – when they required the use of a power tool.

He was drawn to that place for two reasons: he would find spiritual renewal there, and he could look in on an old schoolfriend, Brother Canice. The two were very close. In adult life the monk had become Malachi's confidant. If he ever experienced a crisis of faith – no matter how big or how insignificant – Brother Canice would unfailingly set him on the right path again.

He died on New Year's Day, 2000, a few minutes after midnight. Malachi was glad that his old friend saw a 'little bit of the millennium'.

'He was fascinated by the idea. It meant more to him than most of us. He loved the notion of Jesus going into a third millennium. It's what he'd always prayed for.'

Since the incident in his front garden Malachi had been tormented by memories of the terrible heads. He had nightmares about them, and on occasion would awaken from sleep to find that the horrible vision was still with him, the tableau of the ring of heads appearing suspended in the air above his bed. He prayed often and long for deliverance from them. On a certain September night, when the nightmare had seemed more real – and more threatening – than ever, something roused him.

'I was staring in terror at the heads above me,' he says, 'when I realized there was a figure standing by the bedside. I looked up and saw Brother Canice. He was as real as you are now. He was looking down at me and smiling. I think he had a pair of rosary beads in his hand. When I looked again the terrible heads were gone, and from that time on I never saw them again. That was all due to Brother Canice. I'm sure of it.'

* * *

The attack in June was proving more devastating than Malachi imagined. Not only did his mental health suffer but there was a physical deterioration as well. It was as though something were attacking his entire person, as a virus will enter the body and work its deadly way through the various organs and cell systems. That summer, Malachi was laid low with a raft of minor ailments, from head-colds to muscle pain to inexplicable rashes. He always had a strong constitution and was dismayed to find himself visiting his doctor sometimes twice a week. Dr Moran could find no immediate cause beyond what he called 'the onset of old age'. Perhaps of most concern was Malachi's sudden weight loss. He had dropped nearly two stone in eight weeks.

'"Wasting disease" was what I kept thinking of,' Malachi says. 'I read it somewhere, and those words kept coming back to me. I didn't understand it at all; I was eating the same as I always did – Blenny saw to that. In the end Dr Moran sent me into hospital for tests. I was there two days; they looked at me from top to bottom. Couldn't find a thing wrong with me.'

He was discharged, and advised to have lots of bed rest. But this was to prove impossible. His arrival home coincided with the onset of a series of paranormal events that served to drive him further into despair.

'It was the second night I was home. I was sleeping on my own because of my illness, and I wakened to see something happening to the picture of the Sacred Heart which hung on the wall. It was suspended in the air at the foot of the bed. And as I was lying there trying to figure out if I was seeing things, these two hands appeared either side of the picture and turned it back to front. God, it had a terrible effect on me.'

In Malachi's eyes the sight of the disembodied hands was frightening enough. Yet what caused him the most torment was the idea that Christ was – almost literally, as he saw it – turning

His back on him. Malachi felt that he was being sent a very clear message.

He increased the frequency and intensity of his prayers, but seemingly to no avail. Whatever it was that was haunting him was not to be put off so easily. It stepped up its nocturnal visits.

'I'd see nothing,' Malachi says, 'but I'd always feel an evil presence in the room, near my feet, at my shoulders. I'd get stone cold in my feet and legs, so cold. I couldn't move. I'd wake up and feel it coming into the room. Sometimes I'd feel it on my chest – this terrible weight. One night it was so bad I screamed.'

Blenny Gant awoke with a jolt to find Malachi in a very distressed state. She could not discern a cause; there was nothing out of the ordinary that she could see. The crushing weight had lifted at the same moment Malachi cried out. Not wishing to frighten her, he pretended he had had a nightmare. But Blenny *did* notice something odd: a smell of burning in the room. She described it as being 'like the smell of a fire in a gypsy's camp'.

'From then on, I'd only smell it in the middle of the night when she'd be asleep,' Malachi recalls. 'I'd wake up to the terrible smell and I knew it was the thing again. I knew it was standing beside the bed and I'd just lie there terrified. I felt that if I turned on the light I'd maybe see it, and I just couldn't face that.'

But face it he must, as he discovered. Malachi could just about endure the frightful apparition in the dark of night, but when it began attacking him in broad daylight, his torment became unbearable.

'Sometimes I would feel it moving through the house. God, it terrified me. I always knew when it was coming for me because my body temperature would drop. The temperature in the room wouldn't be any different; it would just be me. I'd start to shiver, and turn blue from head to toe – really freezing cold. God, it was terrifying. I'd concentrate on Brother Canice, sort of talk to him in my head. I'd ask him to help me. I believed his spirit was somehow watching over me, and that was a comfort.'

Nevertheless, the 'presence' in his home refused to leave. Almost every day he had the unsettling, and constant, feeling of being under observation.

'One time when I was driving I looked in the rear-view mirror and felt it on the back seat. I nearly crashed the car with the shock of it. After that I stopped driving. It was just too dangerous.'

Malachi's son-in-law and daughter would take turns in accompanying him whenever he made a long journey. He found himself visiting the monastery less often than he would have liked. At the same time, he sensed a power of some kind attempting to come between him and his religious faith.

'There was a time when I couldn't say my prayers,' he confesses, 'and I was somebody who prayed often. I couldn't say my prayers or read my missal. I'd have the book in my hands and wanted to tear it up several times. I couldn't read anything any more – my missal or anything else for that matter, not even a paper. I felt I was being worn down. Whenever I tried to go to Mass, some kind of force seemed to be preventing me. I'd get terribly agitated and confused on a Sunday morning. Those times I was well enough to go, it would be pushing against me as soon as I got through the church gates. It hated anything holy.'

The last should have alerted Malachi to the true nature of his torment. In fact, he concedes that it did. Yet he was trying to convince himself, in the face of all evidence to the contrary, that it was a battle he could fight alone. He toyed with the notion that his problems were psychological, that it might all be in his head. For all he knew he might be imagining everything. He might even be going a little insane.

He decided to seek medical advice, and went to his GP, Dr Moran. Malachi had been seeing him, off and on, for many years and the doctor was well acquainted with his medical history. He had been unable to ascertain the cause of Malachi's physical decline in the wake of the Sherrin attack. Now his patient was coming to him with a story that was so fantastical it beggared belief. Moran was being asked to make a leap of faith in order to explain the inexplicable.

'I told him everything. He had no trouble believing me because he knew I was a man who didn't invent things. At the end of it all he said: "It's not a doctor you need, Malachi. It's a priest."'

It was a highly unusual statement for the GP to make. Most victims of demonic oppression report that they encounter a wall of scepticism when they confide in their doctors. It is understandable. Few members of the medical profession are willing to allow that a patient's difficulties may have a spiritual, as opposed to a psychological, cause. It is perhaps an indication of enlightenment and insight that Malachi's doctor recognized the presence of something unclean behind the attacks.

So a priest it had to be. Malachi turned to the obvious: the monastery.

It is situated on the outskirts of a small town, no more than a large village, in County Sligo. It is reached from the road by a driveway that meanders between pasturelands where many cattle once grazed but which are now bare, save for a small flock of sheep. In its heyday, the monastery housed a community of over two hundred men; now there are fewer than thirty, the numbers dwindling inexorably with the passing years, as the old monks die off and no young novices come to take their places.

Malachi had a friend drive him there. He had no fears as they negotiated the familiar driveway. He had driven it countless times, knew every bend and pothole. The nearer they drew to the big house, the more at ease he became. On rounding the final bend he caught sight of the chapel with the monks' quarters to the rear. Adjacent was the house itself. It is a fine building in the Queen Anne style, once the home of a prominent Anglo-Irish family. The last heir, a convert to Catholicism, died in 1912 and bequeathed the house and lands to the religious community. Over the past two decades, the monks disposed of much of the original acreage, as well as taking on a farm manager from the area, the first time the business of running the agricultural wing of the establishment had been entrusted to a layman.

There was only one other car in sight as they drew to a halt on the gravel in front of the entrance. It belonged to an elderly woman; she emerged from the little shop which sold religious goods as Malachi's driver cut the engine.

He had a four o'clock appointment with a certain Father Ignatius. He only knew the good man to see, but a younger brother at the monastery had recommended him as an individual distinguished by his purity, his piety – and his reputation as an arch-foe of the demonic.

'But I nearly didn't get to see the priest that day,' Malachi says. 'When I approached the door there was a pressure like a wind. Only it wasn't a wind; it was something like it, trying to stop me from entering. It was like walking against a very strong gale. It was like what I used to experience going through the church gates of a Sunday – but worse, much worse. Something didn't want me to see that priest.'

It is Father Ignatius who urged us to get in touch with Malachi Gant when we expressed an interest in cases relating to demonic oppression. Malachi has been coming to see him regularly throughout the past four years. He is an elderly man, a native of Clare; despite having left the county of his birth some fifty years ago, he never lost the accent. He speaks softly and one has to listen closely to catch his words. Yet his gentle demeanour masks an iron will and a fierce intelligence. There is also an air of another time about him; one could almost believe that the saints and Christian martyrs of antiquity looked and sounded a lot like Father Ignatius.

We are told that men and women from the length and breadth

of Ireland come to see this priest when danger of a demonic hue threatens. They regard him as a spiritual warrior *par excellence*. He is, however, less the crucifix-brandishing exorcist as the monk who spends most of his waking hours in prayer, interceding for the souls of many. He rarely leaves the monastery, yet will astonish the visitor with his almost uncanny understanding of the world beyond its walls. He seems to have even more understanding of the metaphysical regions.

'Father Ignatius thinks that Charlie Sherrin is possessed,' Malachi says. 'He came to that conclusion at once. He asked me about the family, about Charlie's daughters. He was also keen to know about Charlie's father.'

Father Ignatius would indeed have identified, from Malachi's account of his neighbour, several of the hallmarks of the possessed. During the furious sexual assault, Charlie Sherrin revealed what could be construed as evidence of a demonized personality (see APPENDIX ONE, p. 366). Sherrin used the plural pronoun when referring to himself. His face assumed, if only fleetingly, bestial characteristics. He was capable of 'possessed gravity' – that is, of acquiring immovable weight; Malachi likened the weight on top of him to that of 'a plough-horse'. The attacker emitted inhuman sounds: the pig-like squeal. Furthermore, Malachi often felt repulsed by Sherrin's behaviour around his own family: aside from his violent outbursts at minor upsets, he often engaged in lewd talk and behaviour in front of his offspring. In the aftermath of the assault, when he visited Malachi in hospital, he claimed to have no recollection of what he had done.

Finally, there was the hellish vision of the disembodied heads. Not only had the preternatural broken cover during the assault, but further phenomena were continuing to oppress Malachi.

What Malachi recounted in the course of a number of interviews is harrowing – for want of a better word. The events reduced a once-robust man to a nervous wreck, a man who dares not be alone for more than a few minutes at a time.

As we take our leave at his front door, our eyes are inevitably drawn to his garden. There are seven species of rose growing there, in colours ranging from saffron to an almost purple red. Somebody has trained a wilder variety to climb the pebble-dashed wall almost to the first-floor window. Across the way, the green fields have been earmarked for a new shopping development. For now, it is a tranquil place, far from the main road. We hear only a dog barking off in the distance. Malachi nods in the direction of a patch of grass under his living-room window.

'I don't like that spot in the garden,' he says with sadness. 'I only mow it. I thought of digging there last year, to lay a little ornamental pond, but I couldn't do it. I broke out in a sweat at the thought of it. I wouldn't put a spade in that now if you paid me.'

There is a great deal unresolved in this case, yet Father Ignatius has total confidence in Malachi's ability to heal his spiritual self.

'He has come through this ordeal a stronger and wiser man,' he says. 'That is the compensation for enduring great evil. It forces us to learn great lessons. Malachi's faith was always strong, but since this dreadful episode he's had to draw on the power of God more and more. That is the victory.'

Would that the same could be said of Charlie Sherrin.

'Charlie needs an exorcism, but he must want it himself,' the priest says. 'It has to be his decision. And he's not ready yet to make that decision.'

An acquaintance agrees, but feels that the civil authorities should be alerted.

'Malachi ought to have gone to the Guards as soon as that happened,' he says grimly. 'It's a criminal matter as well as a spiritual one. He still can. It's only four years, and the hospital will have records. I have the feeling that more people are in danger. I have the feeling that Charlie's done this sort of thing before.'

Having listened to Malachi's appalling account, and observed his ongoing suffering, we are prompted to ask a very pertinent question. Why does he continue to live so close to the man who caused him such anguish? Surely it cannot be pleasant to look out – every day of his life – at the garden in which the ferocious attack took place. Malachi answers without hesitation.

'Oh, but I could never leave this house,' he says. 'My grandfather built it. It was his home and he was very proud of it. I'd be letting him down if I left. Charlie Sherrin has taken a lot from me but he's not going to drive me out of here.'

When put in those terms, his reasoning is hard to fault. He is a courageous man and his faith is strong. His battle is not yet won but he believes that good will triumph over evil in the end.

'I go to Father Ignatius whenever things get really bad, and he keeps me on the right road,' Malachi tells us. 'I've asked him to do an exorcism but he says I'm not the one who is demonized. He prays with me and for me, and I'm praying the thing won't win. But it keeps on trying. Whenever I go to see Father Ignatius there'll be that same wind again, trying to keep me away from the monastery door.'

He reaches into his shirt and brings out a little silver chain. There is a medal attached; it is circular and displays a bearded saint in a monk's habit.

'It's St Benedict,' he says. 'Father Ignatius gave it to me.' He points to a large cross on the reverse, around which are arranged a number of letters. 'Latin. It means: "Get thee behind me, Satan! Do not tempt me with vain things. You offer evil? Drink your own poison!" Father Ignatius says it's the only Catholic medal with an exorcism on it. He says it's very powerful against evil spirits.'

'I still have the presence in my room at night,' he continues. 'I'll wake up to find the awful stench, that burning smell. I still get the pressing weight on me, but it's not so often now, thank

God! Sometimes when I go to the monastery, I'll be attacked that very night. Father Ignatius always asks me the same question. He asks if I can forgive Charlie and I'm always honest with him. I say, "Father, there are times when I can, and other times when I could kill him and be done with it all." Father Ignatius says those times when I feel the most hatred against Charlie Sherrin are when Satan's in his element. He loves to see us in despair, to give up hope and live tormented. That's his goal, you see: to wear us down so that suicide becomes an option. Father Ignatius says we should love the sinner but hate the sin. And the more I'm able to look at things in that way, the more I'm able to forgive Charlie and feel better. I know he wasn't in his right mind when he did that to me. That's the only way I'm ever going to have any peace. So I pray now for the strength to forgive. And I pray also for his children.'

It is tragic that a man like Malachi has been left in old age to carry such a burden. How could he have known, as he travelled the world with Blenny, that those two glorious years would be followed by four years of torment? In Egypt he accidentally stepped into the path of evil in the form of Walter Ehrlich. No one could have foreseen that, upon the Gants' return, that same evil would manifest itself on the very road where they live.

On leaving Malachi's home, we draw level, some distance farther on, with the Sherrin house. We cannot help pausing to steal a look. In the garden there is a man with his back to us, off to one side, clipping a hedge. At the sound of the car, he turns slowly to stare at us, but we do not linger. The weight of Malachi's testimony proves too much; we have no inclination to examine at close quarters the face of evil.

Little Lucy and the Phantom Family

THE GILLESPIE FARMHOUSE, a pebble-dashed, two-storied structure, sits in thirty or so acres at the end of a narrow, meandering lane in the lake-rich countryside of County Fermanagh. It was built two centuries ago by an ancestor of the present family. The visitor will find nothing remarkable about the property; there is the customary yard with its barns and outbuildings, and farm machinery standing idle or at the ready, depending on the season.

Ian and Linda Gillespie are a handsome, hard-working couple. He is a businessman and farmer; she is a former teacher. Their three children are beautiful, intelligent and well-mannered. The family seem to embody the benefits of wholesome country living. It is hard, then, to imagine extramundane forces intruding upon this idyll; yet that is what occurred in the autumn of 2002. During September and October of that year, the Gillespies' youngest child, eight-year-old Lucy, was the focus of a number of very unusual visitors.

It began one evening when Lucy was playing in the yard with her sister, eleven-year-old Sandy, and brother Darren, aged ten at the time. Their parents were out of doors as well, herding cattle from a back field towards one of the barns.

It was growing late, and all at once Lucy felt the cold. She bounced the ball back to her siblings and instructed them to wait while she fetched her coat. She sped through the open door of the farmhouse and down the hallway to the back room. This room, once a storeroom, had become the playroom; the children would listen to their music and watch videos there.

Lucy's coat was hanging inside the door. It stood open – as it generally did. She stopped abruptly, pulled up short by a most incongruous sight. There was 'a lady' in the room; she was bent over the coffee table by the far wall, her back to Lucy. She seemed to be arranging the videotapes.

The girl was transfixed; she could not move. Not through fear, it must be said, but because of 'something' that held her in the doorway; something that was urging her to take careful account of every detail of what she was witnessing. For Lucy was in no doubt that the lady was not as other women. She knew of the existence of ghosts – or perhaps more accurately the *possibility* of their existence. What child does not? Lucy sensed that she was seeing one; in daylight, in her very own home. She had what she calls a 'clear' view of the lady, though the lady herself was not quite as clear as a normal human being. She was 'fuzzy round the edges'.

Lucy could not see her face but had the impression that the lady was around her mother's age. She was tall, well built and wore a long, grey, straight skirt and a burgundy shawl. The clothes were definitely from another century – even young Lucy knew that. Most bizarrely, the stranger appeared to have no feet. The hem of her skirt seemed to hover about three or four inches above the ground. She was so intent on tidying the tapes that she did not register the presence of the child – not that Lucy wanted her attention. She hurried back down the hallway, coatless and breathless, to relate what she had seen to her brother and sister.

'There's a ghost in the playroom!' she blurted out.

Darren and Sandy, still bouncing the ball back and forth, did not pause their game. Lucy grabbed her sister's arm and shook it hard.

'Sandy, there's a ghost in the playroom!'

'A what?'

'A ghost!'

'Yeah, right!' Darren stopped the ball with his foot and rolled his eyes scornfully. 'And your silly head's a bubble.'

But Sandy was not amused. She was looking quizzically at her sister. It had been instilled in the children from an early age that fibbing was a sin. It was wrong. Sandy sensed that Lucy was telling the truth; her whole demeanour said so.

'Are you sure?'

'Quick, come and see.' Lucy grasped Sandy by the arm and propelled her towards the front door. 'She might be still there.'

Darren, not wishing to be left out, reluctantly followed the pair down the hallway. But when they got to the playroom door, they found it shut.

'It was open the last time!' Lucy whispered desperately. 'She must be still in there.' She put her ear to the door; she could hear shuffling sounds. 'I can hear her lifting the videos. Listen.'

Sandy put her ear to the door. She, too, could hear noises from within. She looked through the keyhole, but saw nothing in the darkened room.

'What are you three up to?' It was their mother. 'Come on: upstairs. Bedtime.'

'Lucy saw a ghost, Mum,' Sandy cried excitedly. 'It's in the playroom.'

'Nonsense!' Linda had had a long, hard day. Ghost stories were the last thing she wished to hear, so close to bedtime. She needed her sleep as much as the children did. A ghost. Such things were known to keep the children awake at night – with all the consequences for her own sleep, and peace of mind. She had to douse this fire right away. 'Nonsense,' she said again. 'There's no such thing as ghosts.'

'But it's true!' Lucy protested, 'She's in there sorting the videos. I saw her, Mum. I'm telling you I did.'

Linda considered her daughter's anxious little face and the earnestness with which she spoke. She felt a slight shiver of unease.

'I hadn't said anything to the children,' she tells us. 'Or nobody else. But the truth of the matter is that I'd had a brush with something myself a couple of weeks before. I don't know if you'd call it a "ghost". I got this feeling there was a presence in the house. It seemed to be a woman's presence, and I felt it most strongly in the girls' bedroom. It was a little bit scary, but I'd kept my fears to myself. I'd no wish to alarm the children.'

'Very well, Lucy,' she said, 'we'll have a look. And if she's there we'll have a wee word and ask her what's she's looking for. And if she's not there, it means that you only *thought* you saw her. Fair enough?'

With that, Linda took her courage in both hands, flung the door open and switched on the light – taking care to keep her eyes averted from the coffee table where the videotapes were stacked.

'There . . . see. No ghost!' She entered the room and spread her arms wide. The children hung back in the doorway. 'See?'

The children's attention was on the coffee table. Young Lucy was pointing.

'But the videos—'

'Now look, there's *nothing* here!' Their mother's tone told them she would tolerate no contradiction. 'Upstairs, all of you, this minute. And I don't want to hear another word about it.'

That seemed to end the matter. Linda got the children to bed and went back downstairs to put the kettle on. She heard her husband Ian come in and switch on the television. He would be catching the nine o'clock news on RTÉ, as was his habit. Before joining him in a cup of tea, she went to check the playroom again. She had been putting it off; but it had to be done, if only to set her mind at ease.

Linda had long given up tidying and putting things away in the playroom. It seemed a futile task. But, at that moment, she found herself fervently wishing for disorder; she prayed that she might see the usual mess: the videotapes strewn willy-nilly over the coffee table. That would prove Lucy's story groundless. She opened the door and switched on the light.

Her heart sank. The twenty or so tapes were neatly stacked – as neatly as a display in a shop. Not only that, but all had been slotted carefully into their individual boxes – boxes which, in the ordinary run of things, Linda would find discarded underneath the coffee table and elsewhere.

With trembling fingers she examined the top row. Each film was in its correct box. There they were, neater even than she would have arranged them herself: *James and The Giant Peach, Babe, Monsters Inc., Muppets in Space.* The fifth box, however – *Harry Potter and the Sorcerer's Stone* – was empty. She looked about the room but could not find it. She went to the VCR and pressed the eject button. The machine was empty.

I don't have time for this, Linda thought. Perhaps the dog carried it out to the barn – he was known to do things like that – or perhaps one of the children had lent it to a friend at school.

Without quite knowing why, she hurriedly removed all the tapes from their boxes, tossed some of the boxes back under the table, and generally returned the playroom to its usual, untidy, state. In the morning the children would see that it had all been one, great joke.

She was not smiling, though; far from it. As she pulled the door behind her, she had the feeling that another door was opening into another place, a place she had no wish to confront, or even consider.

She decided there and then that she would not burden her husband with her suspicions just yet. He had enough to deal with, what with a full-time job from eight to five, and the additional farm work in the evenings. Besides, Ian was a sceptic; he would not take it seriously. She would wait and see how things developed. With luck, there would be no more to it.

* * *

In the days that followed, life returned to normal. The children went to school as usual; Ian went off to work; and Linda, with much to occupy her during the day, tried not to dwell on the strange phenomenon. Being a religious woman, she resolved to pray more with the children at bedtime; it gave her peace of mind, and it seemed to soothe them.

A week later, however, Lucy had her second vision.

It was about four o'clock on a calm, bright Friday afternoon. Linda was in the kitchen doing the washing up. Sandy and Darren were at the table, still busy with their homework, and Lucy, who tended to finish hers before the others, was outside, at play.

The first thing that a visitor to the Gillespie house will notice is the silence that envelops it. It lies some distance from the main road and neighbouring farms, and the silence is potent. Linda, being at home for most of the day, is especially attuned to this quietude. The noises that disturb it are almost welcome: the hum of a far-off tractor, Ian's car as it turns in at the gate, the playful shouts of the children, the barking dog that heralds a visitor.

The scream of a terrified child is something else entirely.

Linda dropped everything and ran outside, with Sandy and Darren close on her heels.

Lucy was racing up the lane towards the house. She fell into her mother's arms, in great agitation. While Linda did her best to calm her, the child kept pointing back the way she had come.

'He was there!' she cried, indicating the wild garden on the left. 'A minute ago, Mummy . . . a man.'

Linda took her by the hand.

'All right, dear,' she said, 'we'll go down and have a look.'

But there was no sign of the mysterious man. He seemed to be as non-existent as Lucy's 'lady' of the previous week.

'Look, there's no one there, sweetheart.'

Linda was perplexed, unsure of what to think. Her daughter

was behaving very much out of character; she rarely, if ever, made things up; it simply was not in the girl's nature.

'There's nobody there, Lucy,' Sandy assured her.

Lucy began to sob. 'But he *was* there. I saw him; I swear he was there!'

Linda could read the child's anguish. She was torn between chastising her for being silly and believing her. She dismissed both as unhelpful. Linda knew that her children were not given to attention seeking. She thought it better for everyone's sake to remain neutral, and simply to allow Lucy to have her say.

'All right,' she said, 'let's all go inside and have some orange juice. Then you can tell us all about it.'

Once settled and calmer, Lucy related what she had seen. As she was skipping down the lane, past the garden, she saw a figure standing just inside the gate: a man. He was of average height and wearing a black, hooded cloak. His hands were clasped chest-high, in an attitude of prayer. He was 'like a monk', Lucy said. He did not move or look at her, but seemed to be gazing fixedly down the lane. The words 'look' and 'gazing' are probably incorrect in this context because the monk had no features as such. A 'peachy haze' – Lucy's charming description – filled the space where his face should have been.

Linda listened with mounting dread. What on earth was happening? Ghosts appearing in broad daylight, inside the house and out of doors. She wanted desperately to discount the whole affair. Yet, of her three children, Lucy was the least excitable: a calm, level-headed little girl. Why this sudden change? Linda was growing very concerned. She resolved to visit her GP and seek his advice.

The doctor's diagnosis held no surprises. Children have fertile imaginations, he told Linda, especially at Lucy's age. They have difficulty distinguishing fact from fiction. What they see in films can sometimes seem very real.

There was nothing new there, but his following words angered Linda. He wondered if the child perhaps felt she was not getting enough attention. The 'visions' might well be her way of refocusing her mother's regard.

Linda could not concur; she treated her children equally. But the visit to the doctor was easing her mind to some extent. Lucy was sleeping well and her schoolwork had not suffered. The GP assured the mother that it was just a phase, that things would settle.

And they did.

'Three whole weeks went by with nothing happening,' Linda tells us, 'but you know, deep down I knew it was too good to last. And the reason I say that is because, even though Lucy wasn't having any more visions, I knew, *I just knew,* that the strange woman was still in the house. I'd sometimes feel her on the stairs, or the landing, but what really worried me was that she was strongest in the girls' room.'

While tidying up in there one morning, she noticed something odd. The children always made their beds before going to school. It did not require much skill: straighten the duvet, plump the pillow and place it on top. But now she noticed that Lucy's bed was made differently. The pillow had been placed beneath the cover. Linda shook her head in mild bemusement, left the room by and by, and thought no more about it.

Until it happened again – and again. She was seeing it every day. She questioned Lucy.

'I always put it on top, Mummy. I thought *you* were changing it.'

The three children were sitting down to tea, having just got in from school. 'Maybe it's the lady,' said Darren, tucking into a slice of cake. He grinned.

'Now stop that! There's no lady in this house – and don't speak with your mouth full.'

'There is, Mummy,' Sandy announced bravely. 'Lucy saw her twice – and we *feel* her in the bedroom as well.'

'What!' Linda was stunned. 'Is this true, Lucy?'

The child nodded.

'Come with me. Take your tea with you if you like.'

She brought Lucy into the front room and shut the door. It was time to have it out with the girl.

'Now, I won't say anything about you being naughty, all right? You just tell me what happened. Right from the beginning.'

The story came out. 'The first time was when I was in the bath on Monday night,' Lucy began. 'She went past the door because the door was open . . . and she . . . She stopped and looked at me, but she had no eyes, Mummy, because her face was all fuzzy like the monk's.'

Linda stared at her daughter and feigned a smile. She had no great wish to hear any more of this, yet knew she must.

'And the second time, dear?' she managed to say.

'The second time was yesterday when I was putting out the bin. She was . . . she was in the backyard. She was praying, Mummy.'

'How do you know that?'

Lucy screwed up her little face, irritated that her mother should ask such a silly question. 'Because she was kneeling behind the wall and she had her hands joined . . . and she had a brooch on.'

'A brooch?'

'Aye. It was gold with a red diamond in the middle.'

'Why did you not tell me this before?' Linda's concern was growing.

'I didn't want to upset you, Mummy.'

'I'll not be upset, Lucy.' Linda tried to keep her voice calm. 'Now promise me, sweetheart: the next time you see a strange woman or man, you must call me immediately. I want to see them as well, and I want to ask them what they're up to.'

Lucy nodded.

'And there's no woman in your bedroom. It's the mirror inside the door.' Linda had placed a cheval mirror that had belonged to her mother in the girls' room. Because of its age, it tended to swing too freely in its bracket. 'Any time I walk into your room, the mirror moves, because it's an old mirror. It's not because of any strange lady. Even a bird flying past the window gets reflected in it, and you'd think it was a person.'

The child seemed content with this explanation. She finished her tea, did her homework and went out to play with the others.

Perhaps the most unusual aspect of Lucy's case is the extraordinary variety of her visions, coupled with the fact that they could appear at any hour of the day: nearly always in broad daylight, and usually when she was engaged in some activity or other. Her encounters appear all the more baffling when one considers that over eighty per cent of ghostly apparitions are seen at night, commonly when the observer is in a relaxed state, having either woken from sleep, or is about to fall asleep. Technically these twin states of consciousness are known respectively as the hypnopompic and hypnagogic. Extensive studies have shown that when in either, an individual can experience odd phenomena. They may take the form of visions and other imagery; a frightening aspect can be a paralysis lasting minutes, or even a loss of speech.

Lucy was, of course, wide awake when she observed her 'ghosts'. Her brain was active and therefore well able to distinguish truth from illusion. Daylight also lent clarity and relative unambiguity.

Her next vision likewise made its presence felt one evening at around seven: once again before night had properly fallen.

Lucy was in the room that she shares with Sandy. Their beds stand about four feet apart. The door was fully open and the landing light was on. Lucy sat down on her bed to slip into her runners. She had just laced them up and was about to rise, when, in her own words, she 'was made to sit down again'.

There was a man standing just inside the door.

She tried to call out to her mother but discovered she was tongue-tied. Again she had the sensation of being 'held' in the one spot.

The man was tall, about six foot; he looked to be in his thirties, and was clad in a dark green uniform with matching beret. About his waist he wore a black belt and across his left breast pocket was a military ribbon rack. Unlike the lady and the monk, there was no 'fuzziness' about this figure: Lucy saw his face clearly. He was stern and very pale, with sharp features – long nose, thin lips and small narrowed eyes – and he moved his head from side to side as if peering from one corner of the room to the other. He did not look at Lucy – at least, not as far as she could tell.

The most significant thing about him, however, was his right arm. It ended at the elbow, and the sleeve was pinned back and secured at the shoulder. Because he was standing behind Sandy's bed, Lucy could not see his feet. But she had seen enough, and at last felt able to shout for her mother. As she did so, the 'soldier' disappeared.

Linda arrived breathless at the top of the stairs, to find a distraught Lucy once more insisting on the veracity of what she had just seen.

Later that same evening, when she had finally got the children settled in bed, Linda decided it was time to tell Ian. Knowing him to be a sceptic, she did not expect much understanding. He was unwinding in the sitting-room after a heavy day, watching the sports channel with his feet up. Bad timing, she thought, but he has to know; I can't shoulder all this on my own. As she had anticipated, Ian saw little cause for alarm.

'After all,' he assured her, 'ghosts never harmed anyone. Lucy will grow out of it. It's just a phase.'

'But, Ian, you don't understand. The visions seem so *real* to her!

We have to do something about them before they go too far.'

'Look,' he said, 'your mother was psychic and you're psychic. Lucy's inherited the "gift". More like a curse, if you ask me.'

Her husband spoke the truth. Linda did indeed share a most unusual 'gift' with her mother: an ability to perceive things that others could not. At times she could almost guess what another was thinking, and frequently knew what a person was about to say before they said it. And Ian was correct: it was more of a curse than a blessing.

'She'll grow out of it,' he said again. 'And anyway, *I* haven't noticed any change in her. She seems perfectly all right to me.'

'But, Ian, you don't see her from one end of the day to the next. I do. And I'm really worried about her. She's just not herself.'

'Well, if it puts your mind at ease, go along and see that parish priest of yours. Priests seem to be good at driving out ghosts and things, if them Hollywood films are anything to go by.'

She was a bit miffed by his flippancy, for it hit a sore spot. Ian is Methodist and Linda is Catholic. When they married, each retained their respective beliefs, but she agreed to the children being brought up in her husband's faith.

'Look, it's not funny!' she said.

'Sorry, love. I know it isn't.' He yawned. 'God, I'm tired. Bed-time, I think.'

Linda knew that there was no point in further discussion. She got up as he switched off the TV.

'It's interesting about that soldier though,' he said as they climbed the stairs. 'That set me thinking, so it did.'

Linda turned, startled.

'Why's that?'

'Well, during the First World War there was an army battalion stationed on this land. My grandfather used to tell me stories about them when I was a wee one.'

Not surprisingly, this information afforded Linda no comfort whatsoever. She knew little about ghosts, had never seen one and, like many people, only half-believed in them. Ian was a doubting Thomas; she herself never shut the door on the paranormal. But one thing she knew of ghosts: they were frequently the souls of men who had met violent ends. As some soldiers do. Lucy's vision was of a battle-scarred veteran; Ian's words were causing Linda to think that the man might well have suffered a violent death on her property.

The notion appalled her. She resolved to go and see Father Lawless the following day. Clearly, this was a case of a restless soul – possibly more than one – and surely a Catholic priest was ideally placed to offer help on the plight of souls.

As it turned out, Father Lawless saw little cause for concern.

'Oh, we don't take such things seriously any more, Mrs Gillespie,' he said. 'Maybe a couple of hundred years ago, but not in these more enlightened times. Children have very active imaginations these days. All that rot they see on TV and the films has a harmful effect. Pray more, and sprinkle some holy water; that's my advice. I'll get you a bottle.'

He left the room and returned a few minutes later with the holy water and a prayer leaflet.

'Now, I'm giving you this Divine Mercy Chaplet to say. It's very powerful altogether. It reminds us that God's love is unlimited and available to all of us. It's good to get into the habit of regular prayer; that way, you'll feel God's protection and won't be too fearful of these paranormal things. The chaplet affords you great security. Say it every day – and have little Lucy say it also. In no time, all this will clear up. You'll see.'

The Divine Mercy Chaplet has an intriguing history, as Linda would learn. Its message and devotion stem from the writings of a Polish nun. Born into poverty as Helen Kowalska, the third of ten children, she would become known as Sister Faustina.

On 22 February 1931, when she was twenty-six, Jesus appeared to her in a most singular vision. He was robed in white; rays of light, some red and others white, were emanating from his heart. An inner voice – she believed it to be the voice of her Saviour – explained that the rays represented 'the blood and water that gushed forth from the depths of my mercy when my agonizing heart was pierced on the cross. The pale rays symbolize the water, which cleanses and purifies the soul.'

The vision continued to reappear. Sister Faustina kept a record of these mystical encounters; it would run to over six hundred pages. The message is always the same: that God is merciful, that He is love itself poured out for us, and that He wants us all to turn to Him with true repentance while there is still time.

The nun was given to understand that she was the recipient of a new mystic image of Jesus and its accompanying message, one that would take its place alongside that of the Sacred Heart. This was a momentous revelation, yet it would be many years after Sister Faustina's death in 1940 before it was recognized and accepted by the Vatican. She herself foresaw its proscription, imposed in 1959 by Pope John XXIII. She wrote that it would remain in place until 'suddenly the action of God will come upon the scene with genuine power, to bear witness to the truth.'

It was not until April 1978 that this decision was reversed. The man responsible was the Archbishop of Sister Faustina's home diocese: Karol Wojtyla. In October of that same year he would become Pope John Paul II. She was canonized in April 2000.

Linda felt better after her visit to Father Lawless. His words had reassured her. He seemed to believe that regular prayer was the remedy. And perhaps it's all that's needed, she told herself: a little more faith and an adherence to the godly.

Back at the farmhouse she decided to perform her own 'cleansing', using the holy water. She had the house to herself; she had the best part of an hour before the children returned from school.

She went from room to room; downstairs first, then upstairs, sprinkling the water and urging the spirits to go to their eternal rest in the peace of God. She left the girls' room until last.

When she entered, she found that the presence of the 'lady' was almost palpable. But it was not unpleasant, not threatening in any way. Linda blessed every corner, sprinkling the water more liberally on the spot where she felt the 'visitor' to be standing. She knew with near-certainty that she was there; it was much the same sensation of another person being in the room. She almost felt she could speak to that 'other'. And no, there was still nothing threatening about the presence, not even when she had sprinkled the holy water. Nevertheless, Linda resented another encroaching on her private space, her home, her children's privacy.

'Go!' she ordered. 'Go in the name of God.' Then, feeling more annoyed than courageous, she said: 'This is *my* house, not yours. Whoever you are, you're not wanted here.'

Linda fetched her rosary, got down on her knees by Lucy's bed, and recited the Chaplet of the Divine Mercy, gazing all the while at the picture on the prayer leaflet that the priest had given her. To her relief, she felt a change coming over the room. There was the sense of a presence departing.

There followed a period of peace and quiet. Lucy saw no more phenomena and Linda inwardly thanked God. Father Lawless's advice had borne fruit. She berated herself for not putting more trust in him; she prayed each morning and night with the children, hoping that the peace would last.

It did not. Three weeks following her visit to the priest, Linda's confidence took a knock when Lucy had her sixth vision. In fact, it was as if the respite had been sent to tease and taunt. Lucy was to experience five more apparitions, a fresh one appearing every other day.

The first three were of an extraordinary nature, and again all were seen during the day, after Lucy had returned from school.

The first occurred when she was once again playing with Sandy and Darren. They were out in the lane, skipping. Lucy and Darren were holding the rope while Sandy took her turn. On the eleventh stroke, Lucy stopped. She had gone a little pale.

'Look!' she cried, pointing to the trailer at the end of the lane. As before, her brother and sister saw nothing.

But Lucy did, and what she saw astonished her. Laid out on top of the trailer, some twenty feet away, was a youth. She was near enough to see him clearly. He was perhaps sixteen, nude, and his body seemed to be outlined in a shimmering, golden light. His eyes were open and, as the girl watched, he very slowly rose, and hovered above the trailer, before disappearing. Lucy says that the vision lasted some thirty seconds.

The next two manifestations did not involve human figures as such. At breakfast one morning, Lucy saw what she describes as a thin 'string of smoke' coming in at the kitchen door. She thought it was dust at first, until without warning it grew denser and thicker, as it formed itself into 'a rope shape' and turned white. This 'rope of smoke' slowly coiled itself about Sandy's head, then Darren's, girdling them in a figure-eight shape. Lucy said nothing, but remained watching, perplexed, as it leisurely uncoiled itself again and disappeared back out through the door.

'Are you all right, sweetheart?' Linda was observing Lucy as she prepared their lunches. She thought the child might be daydreaming, sitting as she was with her spoon poised above her cereal bowl, staring into space. But then again . . .

'I'm fine, Mummy.' Lucy resumed eating. 'I thought I saw smoke round their heads, but it's away now.'

'Nonsense. You know Daddy and me don't smoke.'

'I know.' Lucy sensed that it was probably not the right time to tell her mother what it was she had seen. But later that evening she told all. Linda was dismayed. Whatever it was that had been troubling her daughter was back in earnest – despite her prayers and the sprinkling of holy water.

Lucy's next experience was the most bizarre of all. We will let her describe it in her own words.

'I was in the shower one afternoon and I saw something through the glass door, lying on the floor. I couldn't see it right because the glass was all steamy, so I cleaned a wee hole and I saw this chest, like a man's chest, cut off at the waist with no arms or a head. It was all a pale colour.'

If there was blood present, Lucy did not wait around to check. She was terrified; she jumped over the ghastly torso, and ran naked and screaming to her mother.

Linda was desperate now. Up until then, Lucy seemed to be coping reasonably well with the phenomena, but the torso had truly frightened her. What on earth might the child see next? Linda decided not to bother Father Lawless again. There was another man of the cloth who might be able to advise her: Dr Nigel Lomax, the minister attached to Ian's church. She went to see him that very evening.

Dr Lomax was distressed to hear of Lucy's predicament; she was one of his favourite parishioners, and he was eager to do all he could. Yet he confessed to having very little experience of what he termed 'the paranormal'. He did, however, know a man in Newcastle who perhaps could help: Reverend Charles Cartwright. He gave Linda an address and telephone number, and wished her well.

That night, little Lucy slept fitfully. Her mind was replaying over and over the horrid shower scene. Sometime close to midnight, she eventually gave up her attempts at sleeping; her darkened bedroom, with its shadows and hints of danger, was making her uneasy. She slipped into her parents' room and roused her mother, who made space for her in the bed. Eventually she drifted off to sleep in the comfort and security of Linda's arms.

But at about six o'clock, she found herself wide awake. Light was peeping in at the window and she no longer felt sleepy. She eased herself quietly from the bed and padded to the door.

She checked on her brother and sister and was disappointed to find them fast asleep. Lucy was at a loose end. She had no wish to return to bed, sensing that she would be unable to sleep. She was hungry, but was reluctant to go down to the kitchen. The downstairs bathroom, where she had seen the gruesome body part, lies just off the kitchen and she was afraid of going near there. Were she to see the torso again, at that hour of the morning, she knew she would scream and wake everyone up. She put on her bunny rabbit slippers and went to one of her favourite places: the top of the stairs. Ever since she was a toddler she had chosen to sit there, where she could watch people coming and going down below.

All was quiet, save for the snores coming from the open door of her brother's bedroom. Through the glass-panelled front door, the dawn sun was gradually filling the hall with a golden light, bringing the house's interior to life. Lucy felt safe. She put her chin in her hands and gazed down at the phone table, the coat stand, and the door jamb of the parlour door at the foot of the stairs, its high-gloss varnish reflecting the light. All those familiar things were real, and therefore comforting. They would not suddenly vanish, to manifest again and upset her.

It was while Lucy was gazing at the jamb of the parlour that something magical occurred. Without warning, a little girl's head popped out from behind the door, smiled up at her and disappeared back inside.

Lucy was not scared; she was fascinated, and wanted to see the little girl again. Her wish was granted; seconds later, the child reappeared. But this time she stepped out from behind the door, and went to stand on the bottom step of the stairs.

'She was like a wee Victorian doll,' Lucy says, 'because she had on a pink frilly dress and, like, frilly legging things. Maybe she was about four or five, and' – Lucy giggles at the memory – 'she started playing peek-a-boo, jumping off the step and covering her eyes, and popping in and out from behind the door.'

She was delighted. Since Darren's room was closest, she called out to him to come and see what she was witnessing. There was no response. Well then, it was Darren's tough luck for being a sleepy-head and missing all the magic. Lucy returned her attention to the little girl.

'But when I looked again,' she recalls, 'I saw this big hole, like a big oval shape opened in the wall on the stairs, and it was all filled with fuzzy bright colours. And I saw the wee girl coming up the stairs and standing beside it. Then she just went into a mist, like a smoky thing, and the smoky thing went into the fuzzy hole in the wall, and then everything went away, so it did.'

Like Alice through the looking-glass.

Lucy was saddened by the disappearance of her spectral play-mate; she felt cheated; the little girl was the only apparition that had actually engaged with her in any way.

Or had it? The ghost appeared to Lucy to have been aware of her, had played peek-a-boo with her. And yet, on consideration, all Lucy had observed was an apparition that *seemed* to be looking at her, as if the ghost were seeing her too. The question therefore arises: Had Lucy not been sitting on the top stair, might the phantom child have appeared in any case, and gone through the same motions as she had done with Lucy? In other words, there is no good reason to believe that this new apparition was in any way different from the others Lucy had seen.

Two days later, on the evening of Thursday, 17 October 2002, Charles Cartwright was scheduled to perform his cleansing of the Gillespie farmhouse. On that very morning, Lucy was to see her ninth, and final, ghost.

Unlike the other manifestations, this one appeared to her short-ly after she had woken up, at roughly 7.30. Sandy was still asleep in the adjacent bed, but standing behind the bed was a figure.

'She was like a maid,' Lucy tells us, 'because she had on a black dress and a white apron and a frilly cap, and she was carrying a big silver tray with cups on it.'

While Lucy stared in wonder, the maid began to move. As she did so, a pool of gold appeared to advance before her. Lucy de-scribes the pool as a circle of gold, 'like the sun, but you could look at it, because it wasn't dazzling.'

'Sandy, Sandy, wake up!' she yelled. 'Quick, wake up!'

Sandy sat up in bed, startled. Her sister was pointing at the wardrobe. It was to be the only time that she would share one of Lucy's enigmatic experiences. She saw 'a black-and-white cloud', almost like the static seen on a badly tuned television set. It hov-ered for a moment or two above the wardrobe, then vanished.

Thus did the final day of phenomena begin.

We thought we might test Lucy by asking a trick question. Ear-lier, she had told us that the maid appeared *behind* her sister's bed. What, we asked presently, was the maid wearing on her feet?

Lucy threw her eyes heavenward, and replied immediately: 'I told you, didn't I, that she was standing behind Sandy's bed, so I couldn't *see* her feet.'

It has to be said that, throughout our conversations with little Lucy, we were impressed by her absolute honesty. She neither em-bellished nor exaggerated, even when pressed. The most skilful prosecuting barrister would doubtless be no match for her.

We came away from the Gillespie farmhouse in the conviction that we had made the acquaintance of a very special young girl.

'The Gillespie case,' Charles Cartwright says, 'was extraordinary because of the number of manifestations, and the fact that they were so unusual. But there was nothing evil about them, thank heavens. One of my less disturbing cases, I'd say.'

He goes on to explain that little Lucy's phenomena seemed to conform to what is known in psychical research circles as a 'residual' or 'mental imprint' haunting. The manifestations generally occur at the site of a highly charged emotional event – for example a battle or a murder. It is believed that the discharge of enormous amounts of emotional energy by such events can cause the scene to be imprinted on its surroundings. At significant times – for instance on the anniversary of the death or deaths of those involved – the occurrences may somehow be re-enacted. One can think in terms of a three-dimensional film, in effect a moving hologram, the images being projected not onto a flat screen but onto the very air itself.

A number of other factors seem to bear out the 'residual imprint' hypothesis. Such hauntings tend to occur in old houses or historical buildings. The Gillespie farmhouse is over two hundred years old. Lucy's ghosts tended to hover a few inches off the ground and walk through walls; it might be conjectured, then, that they continued to follow floorplans that existed in earlier times. They seemed oblivious to the presence of the living – even though it could be argued that the little girl on the stairs was attempting to interact with her. It is believed that the psychic energy such apparitions emit can be picked up by individuals who are psychically 'sensitive'. Lucy's mother is of the opinion that her daughter is psychic, and that this gift, or indeed peculiarity, has been passed down the maternal line.

'Such phenomena usually disappear over time,' Charles Cartwright asserts, 'although there is the risk that repeated sightings by the living can revive the psychic energy that keeps them going. There is also the danger that evil entities will use the opportunity to gain access, and cause great distress and upset. So it's always best to cleanse the site as soon as possible.'

We are curious to know what, in his opinion, triggered the

manifestations in the first place. Prior to Lucy's experiences, there was no history of sightings. We wonder if it was a case of somebody dabbling in the occult. It is accepted wisdom that anything connected with the occult – ouija boards, horoscopes, séances, tarot cards, fortune-telling, witchcraft, etc – can sometimes serve as a portal for spirits to enter an individual's life.

'I'm glad you asked that,' the rector says. 'Yes, something the mother told me set the alarm bells ringing. Two things, in fact.

'Mrs Gillespie's own mother had died in April of the year the manifestations started. They had made a pact, you see. While the mother lay dying Linda asked that, when she got to the other side, she send her a sign that she was all right. The mother agreed. When a month passed and nothing happened, Linda became anxious and started ringing psychic phone lines, hoping that a fortune-teller could tell her something.

'What she heard from one of them was very strange. The medium asked her to go outside, because she saw the mother in the yard standing beside an orange duck. Linda thought this was bizarre. The family did not keep ducks, but she decided to check anyway. She found Lucy outside and, odd as it seems, the orange plastic duck which she played with at bath times was lying at her feet. Lucy claimed she hadn't taken it from the bathroom and her mother had no reason to doubt her.'

Did this occurrence confirm for Linda that her mother had indeed made contact?

'No. She said the experience upset her, but that same evening something else happened which satisfied her that her mother had succeeded. She was resting on the sitting-room sofa when a circle of golden stars appeared in one corner of the room, whirled around for a few seconds and then disappeared.'

'I didn't like the sound of any of that,' Reverend Charles continues. 'Even though Linda was acting with what she believed were the best intentions – caring about where her mother might

LITTLE LUCY AND THE PHANTOM FAMILY

be. Make no mistake: such naiveté can be used by discarnate entities to disturb and disrupt lives. It was after that occurrence that
Lucy began having her visions.'

The rector goes on to cite the incidents in Scripture which
record the living making contact with the dead. He views those
examples as warnings, and holds that they are as pertinent today
as they were in biblical times.

In the First Book of Samuel, King Saul requests that the witch
of Endor, a woman possessing a familiar – a demon that does
her bidding – commune on his behalf with the spirit of the dead
Samuel. She succeeds, to her surprise, and it seems that it was the
demon that made the contact possible. It is also interesting to
note that Samuel is none too happy at his rest being disturbed.

Also, in Luke's Gospel, Jesus tells the story of the rich man and
Lazarus. The former is suffering in hell and asks that Lazarus, the
poor man residing in heaven, be sent back to earth. The rich man
fears for his five surviving brothers, and asks that they be warned
of the torments that await them if they do not mend their ways.
His request is refused on the grounds that the living have the
word of Moses and the prophets to persuade them. They should
have no need of the testimony of dead men.

And this is the nub of it, according to Charles Cartwright.
Those who turn to the occult for answers are demonstrating a
lamentable lack of trust in God. He reminds us of a passage in
Deuteronomy: 'Let no one be found among you who practises
divination or sorcery, interprets omens, engages in witchcraft, or
casts spells, or who is a medium or spiritist or who consults the
dead. Anyone who does these things is detestable to the Lord.'

They are also asking for trouble, the rector feels. Doors into the
unknown can open. The Gillespies were fortunate that their particular door seems to have opened onto one of the more benign
regions of extraphysical existence.

* * *

We are interested in the nature of the exorcism itself. It is our understanding that it was more a cleansing of the house than a deliverance of Lucy.

'Yes, indeed. One can speculate that the lady whom Lucy had seen three times had possibly the greatest emotional attachment to the place. Probably suffered a good deal during the war. The armless soldier could have been the husband; the body part in the shower, the naked boy, possibly sons who died violently. Interesting that Lucy first saw the mistress tidying the videotapes. Asserting ownership I'd say, then her praying by the wall and the monk praying also . . . trying to come to terms with the tragedy.'

We wonder if any of Lucy's apparitions congregated for the blessing; whether the rector was aware of any 'presences'.

He shakes his head. 'I did feel a presence, which I suppose could have been that of the mistress. I sensed that if I laid her to rest, the others would follow in due course. I celebrated a Eucharist with the family and prayed that she'd go in the peace of the Lord, where she could meet her loved ones again in the light of God's love. Then I blessed each room in the house and the out-buildings as well.'

'So all in all, everyone was happy,' he concludes. 'It is wonderful to participate in such a healing victory. Experiencing the power of God's love in these situations is something neither I nor those afflicted ever forget.'

The Good Presbyterian
and the Succubus

BY FAR THE MOST POIGNANT case we encountered in the course of our research was that related by a Presbyterian minister. His is the sole account on record. The victim in question died in 2003 before we had an opportunity to interview him. Nevertheless, we are confident that the following account is reliable, obtained as it was from a man whose credentials – both academic and spiritual – are of the highest order.

We arranged to meet Dr Bernard McElliot in his office in the church hall. His ministry is part of a prosperous Dublin suburb; it answers the spiritual needs of a congregation which, though dwindling in numbers, remains steadfast in its faith and in its sense of community. There is a strong tradition of pastoral care. At the start of our meeting, Dr McElliot courteously sought our permission to take a phone call; the caller appeared to be in some distress and his gently spoken advice brought her comfort. He is a caring man, perhaps sixty, with an easy manner. His office is that of an academic: the many bookshelves are lined with scriptural exegesis, concordances, and works relating to church business and administration. He instructed his secretary to hold all further calls. He was eager to discuss the strange case of Peter Rickett.

Rickett, we learned, was eighty-nine at the time of his death. Born at the outbreak of one world war, he had survived another. Seeking adventure, he went to England in 1933, where he en-listed in the army as a non-commissioned officer. Peter's regiment was part of the Expeditionary Force sent to aid the French when Britain entered the war against Germany in 1939. He was among those evacuated at Dunkirk, during which action he sustained a leg injury from a ricocheting machine-gun round. The injury was to cause him chronic discomfort in later years, although it did not prevent him from reporting for active service as soon as he was discharged from hospital. In 1944, he found himself in Italy, as Allied forces sought to liberate that country. Again Peter Rickett was wounded in action, this time very seriously. A shell fired by the retreating Germans at Monte Cassino tore away a large part of his stomach. He nearly died. He sat out the rest of the war in a nursing home in Buckinghamshire.

He returned to Dublin in 1946 and used his severance pay to fund a degree course in engineering at Trinity College. Almost immediately upon graduation, he secured a position with Dublin Corporation. He had a hand in many important civil engineering projects throughout the 1950s and 60s; several of the most prestigious and innovative public works carried the Rickett stamp.

He retired in 1982. He had looked forward to enjoying his twilight years in the company of his wife Mary, but that was not to be. She died of cancer in 1991, leaving behind five grown-up children with families of their own.

With Mary's passing, Peter Rickett lost more than a wife. The couple had been a shining personification of the dictum that love conquers all. They had overcome some of the worst religious intolerance imaginable in order to be together.

At the heart of their difficulties lay Mary's Roman Catholicism. The couple met and fell in love in 1953, in a time when Ireland was only nominally a secular state. They decided to marry and a date was set. Peter had always known that a 'mixed' marriage would pose problems, yet had been naive enough to believe that those problems would be minor. Neither was prepared for the response from both sets of parents.

Peter's people had always believed he would marry a Presbyterian. His grandfather was a Belfastman who had come south largely for reasons of economic expediency. He had brought with him a faith that was as unshakable as it was narrow, and reared his children to view the Roman Church with suspicion. When Peter announced his intention of marrying Mary, his father was appalled. He saw this 'betrayal' as the thin end of the wedge that would come between him and his faith.

To a certain extent he was justified; the 1950s were a time of great repression in Irish society. With the founding of the state, de Valera had made no secret of his pact with the Catholic hierarchy; Rome would enjoy a 'special position' within Irish affairs. The discriminatory *Ne temere*, decreed by the Vatican in 1907, was also in place – and nowhere else was it enforced with the same rigour as in Ireland. Under this ruling, a non-Catholic marrying a Catholic would have to agree that any children of the marriage would be brought up as Catholics. Understandably, the non-Catholics of Ireland saw this as a means by which their numbers – already reduced since the 1920s – would decline further.

As if this was not obstacle enough to the young couple's happiness, Mary's family also bitterly opposed the match. Her parents were staunch republicans. Both her grandfathers had taken part in the Easter Rising, and her great-grandfather's family were victims of 'souperism', the unethical methods of proselytizing used by a small number of Protestant clergymen during the Famine years. For Mary to marry into a Presbyterian family would, in her parents' eyes, bring undying shame on their house, and sully ancestral memories.

For many months, blazing rows were the order of the day in both households. Neither set of parents would yield; the family honour was going to take precedence over love. Peter and Mary alike were threatened with disinheritance; every form of emotional blackmail was brought to bear. They would be ostracized, they learned; the children of the marriage would never know their grandparents.

Perhaps it was the very vehemence and spitefulness of the

anger thus unleashed that drove the pair to take the course they did. They left Ireland entirely. With the help of an old college friend, Peter secured a fine position as an engineer with the London Board of Works. Within months of their engagement, the couple had bought a house in Wimbledon, married without difficulty in a registry office, and enjoyed a wonderful honeymoon in Bognor Regis. On their return it was discovered that Mary was pregnant with their first child.

The girl, whom they named Emily after Peter's aunt, was in time joined by four siblings. By 1961 all were attending the same school in the west-London suburb the family had moved to. The school was non-denominational, a situation which admirably suited the parents.

That is not to say that Peter and Mary did not care for religion. In fact both were exceptionally devout. Neither had allowed their parents' narrow thinking and prejudices to cloud their judgement. They had reached an agreement shortly after marrying: they would allow the children themselves to choose the religion they wished to follow. To everyone's surprise – and to Mary's dismay – all but Emily chose the faith of their father. There does not seem to be a good explanation for this and, if there is, Reverend McElliot was not informed of it.

'I only know what Peter told me,' he says. 'And this was in later years, when he and Mary had returned to Dublin. This would have been in the early eighties. All the children were grown up by then and gone their separate ways. Two went to Canada; the others stayed in England.'

By that time Ireland had become a very different society from the one the 'eloping' couple had left. A spirit of ecumenism was blowing across the Christian divides; old enmities were forgotten or allowed to die. Peter's parents were elderly by then and time had mellowed them. There was a reconciliation with their wayward son. Mary's parents, however, stood firm; in their eyes she had disgraced the family. Both died without ever seeing either their grandchildren or great-grandchildren.

Peter had envisaged starting an engineering consultancy in Dublin. He had already leased premises and secured his first contract before concluding that it was not for him. He was sixty by then, close to retirement age. He dropped the idea in favour of something radically different: he decided to open a restaurant. They were both fond of cooking, had always enjoyed having friends round to dinner and trying out new recipes on them. They took over the lease of an existing restaurant and used their savings to renovate it to conform to their own ideas. It was a success, although not as successful as the couple had hoped. In time they hired a chef and took a back seat.

'It was about this time that they moved here,' Dr McElliot says. 'They no longer had to travel to the restaurant every day so they could live wherever they liked. Peter showed up one Sunday out of the blue and that was that. We saw him regularly at worship from then on. A fine man, very open and friendly. He fitted in very well. I think everyone thought he must be a widower or a bachelor. It was only after a time that he told me about Mary and what happened back then. He was still very cut up about it, and who can blame him?'

In 1991 the greatest tragedy of all would befall Peter. He lost his darling wife.

'Cancer,' Dr McElliot says simply. He discloses nothing of its nature. 'Thank the Lord it was over rapidly. Within two months of its being diagnosed she was no longer with us. She did not linger, as so many sufferers do, and neither of them had to witness the terrible deterioration that usually accompanies cancer. There was no chemo or radiation; it was too far gone for that. That, I expect, was a blessing.'

Her family showed for the funeral, stayed on for an hour or

two to offer condolences, then were gone. Peter would never see any of them again.

His youngest daughter Renee, who by then had a grown-up family, very kindly remained to look after Peter for a month or two. Her husband returned to their home in Sussex; he would visit every other weekend.

The truth was that they feared for Peter's sanity. He had taken Mary's death very badly. He was inconsolable.

'I've never seen a man so cut up over the death of a loved one,' Dr McElliot says. 'I was half-afraid we were going to lose him as well. If it wasn't for Renee I'm certain we would have. She was wonderful altogether.'

He goes to a filing cabinet and returns presently with a newsletter. Crude, it seems to predate desktop publishing and modern printing techniques. He opens it on the desk before us; there is a group photograph taken at some congregation event or other. Renee is a striking woman: tall, fair-haired, good bone structure.

'I'm showing you that because she's the image of her mother,' the minister says. 'They might have been sisters. Anyway, Renee was such a comfort to him during those first bleak weeks. Peter wished to mourn in private, and of course my wife and I respected that. After a time, though, I'd look in on him, maybe bring him a little something my wife would make. He liked that. But he was taking it very badly. Renee couldn't get him to eat anything. One could see his health getting worse by the week. He spoke of suicide. That was what worried me most of all.'

Dr McElliot's visits to the Rickett house grew more frequent and prolonged. Very soon the visits were following a pattern. Renee would make supper for the men and retire; Peter and Dr McElliot would talk long into the night, the widower pouring out his heart to the minister. It was during one such session that Peter spoke of his wish to end it all. He saw no point in continuing; with Mary's passing, the bottom had fallen out of his world. She meant everything to him. He saw no reason why he should not join her in the afterlife.

'I don't mind telling you that was a tricky position he put me in,' the minister confesses. 'Peter's arguments made perfect sense – that is, if one looked at them in the cold light of reason. He and Mary had been inseparable while she was alive. Why should he not be allowed to join her in death? Particularly when his life without her had no meaning, as far as he could see. I put it to him that perhaps the Lord had a special purpose for him, one that Peter was unaware of but would be revealed in time. "Bernard," he said to me, "I'm seventy-eight years of age. If I haven't discovered my mission on this earth by now, I never will. What use am I here? Would I not be better off with Mary?"'

'I had to bring a little theology to bear,' Dr McElliot continues. 'And I tell you those are the hardest moments of all: when you have to assure a suffering fellow-Christian that the Divine plan is greater than the human one, and that we must accept it. We must accept that God knows what's best for us, not in the temporal sense but in the long run, in the sense of what's best for our immortal souls.'

The minister pauses. He is choosing his next words carefully.

'There is of course the difficulty that nowhere in Scripture does the Lord actually *forbid* us to take our own life. But Paul told the Philippians that "to live is Christ and to die is gain". He went on to say that his "desire is to depart and be with Christ, for that is far better, but to remain on in the flesh is more necessary for your sake," meaning the sake of the people he was trying to convert. I interpret that as an allusion to a God-given duty to our fellow men. In the end I told Peter that the commandment that forbids us to kill must be interpreted as forbidding *all* killing, including killing ourselves.'

And so it went for several months: Peter Rickett plunging into black moods of despair and the minister pulling him out of them again. It did not help when Renee returned to Sussex, but that was an inevitability; her own family came first. Peter simply had to learn to cope with his loss, as all bereaved persons must.

As more months passed, it did seem that the truth of the old adage of time healing all wounds was borne out. He retrieved some of his former *joie de vivre*, could laugh and smile again – if only infrequently. On Dr McElliot's urging he began to take more of an interest in the congregation's affairs. He joined a group of elders who made it their business to actively support the aged, the sick and the dying. They visited hospitals and hospices, making the final days of elderly patients a little more comfortable and dignified. Such proximity to the death of others seemed to take Peter's mind off his own grief.

Dr McElliot was pleased. He felt that progress was being made. Peter's thoughts were no longer morbid. He would still speak often of Mary, but now it was in a more positive and healthy way – up until the morning, a little over two years following her death, when he called unexpectedly to the minister's home, before the good man had finished breakfast. Peter was flustered, wild eyed. Dr McElliot feared he might have a seizure of some kind.

'Bernard, Bernard!' he gushed. 'You'll never guess. Mary came to me last night! She wants me to join her.'

Dr McElliot is of the old school of Presbyterianism. He does not hold with ghosts. He mistrusts them. He will speak of 'a chasm which divides this world from the next', and will refuse to countenance the possibility of the dead returning. He explains that there is no call for it, that the Lord Jesus Christ is the only mediator we need, and that Leviticus expressly forbids necromancy, the communication with the dead by way of spiritists.

'Sit down, Peter,' he said gently, 'and tell me all about it.'

Over a cup of tea the elderly man spoke of his extraordinary experience. He had gone to bed at roughly 2 am, as was his habit;

he was finding that he needed less and less sleep. An hour later he awoke to find a figure standing at the foot of the bed. It was his beloved Mary. She looked to be 'not a day over twenty', according to Peter. In fact, she appeared exactly as she had the day they met, all those decades past.

As apparitions go, it seems to have been small beer. Mary's spirit was not quite solid, but nor was she ethereal. Peter described her appearance as being 'like a black-and-white film'. He estimated that she remained visible for no more than a minute and a half. In that time, though, she managed to convince him that she had survived death and that she missed him terribly. She seemed sad. Peter recalled her exact words.

'I am lonely, so lonely here,' she said. 'My dear, I need you by my side.'

The minister considered the man before him. He had come to him with a story which may or may not have contained truth. Dr McElliot does not dispute the possibility of ghosts; neither does he give credence to every sighting of a 'spirit', no matter how trustworthy the witness may be. His first thought was that Rickett had imagined it, that an obsessive mind was somehow enabling him to fulfil his dearest wish: that he and his beloved wife be reunited. The minister elected to believe this latter explanation. It was important, too, that Peter should come to terms with the reality of his situation, hard though it might be.

He gave what guidance he could. He suggested to the widower that he was perhaps better off investing even more time in the welfare of the congregation's less fortunate, as well as placing a little more trust in the Lord.

Dr McElliot was confident that his advice had fallen 'into good ground'. He was mistaken. The following week Peter called round in the evening, and, having taken supper with the McElliots, joined the minister in his sitting-room. He had important news. On the commendation of a friend, he had paid a visit to a group of spiritists who met in a house on Orwell Road, Rathgar.

'He told me about the séance,' the minister says, 'and no detail was spared! I had to keep myself from smiling because it was as if he was telling me about something from Victorian times. From the way he described the house, I got a picture of an old rambling place with heavy dark furniture and velvet curtains. One could almost see men with wing collars and the women in bonnets. Peter wasn't sure if somebody actually lived there or it was owned by the group. There were nine of them that evening, he told me, including Peter: three gentlemen and six ladies. Most were elderly with the exception of a young man, a first-time visitor like Peter. The poor fellow had apparently lost his wife in a drowning accident. He was hoping to be able to contact her.'

Peter joined the others in a room on the first floor. He remembered it as having heavy curtains, which were already drawn even though it was early on a summer's evening. There was a small table in the middle of the room, only a little bigger than a card table, but circular, with chairs arranged about it. Peter and the others took their seats.

All except the young man and he were relaxed and talkative. They discussed such matters as 'spirits', 'channels' and 'the other side', relating as they did the words and deeds of their ethereal interlocutors as others might comment on a recent episode of a soap opera. Someone revealed how a spiritist group in Edinburgh had made a breakthrough of some significance that very week, apparently involving an 'apport'. The others were impressed.

Peter wondered when the medium would join them. They had been seated in the room for a half hour or more and there was no sign of her – he assumed the medium would be female. He was taken aback when one of the ladies present, the most unprepossessing of the three, abruptly requested that the main light be dimmed, and announced she was 'ready to begin'.

She invited the participants to link hands around the table and

THE GOOD PRESBYTERIAN AND THE SUCCUBUS

called for all talk to cease. Peter had paid no attention to the windows when entering the house, but decided then that those in that particular room must be double glazed; there was only the whisper of sounds from the road. The light was fading. He was sitting almost directly across from the medium. He watched in curiosity as her head drooped slowly down onto her chest, until she appeared to have fallen asleep. But she had not. To his consternation, she began to growl.

'Not really a growl in the sense of an animal, a big cat or something,' Dr McElliot says. 'Peter described it as being more the sound of somebody clearing their throat, but drawn out. He did an impression for me. It was not really threatening; more like somebody grunting with satisfaction.'

Almost at once, something utterly out of the ordinary occurred. Peter had been expecting a gradual preamble, perhaps the medium's renewing acquaintance with 'spirit guides' and what not. This he had been prepared for, he said. He had come to the séance with mixed feelings, the Christian side of him finding the idea of necromancy faintly repugnant, his despairing side ready to grasp at straws. The last thing he expected was that the proceedings would commence with his own circumstances; he was startled when the medium spoke his name. But the voice she used was not her own. It sounded uncannily like that of Mary Rickett.

'Peter,' she said. 'Oh, Peter!'

He was dumbstruck. To be sure, he had come to the house in Rathgar with the express purpose of receiving confirmation. Confirmation that the soul does indeed survive death. Confirmation that his lost love was not entirely lost to him. Confirmation that she it was who had visited him in the early hours of morning, and that she would visit him again. But, for all that, he was awed and afraid when Mary's voice came issuing from that mouth, from the lips of a complete stranger, from a woman who never knew Mary in life and could not possibly know her in death.

Or so it seemed to an utterly bewildered Peter Rickett.

'Pray for me, my darling,' she said. 'Will you promise to pray for me?'

He could not answer her.

'I am in a cold place,' the voice said, issuing perplexingly from the woman slumped opposite. 'There is no warmth here, Peter. I am so cold, so alone. That is why you must pray for me. Will you do that?'

He found his own voice at last.

'Yes – anything, Mary,' he croaked. 'Anything for you.'

'Thank you, Peter. I will come to you again, my darling. I'll come to you when you pray for me.'

With those words, the spirit of Mary Rickett evidently departed, to be replaced by that of another woman. The intonation was different, and she introduced herself as 'Paula'. There was a gasp from the young visitor. It seems that his drowned wife had manifested by way of the medium.

According to Dr McElliot, it was with the plea for prayer that Peter Rickett had most difficulty. He presented himself at the church hall the following day, looking the worse for wear. He was unshaven and his hands were trembling a little. The minister suggested a stroll in the nearby park.

'Peter was most disturbed by the idea of praying for the dead,' he said. 'It was the one thing Mary and he could never see eye to eye on. It seems that she was forever popping into a church and saying a little prayer for some deceased friend or relative. Lighting candles, that sort of thing.

'Peter did not hold with that at all. He could accept many things from Roman Catholic belief, including the assumption of the Virgin into heaven, the transubstantiation during the Eucharist, but he always drew the line at praying for the dead. He was a good Presbyterian and believed with heart and soul that we can only be saved by faith and by the Grace of the Lord, and that we go to our deaths either saved or not saved. So no amount of prayer said after his death will benefit a man if he has not found salvation within his lifetime. Peter never wavered in that belief. Not until that moment.'

The séance had done more to upset Peter Rickett than he first supposed. In the days that followed, he grew steadily despondent, torn as he was between allegiance to his religious faith and love for his dead wife. It seemed to him that the old demons had returned: the doubts that tormented him all those years before, when he was forced to choose between his parents' wishes and the dictates of the heart. It was unbearable. He found himself slipping into the church every day, and praying to Jesus for guidance. But, although he prayed long and hard, he resisted the temptation to pray for Mary.

At the end of seven days, the anguished man was no closer to resolving his dilemma. That night, a Saturday, he went to bed earlier than usual: a little after midnight. He was exhausted; he feared for his health. He was beginning to believe that nature was about to take its course – and thereby neatly solve his problems. He need think no more of suicide; he felt that death was about to overtake him. And he need have no qualms of conscience about not responding to Mary's plea for prayer, for he would be joining her soon anyway. With those consoling thoughts uppermost, he drifted off to sleep.

He dreamed a dream the like of which he had never before experienced. Mary was in it. To his joy, she resembled the Mary who had appeared at the foot of his bed, the apparition which had spurred him into visiting the spiritists in Rathgar. This Mary was radiant; she was the Mary he had fallen in love with when both were so young and vital. And, in his dream, Peter was likewise magically rejuvenated. Although he saw nothing of the body he was occupying, it *felt* young. In his dream the years fell away and he revelled in the wonder of life, the *potentiae* of it all, the sense of marvellous things to come. In his waking state, he had forgotten how that felt; in his dream, it was as though such emotions had never left him.

Mary came to him in a place that resembled the Dublin suburb of his youth, with its pleasant parks and leafy avenues; yet it was different in subtle ways. The colours were more vibrant than anything in the real world. Peter would describe it to Dr McElliot as 'like the Technicolor you saw in the old films; like *The Wizard of Oz* or *Chitty Chitty Bang Bang*.' Grass was greener, the sky belonged more in the tropics.

All at once, his dream girl was in his arms. Time had rolled back. Then passion seemed to take over.

Even in his dream, Peter knew that this was somehow wrong. The couple had never behaved thus in real life. Never; not even when joined in wedlock. Mary had been decorum itself. This other Mary bore no resemblance to *his* Mary. There was something wanton about her, something lascivious.

'Pray for me, Peter!' she cried. 'Oh, pray for me, my darling. You must pray for me; you must save me. I must be saved!'

He woke up.

He lay there gasping, hearing his heart thudding at twice its normal rate. He was sweating copiously. He could feel it running into his eyes. Not since the horror of Monte Cassino had he experienced such fright. He felt close to death.

'And this is the delicate part,' Dr McElliot says, lowering his voice. 'Peter could not say this in so many words. He was a very private person, in ways a man out of time. He could never find it within himself to discuss matters of a sexual nature. I had to read between the lines, as it were. When he told me that he felt close to death, I knew he was actually referring to the *little* death.'

The minister explains as delicately as he can that Peter Rickett woke from his unusual dream in a state of sexual arousal. It was deeply embarrassing for the widower, yet he felt obliged to confide in his friend and spiritual adviser.

'I told him not to be concerned, that it was a natural thing, nothing to be ashamed of. "We're not responsible for what we do in our dreams, Peter," I said. "If that were the case, then more than a few of us would be behind bars by now. I know *I* would be." That got a smile out of him at least.'

Unfortunately it was no laughing matter. That dream was the first of many such dreams. Mary came to Peter in each of them, always radiant, always young. In each dream she would initiate acts of passion that grew progressively more salacious. And each time, Peter would awaken in his bed, drenched in perspiration, in a state of arousal, his heart pounding. Each new dream was worse than the last. And each time, his dream would end abruptly when the phantom Mary posed the question: 'Peter, will you pray for me?'

He could stand it no longer; he must give in. And did, on the twelfth occasion. Setting his beliefs to one side, he dropped to his knees by the bed and prayed for the soul of his dead wife.

His relief was immediate. He rose with the sense of his prayer's effectiveness, the sense that somewhere in that vast, unknown territory beyond the grave, his message had been passed on, and that Mary would benefit in due course.

However, in daylight it was otherwise; a sense of betrayal overcame Peter. He went to the minister's office, waited patiently until some congregation business or other was completed.

'He put such store by faith in the Lord,' Dr McElliot says. 'He felt that in helping Mary he was betraying Jesus Christ. What could I say to him? Peter had lived his life by his Christian beliefs. Now, in his twilight years, he felt that he could no longer be considered among the saved. I told him that the Lord would understand, that He would look lightly on all this; that, in any event, his salvation was still a grace bestowed by God. Peter's actions would not influence the Divine will, that it was human arrogance to believe otherwise. Peter wasn't convinced. We argued for hours. It was an absurd situation; the roles were completely reversed. *I* should have been the one defending doctrine; instead, it was Peter.'

The minister lost sight of Peter for a time. He no longer showed for worship or Holy Communion, and could be reached neither by telephone nor by calling to the house. It was almost a repetition of his mourning days, when he was displaying suicidal tendencies. The minister and the elders were concerned. They took turns in checking the house, by day and in the evening. It was feared – considering his age; he was approaching eighty – that the worst had happened, or that he might be lying helpless, having sustained a fall. Anything was possible with a pensioner living by himself.

But elders would report Peter's radio playing, his lights being on or off at appropriate times. The conclusion was reached that he simply wished to be alone.

No one was more surprised than the minister when, nearly three weeks following what he calls the 'theological argument', he received a phone call from Peter Rickett. The elderly man sounded odd, distant, disorientated, as though he had been roused from a deep sleep and was not yet fully awake. Could the minister come and see him? It was urgent, he said; very urgent.

'I dropped everything and drove round there at once,' Dr McElliot says gravely. 'He was only five minutes away. This would have been about ten in the evening. It was in early October.'

He goes to a filing cabinet again, a different one, and returns with a sheaf of papers. They are handwritten pages.

'I made notes,' he says. 'I had to. I felt it was important to set down on paper a good account of that evening.'

He sensed that something was terribly wrong as soon as Peter admitted him. The minister is not given to exaggeration but says that he felt a strange 'atmosphere' on entering the house. It was indefinable, yet gave him a sense of unease. There was something oppressive about it.

The house was in disarray. It was not quite the shambles that Fintan Donnelly encountered in the priest's house in Kilkenny (see p. 144) yet bad enough to dismay the minister. Peter Rickett was an orderly man. He took pride in his appearance, never appeared in public or in company without being properly attired. His home had always reflected his disdain of slovenliness.

He had a woman come in twice a week to tidy and clean. Now the minister saw that Peter had evidently dispensed with her services. The floors looked unswept; there were cups and saucers and plates on tables in the sitting-room, magazines and newspapers lying discarded and unfolded. Peter himself was tieless and there was a day's stubble on his chin. He was holding a mug of coffee.

'Would you like one?' he asked.

'No, thank you, Peter.'

The minister moved some newspapers aside and seated himself on a sofa. Peter set his mug down, made himself comfortable and began his account of all that had occurred in the intervening weeks.

He did not dream on the night following his talk with the minister. Instead he woke in the early hours, as he had done the first time. Mary was again standing at the foot of the bed, and as before, youthful and beautiful. But she looked inexpressively sad. He sat up. She spoke to him, and her voice seemed to come from inside his head, although her lips were moving.

'Thank you for the prayers,' she said. 'I am so grateful.'

He could only nod.

'I am in this cold place,' she said. 'Your prayers have eased my pain. Please, continue to pray for me. But only your love can release me from my suffering, Peter. I want you to know that.'

She seemed to drift closer to him. Her discarnate body was so close that he swore he could make out the colour of her eyes. They seemed darker than they had been in life. Her lips seemed fuller too; they looked black in the faint light, as though she wore heavy lipstick; in life she had shunned make-up. The lips were more voluptuous than he remembered.

Then abruptly her face filled with anger.

'They lied to us, my darling,' she said. 'They all lied. The priests, the bishops, your minister. All a pack of liars. Nobody can save you. Not Jesus, not the prophets. There is no Messiah. We're all alone. All we have is ourselves. All we have, Peter, is our love. Love is everything. It holds the universe together; it's the glue that binds the stars. Without love, we're lost.'

Peter was horrified. This was blasphemy of the first order. He knew that; it went against everything he had been brought up to believe. And yet he found himself weighing Mary's words carefully. In his confused state – sitting up in bed in the depth of night, communing with a ghost – he was coming to believe that her words made sense. Did not Jesus preach of universal love? Did He not teach us that we must all be brothers?

'We must *love*, Peter!' the ghost was saying. 'We must harness the power of love. In this way we can overcome death itself. We can be immortal, you and I. We do not need the Lord's grace for our salvation. All I need is your love for me.'

'But you're dead already, Mary!' he countered. 'Why would you need to overcome death?'

'Not the death of the body! That is meaningless where I am. I mean we can overcome the death of the soul.'

'I didn't think the soul could die. . . .'

'You are wrong! Without love the soul dies.' She moved even closer. 'Sleep now, my darling,' she said gently, and he felt his eyes growing heavy. 'In sleep you will understand.'

No sooner had he fallen asleep again than Peter began to dream.

Once again, he was with Mary; it was as though the dream were a continuation of his vision. In his dream he began to wonder if the apparition had not been a dream also.

Mary fell into his arms, as before. Her passion was, if anything, even stronger. In his dream she was pushing him down upon the too-green grass. He could not resist her.

Peter woke for the second time that night in a state of confusion and despair.

'That was the story he told me that evening,' Dr McElliot says. 'I recognized the voice of nihilism straightaway. The voice that lies at the heart of all demonic assault, the idea that nothing has meaning. This demon, posing as Mary, was not talking about the nature of unconditional love, as that preached by Our Lord Jesus Christ. It was implanting in Peter's mind the idea that freedom and real meaning lie only in the gratification of the senses, in other words: sexual love.'

The episode was the first of many. Each night, Mary would come to him as an apparition, send him to sleep. Each night, he would have the lucid dream. He was torn between the excitement of her embraces and his sure conviction that it was terribly wrong. He feared for his soul, feared that he was putting himself beyond salvation; that if the Lord had ever bestowed that grace upon him, He should surely rescind it now.

Peter cut himself off from the congregation. He came to believe that his sin would be visible to all, like some ghastly mark of Cain; that all would see the change in him. He learned to both dread and welcome the night, by turns anticipating Mary's visits and terrified of the power she was exercising over him. When he did sleep, it was to be tormented and shown ecstasy, over and over again, night after night.

At last he summoned the courage to phone the minister. He felt that he was losing his mind.

* * *

'He fell foul of the demon known as the succubus,' Dr McElliot says. 'What you might call a she-devil.'

He has examined the subject in some detail, no doubt as a consequence of the haunting of Peter Rickett. Belief in the succubus, he is at pains to clarify, has no place in orthodox biblical teaching. It is not even Christian in the accepted sense. Some hold that its roots lie in Sumeria and can be traced to the legend of Lilith, the first wife of Adam.

In CS Lewis's *The Lion, the Witch and the Wardrobe*, the children are curious about the provenance of the eponymous witch. The character known as Mr Beaver tells them that the wicked woman is descended from 'your father Adam's first wife, her they called Lilith'.

Lewis had come upon the story in *Lilith*, a dark fantasy novel by George MacDonald, a theology scholar and thinker whom he much admired. MacDonald's Lilith is a demon princess loosely based on a Judaic entity of that name.

Lilith is first mentioned by name in a curious work, *Sepher Ben Sira*, also known as the *Alphabet of Ben-Sira*, written at an unknown date but certainly after AD 700. The original is thought to be a copy of an earlier work; it was written in Aramaic and Hebrew, and translated into several languages.

The legend offers a strangely modern, feminist explanation for Adam's marital difficulties.

> After God created Adam, who was alone, He said, 'It is not good that the man should be alone' (Genesis 2:18). He then created a woman for Adam, from the earth, even as He had created Adam himself, and called her Lilith.
>
> Adam and Lilith at once began to quarrel. She said, 'I will not lie beneath thee,' and he, answering, said, 'I will not lie beneath thee, but only above. For

thou art created to be subordinate, whilst I am to be the superior one.'

Lilith responded: 'We are equal to each other inasmuch as we were both created from the dust of the ground.' But they would not listen to one another. When Lilith saw this, she pronounced the Ineffable Name and flew off into the air.

Adam stood in prayer before his Creator: 'Sovereign of the universe!' he said, 'the woman whom thou gavest to be with me hath fled.' At once, the Holy One, blessed be He, sent three angels to bring her back.

God offered Lilith a choice. She could return to Adam or could have one hundred of her children die each day. She refused to return. The angels pursued her to Egypt. Still she refused to return, and they threatened to drown her.

Finally, Lilith made a pact with them:

'Leave me!' she said. 'I was created only to cause sickness to infants. If the infant is male, I have dominion over him for eight days after his birth, and if female, for twenty days.'

Lilith would have no power over any infant protected by an amulet bearing the name of an angel. From that time on, a sick child thus protected would recover. She swore an oath that she would keep her word.

And so grew the legend of Lilith. Over time her name was given to an array of she-devils, and came to be synonymous with evil. Legend identified her as one of the succubi – in Latin, 'those who lie under' – an order of demons whose infernal task was to seduce a man while he slept. In medieval times it was believed that a succubus would harvest a man's sperm, and use it to impregnate an unsuspecting woman. Such tainted seed, it was held, would inevitably produce a child who was susceptible to demonic influence.

Dr McElliot shared his suspicions with Peter Rickett.

'He was horrified by the idea of the succubus,' the minister says, 'but he agreed with me that it seemed to fit what he was going through. Poor man. He believed that he'd brought it all on himself, that he'd allowed evil to gain a purchase on his life. He believed that he had damned himself.'

The minister appreciated at once the extreme gravity of the situation. Weighing all in the balance, he asked himself if he had not already allowed matters to get out of hand, if he could do what he had to do alone. For he was in no doubt that something evil had entered Peter Rickett's life. He prayed that he was not too late to banish it.

'Let me say that deliverance is not something I do every day of the week,' the minister is at pains to point out. 'In fact, it's very rare that I'm called upon to do anything of the sort. On the odd occasion, I'll be called out to help somebody with a crisis of faith, and that person will insist it's the work of demons. But nine times out of ten it's nothing of the sort, nothing that some judicious counselling won't cure. Peter's case wasn't like that.'

The following day, he turned to colleagues for advice. Some-one suggested that he get in touch with a Presbyterian minister in Edinburgh, a man who, it was said, had dealt with a case bearing some similarities. This was not strictly true. At the same time, Dr McElliot received some excellent advice on how to proceed.

'I was told not to attempt anything on my own,' he says. '"Whatever you do, Bernard," he told me on the phone, "have somebody else along. Just in case."'

The minister laid his plans. That same day, he called round to see Jack Millward, an old friend. He was perhaps the most reliable elder in the entire congregation, and was also on excellent terms with Peter Rickett. He had sought to lessen his grief in the early stages of bereavement.

'I knew I could count on Jack,' the minister says. 'But it took a lot of persuading, I can tell you. He's a level-headed man. I had to go very carefully over the idea of the succubus, and I think he imagined I'd lost my marbles. But in the end he said: "You're the expert in these matters, Bernard. If you believe that's the case then count me in. Only let's keep it between ourselves, fair enough?"'

Dr McElliot judged that swift action was called for. He believed that Peter's situation had deteriorated so rapidly that not even another night should be allowed to pass. That evening, Millward and he went to the house. There was no change; if anything, the persecuted man was more unkempt than ever, his home in even worse disarray. Without further ado the minister instructed him to prepare to leave. Minutes later, he was dressed and shaved.

Dr McElliot let himself into the church by a side door, not wishing to attract the attention of the caretaker, who lived opposite the main entrance. Jack and Peter followed. The minister switched on a single lamp in the sanctuary. It gave off a dim light, sufficient to work by, but unseen from outside.

He began at once. He had Peter kneel before the cross and urged him to focus his thoughts on the Passion of Christ, how He had died to save us. He asked Jack Millward to fetch two Bibles.

'Let us read from the fifty-first Psalm,' he said.

In the quiet of the church, two voices spoke aloud the lines handed down by royal David, the sweet singer of Israel, ten centuries before the birth of Christ.

> Have mercy upon me, o God, according to thy loving kindness, according unto the multitude of thy tender mercies blot out my transgressions. Wash me throughly from mine iniquity, and cleanse me from

> my sin. For I acknowledge my transgressions, and
> my sin is ever before me. Against thee, thee only,
> have I sinned, and done this evil—

Dr McElliot was forced to stop in mid-sentence. Jack stopped too. Their eyes met. A strange atmosphere was stealing over the sanctuary.

'It was so alien,' the minister says, 'so utterly alien to anything I'd ever experienced. I felt as if I was standing at the edge of an abyss, and that very soon something was going to push me over, off into nothingness – totally annihilate my whole being, body and soul. I had to struggle to resist the urge to give in to it. My very faith was under threat.'

He saw that Jack was feeling it too; at least he surmised as much, judging by his companion's expression. Later he would learn that their experiences were similar. Oddly enough, the elderly man kneeling before them seemed not to be affected. The minister shivered, found his voice again and resumed praying.

> Behold, I was shapen in iniquity, and in sin did my
> mother conceive me. Behold, thou desirest truth in
> the inward parts; and in the hidden part thou shalt
> make me to know wisdom. Purge me with hyssop,
> and I shall be clean: wash me, and—

He had to stop again and take a deep breath. Perspiration was running down his face.

'I was burning up inside,' he tells us. 'Not only physically but mentally as well. Suddenly the words of Scripture sounded hollow and meaningless. I had the urge to drop the Bible and just run out of the church, and keep on running.'

The minister shut his eyes and silently implored Jesus to come to his aid. As he did so, he heard a little gasp from the kneeling man, followed by a groan. He ignored this and continued.

The sense of despair and hopelessness began to dissipate, to be replaced by a sense of calm. The minister kept his eyes closed.

'The Lord was fortifying me for what was coming next,' he says. 'It was terrifying, but I knew that I could confront it. I was no longer afraid.'

> Make me to hear joy and gladness; that the bones
> which thou hast broken may rejoice. Hide thy face
> from my sins, and blot out all mine iniquities.

'Bernard!'

It was Jack. Ashen-faced, he was calling the minister's attention to the door on their right. Into the church, from under the door, there eddied and swirled something with the appearance of black smoke.

'I had never witnessed it myself before, thank the Lord,' Dr McElliot tells us, 'but I sensed that it was the thing that's known as the Shadow. I believe it's common to many hauntings of a diabolical nature. "Frightening" doesn't even begin to describe the sight we witnessed that night.'

The minister and the elder watched grimly as the smoke began to assume form. It issued up from the floor, swirled about as a swarm of tiny insects might, and coalesced into a dense formation, to resemble the figure of a very tall man. As the minister looked on and prayed fervently, the manifestation moved slowly across the church, its unclean form approaching the sanctuary. As if sensing its coming, the man who knelt beneath the cross turned his head.

'Mary!'

Peter Rickett was staring at the apparition and getting to his feet. The minister quickly laid a hand on his head. Jack Millward placed his own hand on the widower's left shoulder. Peter tried to stand, but the minister and the elder restrained him.

'Don't, Mary!' Peter cried suddenly. 'Not here. I beg of you!'

Mary? Dr McElliot was perplexed. For there was no Mary, not anyone or anything remotely resembling her. There was only the column of black smoke in the vague shape of a tall man. It seethed and writhed dangerously close at hand. It seemed to the minister that there was an invisible line drawn in the sanctuary, one which the entity was forbidden to cross.

Dr McElliot needed no book. He knew the appropriate verses of Luke by heart. In a loud voice he recited them.

> Lord, even the devils are subject unto us through
> thy name. And he said unto them: I beheld Satan as
> lightning fall from heaven. Behold, I give unto you
> power to tread on serpents and scorpions, and over
> all the power of the enemy: and nothing shall by any
> means hurt you.

'I sensed what was happening,' he tells us. 'Peter was seeing what Jack and I could not. We saw the black shape; he was seeing the ghost of Mary again. Except that by then I knew it to be an imposter – *the* Imposter.'

'Begone, demon!' the minister cried. 'Leave this sacred place. You have no business here. The Lord Jesus Christ commands you to leave this holy church and to leave His just servant Peter in peace. Go!'

But Peter was straining to rise. Jack and the minister had difficulty keeping him on his knees. For all his years, the widower seemed to have acquired a formidable strength.

'I was sure that if he went near that thing it would have power over him,' Dr McElliot says. 'He was imploring me to leave Mary in peace. I tried to convince him that it wasn't Mary. But he was growing hysterical. He thought I could see what he was seeing but of course I could not. Nor could he see that terrible black thing. He obeyed me, even though he looked frightened to death.'

Throughout, the dark Shadow had seethed at the edge of the

sanctuary as a single entity. Now it divided itself up into six amorphous black gatherings, and began to swirl about the ceiling.

He later heard from Peter that he saw them too. Gone was the earlier pretence of Mary's likeness. Whatever it was that visited the church that night had given up its masquerade. In the face of such evil, the minister knew of no other course than prayer.

'We said prayers together: prayers Jack and Peter would know intimately. The Lord's Prayer, the Prayer of Confession. The more we prayed, the vaguer the black shapes became. I have never seen a man so terrified as Peter was that night. I honestly thought we'd have a corpse on our hands.'

The minister lays the sheaf of papers aside and steeples his fingers. He is marshalling his thoughts.

'To this day, I can't be certain that anything I saw or felt in the church that night was real,' he says at last. 'I know enough about the power of suggestion to know that I could simply have imagined everything: the psychological attack on my senses, the atmosphere of wickedness. It's perfectly possible. I have no proof that Peter saw anything out of the ordinary; not then, or when he was alone in his bed at night. At the same time, I knew him to be a particularly sensible gentleman. I trusted his judgement. He was a scientist, an engineer. He was nobody's fool.'

Dr McElliot wishes to go on record as being a man who accepts the orthodoxy of his Christian faith, and who dismisses anything that lies beyond those boundaries. There is no place in his belief system for superstition. We are curious as to how he interprets the notion of the succubus.

'I don't know if I can go along with the idea at all,' he says. 'It's probably a lot of nonsense. Who knows but it wasn't something invented by the rabbis of old to keep wayward men on the straight and narrow. The Bible tells me that Adam only had one wife, and I believe implicitly in the Bible. If I did not, I wouldn't be a minister of God.

'Instead of placing any credence in the succubus theory, I'm prepared to believe that Satan, that great deceiver, took the guise of the wife of a lonely old man, that he might lose his faith in the Lord. And Peter did waver for a while. But after that night, he never did again.'

Dr McElliot seems troubled. Throughout our meeting he has been very candid and forthcoming. After much hesitation, he seems to make up his mind about something.

'Here's the thing,' he says. 'Peter wasn't the only one affected by that night. We were two hours together in the church, although at the time it felt no more than fifteen minutes. The three of us prayed harder than we'd ever done in our lives, and after a time I could feel the atmosphere change. The smoke left. I didn't see it leave and I don't know if it went the same way it came. But I was deep in prayer by then, and when I looked up it was gone.'

'The smoke came back, though,' he continues after another silence. 'It came to visit me at home. On two occasions. I was alone both times, luckily; it was the last thing I'd have wished my family to see, I can tell you. I was in my study both times, and it crept in under the door, just like in the church. I prayed very powerfully then, and it never bothered me again, thank the Lord.'

What does he think it was?

'In my house? I believe it was a last-ditch effort by something ungodly. Maybe it was testing me, seeing how far it could get with me. Who can say?' He smiles. 'But it's unimportant.'

'When Peter Rickett left the church with me that night, he was clinging to me like a man just rescued from drowning,' Dr McElliot says in conclusion. 'And I suppose in a way that is what he was. He was rescued. He was saved again. And he died a few years later in the full knowledge that he was saved – and in the knowledge that he would be reunited with his beloved Mary.

'The genuine Mary.'

THE BOY WHO COMMUNES
WITH DEMONS

WHEN GARY LYTTLE was ten years old he met the Devil. To be sure, the Devil did not introduce himself as such and the boy was too young to recognize him for what he was. Satan, the fallen angel of Revelation, is believed to come in many guises, assuming many names. Most churchmen hold that the Devil, the Adversary, presides over a host of lesser demons, and that each demon has its own diabolical attributes, its own means of corrupting souls. Whatever the truth, the following is an account of how an evil entity appears to have gained a foothold in a young boy's life.

Gary lives in a sleepy town in County Donegal. Not much happens there, which is no bad thing. There are no murders, rapes or random acts of cruelty and mayhem. Pensioners do not feel threatened, and the Gardaí are rarely called upon to investigate serious crime. The other side of the coin is that the town has little to offer an adolescent boy who craves excitement in his life.

In the spring of 2004, Gary was making his way home from school. As usual, he took a short cut that involves an unpaved footpath which cuts under a bridge and leads alongside a small river, before joining another road. The path is in frequent use – by schoolchildren, young lovers, and the occasional angler trying his luck at the bream and carp that can still be found in the river, despite the light pollution generated by a chemical plant some four miles upstream.

Gary does not know why he chose to venture away from his customary route homeward, but had the distinct impression that something was 'telling' him to leave the track and inspect a sandy patch of earth and undergrowth. There were objects strewn there, many unfamiliar. He thought at once of 'treasure'. Not treasure in the sense of booty, though; more the sort that enriches a boy's imagination. But a quick examination told him that he had chanced upon an illicit dumping site. It was not unlike the rubbish to be found in much of rural Ireland: broken household appliances, old shoes, items of clothing, and other detritus dumped by the inconsiderate. Somebody had buried the lot, but it seemed that another had tried to dig it all up again. It might also have been a scavenging dog, lured by an odour still clinging to a cooking utensil. Gary was disappointed.

Until, that is, his eye was drawn to what appeared to be a large rectangle of wood – a slim panel – half buried in the ground.

He shrugged off his schoolbag and hunkered down to inspect his find. He frowned. It resembled some kind of household ornament, a picture done on wood. But it might equally well be a board game, he thought – one of the old-fashioned kind he had seen in a friend's house. He tugged at the panel and it came loose.

Gary was thrilled. It was a ouija board. This he knew because he had seen them in films. He recognized it by the arrangement of numerals and letters, the words YES and NO. It seemed to be very old and was decorated with engravings. There was a sun and a moon, both drawn 'with funny faces'. At the bottom of the board, to left and right of the word GOODBYE, were 'dark ladies'.

'There were two black babies floating behind them,' Gary says, 'and angels with wings'.

The schoolboy is unclear as to what happened when he pulled the board free of the earth. He claims that something 'flew up in the air'. But the object refused to obey the laws of physics; instead of falling to earth at once like a tossed stone, it remained suspended in the air for a few moments, before floating gently down and settling on the board.

The object turned out to be the *planchette*, or pointer, belonging to the ouija. It was made of the same wood as the board, and shaped like a triangle with rounded apexes. There was a circle of clear glass in the centre. Gary picked it up and wiped away the soil.

He returned his attention to the ouija board, laying it flat on the ground. Carefully, he cleaned it of all traces of dirt, intending to bring it home with him in his schoolbag – if it would fit, that is. He glanced about him. He was alone by the river. By this time, all the other stragglers from school had disappeared; there was no sign even of a hopeful angler.

Then, without warning, as Gary sat innocently gazing at the board, something incredible occurred. He experienced what can only be called 'a vision'. In the earth beneath his feet he felt a violent tremor. When it ceased, he heard voices: men and women's voices moaning and shrieking under the ground. Some were crying out.

'They were all shouting something like "bim eye ah",' Gary says. 'Or it could have been "bam eye ah". I didn't know what it meant.'

The boy was terrified and attempted to get up, but instead, was thrown back into a sitting position. He was being held captive for a reason. Slowly, the ground in front of him began to open up, and Gary found himself on the rim of an enormous cavern-like space. Down in its depths he saw a throne. There was a figure seated upon it, but Gary insists that 'it wasn't the Devil', that it was an entity that would make itself known to him by and by.

But his attention at that moment was not on the throned figure, for from all parts of that great cavern, beings with wings began to rise. He identifies them as 'demons'. They were flying up towards him: hundreds of them. Even at that great distance, the boy could make out their eyes; all seemed to be focused on him, as though a signal had been given and all were launching themselves simultaneously into the attack.

It was an apocalyptic vision such as those experienced by mystics throughout history. In 1550, St Teresa of Ávila recorded a scene displaying many similarities. No one can say with certainty where such visions emanate from – whether they are a by-product of our upbringing, memories of illustrations seen in sacred books, stained-glass windows and the like. Or even, in Gary's case, images recalled from straight-to-video horror movies.

The last explanation would be perhaps the most obvious and plausible, were it not rendered null and void by what was to happen later that day. Gary tells how he recovered from his 'trance', seeming to reawaken many minutes later in the same spot. There was no longer a fissure in the earth, no more moans and shrieks from souls in torment. There was only the ouija board, lying where he had dropped it, amid the illegally dumped household rubbish. He picked up his schoolbag and took to his heels, running home as fast as he could.

This is Gary's version of events. He is supposed to have fled the scene, leaving the board behind. But, as his account progresses, so also does the likelihood increase that he either took the ouija board with him or concealed it by the river.

Elsewhere in this book we examine the disturbing repercussions of ouija, principally the case of Julie Neville, the County Antrim woman who was tormented by a demon for fifteen years. There are a great many such tales of misadventure. For instance, it is not widely known that the 'talking board' figured large in the true-life case on which William Peter Blatty based his novel, *The Exorcist*. The demonized youngster was in reality a boy named Robbie, and the exorcism took place in 1949 in his home-town, Cottage Hills, a small community in the state of Maryland. The boy was thirteen at the time.

The family were from St Louis, Missouri, and an aunt would visit from time to time. She was a medium who, among other things, used the ouija board extensively to contact the spirit world. Robbie learned the 'art' from her, and continued to employ it without adult supervision. When his aunt died suddenly in January 1949, the boy tried to communicate with her. That was when the manifestations – those that would lead to his demonization – started in his parents' home. Minor and seemingly innocent at first, they grew in time to be unmistakably malignant.

This appears to be a common pattern where ouija is concerned. Most modern commentators on the use of the boards will warn that they should be approached with extreme caution. One churchman likened playing ouija to allowing a child to build sandcastles on a beach primed with landmines. The sensible advice is perhaps to avoid ouija altogether. The boards have too much of an unfortunate history.

It was not too long ago that the board was freely available in Ireland. The producer of the most popular version was the Waddington toy company, based in Leeds. But the company withdrew it from the market in 1970, principally because of a petition drawn up by a number of Christian churches. It was found to have disturbing effects on those who used it. At the time, the Reverend George Tarleton of South Woodford Congregational Church, London, voiced the concerns most vehemently.

'Ouija always affects a person spiritually,' he stated with conviction. '*Always*, without any shadow of doubt.'

A Leicester toy manufacturer took over the distribution of the controversial board-game, despite the protestations of British clergymen and concerned parents. There were calls for it to be banned, especially when a survey taken by a Leicester vicar, the Reverend Peter Anderson, revealed that eighty per cent of the schoolchildren interviewed had consulted ouija at one time or another. He pointed to a tragic case of a young boy who threw himself from a fire-station tower following extended sessions with the board. The dead boy's father subsequently left home and his mother was declared insane. It was revealed that both had consulted ouija on numerous occasions.

The British tabloids had a field day with the sensational findings, and it could not be long before the Irish media picked up the story. The resulting furore, while not leading to an official ban, ensured that ouija in any event disappeared from the toy shops. The 'game' had lost all pretence of innocence.

It was going to fall out of favour anyway. By the mid-1970s few boards were being produced in these islands. Grown-ups and children were making alphabets from pieces of paper instead, and using an upturned glass to move between the letters. It would not be until the 1990s that the traditional 'talking board' began to make a comeback.

A new generation would come to recognize ouija from its recurring appearances on the big screen. Among them was Gary Lyttle. Those who approach his story with the intention of obtaining evidence of falsehood or fraud, however, may well come away empty-handed. While it is true that Gary *might* have been acquainted with the case of Robbie 'Doe', the boy who inspired *The Exorcist*, it seems unlikely. Book and film date from the 1970s. Nor is it likely that he could have faked what was to follow.

Gary arrived home in great distress, according to his mother. He went upstairs to his room, and when he came down again a half hour later, he was still nervous.

'What's wrong with you?' she asked.

'Nothing.'

'Don't tell me there's nothing, Gary. You're as white as a sheet.'

She had a thought. 'Were you fighting with somebody? Is that it?' She inspected his face for bruises. It would not be the first time he had come home from school bearing the scars of 'battle'. Nothing serious; simply boyish exuberance. 'Did somebody pick on you?'

'No. I'm going to do my homework.'

He left the kitchen and she heard him climbing the stairs again. She was shaking her head in resignation when she heard a scream. It was so shrill and so unexpected that she hardly recognized it as having come from her own son.

She found Gary halfway up the stairs. He was gripping the rail as if his fingers were welded to it, and staring open-mouthed. She had never before seen him looking so terrified. Kelly, her eight-year-old daughter, was immediately at her side.

'Gary?' she called out.

But Gary seemed unaware of her presence. His eyes were directed at something at the top of the stairs. Whatever it was he was seeing, it was frightening him to such an extent that he could not move.

'What is it, Gary?' she asked again.

But he shook his head, refusing to answer.

His young sister giggled. Gary turned at the sound and fixed the girl with a look that Jessica had never seen before – at least, not in Gary. It was a look that took her back to the bad old days of her failed marriage, when her 'differences' with her husband had become truly irreconcilable. It was a look of hatred and contempt, and it had no place on the features of a ten-year-old boy. She hardly recognized her own son.

Jessica is quick to point out that, in the past, Gary never gave her cause for concern. She was forever thankful that he had turned out so well, so 'normal'. To meet him is to confirm this seeming normality.

There is very little about Gary's appearance or demeanour that marks him out as unorthodox, or even unusual; one could pass him in the street without a second glance. He is of average height, with green eyes and tightly cropped black hair. Already there is the promise of his growing into a handsome and athletic young man. He shares the interests of most boys of his age. He enjoys football, is developing a liking for rock music, plays computer games and watches DVDs whenever he can. Of the last, his tastes lean towards science fiction, as well as the gory and macabre – in his own words: 'scary movies'. Also in this respect he is no different from so many pre-teen boys.

For these reasons, Jessica had never considered her elder child to be 'a worry'. She was grateful that he had avoided bad company, had never been in trouble with his teachers, and there had likewise been no visits by Gardaí to report a misdemeanour – as is often the case with other young boys on the estate. Gary was turning out to be a model son; Jessica was proud of him, and not a little proud of herself too, for having done such a fine job in rearing him.

Now he seemed so different; she felt she no longer knew him. She glanced from one child to the other. Without knowing why, she took little Kelly roughly by the hand and rushed her back to the kitchen. Gary had frightened her, filled her with an inexplicable and nameless fear.

The little household fell back into its everyday routine. One week following the incident, Jessica had forgotten it, and Gary seemed to be his old self again. It was with great surprise, then, when Jessica heard the row from upstairs.

'Get the f*** out of here, Kelly! Get out or you're dead!'

She hurried up the stairs. On the landing, her younger child stood with tears flowing freely down her cheeks. She was nursing her left arm.

'What on earth . . . ?'

'Gary twisted my arm,' Kelly wailed. 'He *hurt* me.'

She found Gary in his room, sitting on his bed with his headphones on. He looked at her without interest. She raised her voice. He seemed to be defying her. She went to the bed. Gary must have sensed her fury because he snatched off the headphones.

She could hear faintly the upper registers of a heavy-metal power solo.

'Did you hurt your sister? Did you twist Kelly's arm?'

'No.' More defiance.

'She says you did.' Jessica was unaccustomed to lies from her children. 'What's going on, Gary?'

'Nothing.'

She hauled him from the bed and marched him to the landing where Kelly still stood, tearful and nervous.

'Why did you do it?'

'She was annoying me.'

'How, annoying you? She's never annoyed you before.'

This was true. The two got on exceptionally well. The incident was a new development and Jessica did not like it one bit.

'Tell her you're sorry.'

'I'm . . . er, sorry, Kelly.'

Kelly did not seem convinced. She was looking at her brother with something close to fear.

'Tell her it'll never happen again.'

'It'll-never-happen-again.'

But it did. Two days later Jessica heard another commotion from upstairs, and more wailing from Kelly. This time Gary had punched her, almost dislodging the last of her milk teeth. It was about to come out anyway, and Kelly was expecting a bigger reward than ever from the tooth fairy. Instead she got *this*.

'What has got into you?!' Jessica screamed at her son.

As before, he glared at her in defiance. She lost her temper, and did something which she seldom had to resort to. She slapped him hard across the face.

What next occurred astonished Jessica. Gary pulled back his fist and made to hit her. His face was dark with anger. She was genuinely frightened of him.

But the moment passed as quickly as it came. Gary quietened

down and seemed to revert to his usual affable self.

It was a false dawn. Next morning at the breakfast table Gary suddenly convulsed. In front of his startled mother and sister, he fell from his stool and onto the hard kitchen tiles. His limbs began to jerk violently, writhing and twisting like those of an upturned beetle seeking to right itself. Within moments, the fit subsided and the boy went rigid, as though paralyzed; his eyes were staring straight up at the ceiling. He looked terrified.

'Gary!'

Jessica bent over him, cradling his head in the crook of an arm. His eyes were still open and staring; they seemed to be glazed over. She gently slapped his cheek. There was no response.

'Is he dead, Mammy?'

'Run next door to Mrs Sharkey, will you, Kelly? Ask her to come quick.'

The neighbour was there within seconds, and was startled to see Jessica attempting to bring Gary round. There was no change in him.

'Has he fainted?'

'Aye. Can you ring Dr Flynn, Carmel?' Jessica pleaded. 'Say it's urgent.'

But when the doctor arrived some thirty minutes later there was still no change in Gary. He was reluctant to move the boy, fearing that any sudden motion might trigger a fresh seizure. At last he removed his stethoscope and turned to Jessica.

'I'll have to send him in for tests, Mrs Lyttle.'

'What is it? What's wrong with him?'

'I'm afraid I don't know. It could be a mild form of epilepsy, but it's too early to say. We'll know when we get him to the hospital.' He looked at his watch. 'My brother-in-law is the neurologist there. I'll give him a ring now and make sure he's there to take the lad as soon as he arrives.'

That day, Gary was subjected to a series of tests. They included a blood test, which might have shown low blood-sugar levels, or even diabetes. The neurologist ruled out both. He considered the possibility that the boy might have a weak heart, but a cardiogram showed otherwise. Gary had a robust constitution.

There remained the final possibility: epilepsy. Jessica was truly alarmed by the prospect. Even though she knew very little about the affliction, she understood the dreadful implications. He was just a child; what sort of a future would he have? It was too hard to even think about.

There are two principal factors that can trigger epilepsy; it can be inherited or can result from brain dysfunction, commonly called a seizure. As far as Jessica knew, there was no history of epilepsy in her family; and it was likewise unknown in her ex-husband's line.

The neurologist ordered an electroencephalograph (ECG) test. If there were patterns of abnormal electrical activity in the brain – epileptiform abnormalities and the like – then epilepsy was a distinct possibility. But the scan revealed no such irregularities; the boy's brain was completely sound. Epilepsy was therefore ruled out. But it was never going to be a serious contender as the cause of Gary's attack. An epileptic fit is usually of short duration, on average five minutes. Gary's lasted almost an hour.

When he was discharged the following day, no one was any the wiser as to what had happened to him in the kitchen. He himself had very little memory of the seizure. All he could call to mind was being seized by a great fear. Then he blacked out, to regain consciousness in the hospital. He thought of it as a great adventure – especially the brain scan. He had likened the huge machine to something he had seen in an episode of *Star Trek*.

'Like the Borg were experimenting on me,' he told his mother excitedly.

'If you say so, darling. You just try to rest now.'

Understandably, Jessica was beside herself with worry. She

suspected that something was terribly amiss with her son but could not even guess at the cause. Her thoughts returned to that day, a fortnight before, when she found him seemingly in a trance halfway up the stairs. She was not satisfied with the explanations he had given; she wished to learn the truth.

She waited until Gary had recovered from his ordeal, and was back to normal – insofar as she could ascertain. School was out of the question; he would not return for another two weeks, on Dr Flynn's orders.

'Gary,' she began, 'we have to talk, you and me.'

She switched off the television, much to little Kelly's annoyance. She slunk off to her room.

'Gary, I want to know what happened that day – the day you saw something on the stairs. Would you like to tell me now?'

'It wasn't anything.'

'Yes, it was. And I want to know what it was. When they were treating you at the hospital, Dr Flynn asked me if you'd had this sort of thing before, and I told him about that day. He says the two things must have something to do with each other. Now, have they?'

Gary shrugged, unable to meet his mother's eye. She pressed on.

'Kelly says you have a new friend. Is that true?'

'Yes. And it's none of her business.'

'Is that why you were fighting with her? That wasn't nice. You never used to fight with Kelly.' She sat down next to him. 'Who is this boy? Do I know him?'

'What boy?' Gary asked, in seeming innocence.

'Your new friend!'

'He's not a boy. He's a man.'

Jessica swallowed hard. This was the last thing she wished to hear. Only that week there had been extensive media coverage of a child-abuse scandal in England. Thoughts of how an adult could manipulate a child – she remembered they called it 'grooming' – were still strong in her mind. The reports had alerted her to the vulnerability of children; that it could happen to anybody's children. Even hers.

'What's this man's name, darling? Do I know him?'

'His name's Tyrannus.'

'Tyr— What sort of a name is that?'

'I dunno.'

'Where did you meet this man?'

'At the river; it was the man I saw on the throne,' he said, his words tumbling out in a torrent, 'the one that was like the Devil, only it wasn't the Devil; it was Tyrannus; he was on the stairs, and he was huge; he was ten times bigger than me.'

Jessica could only stare. Tyrannus is not a name one comes across very often. One of the films in the *Star Wars* series had a minor villain named Darth Tyrannus, and a recent television series set in ancient Rome featured a gladiator named Tyrannus. Jessica was familiar with neither character. To the casual eye, Tyrannus seems to contain elements of 'tyrant' and 'tyrannosaurus'; it could be argued that both words would hold a fascination for a ten-year-old boy. In fact, Tyrannus is a Latin name, derived from the Greek *tyrannos*: 'sole ruler'. It is not difficult to see how 'sole ruler' could come to mean 'cruel despot', as 'tyrant' does today.

In literature we encounter the name in a play by the Greek tragedian Sophocles: *Oedipus Tyrannus*. It is more generally entitled *Oedipus Rex* or *Oedipus the King*. What is not widely known is that a man named Tyrannus is mentioned in the New Testament. Paul the Apostle had been preaching in the city of Ephesus:

> But when divers were hardened, and believed not, but spake evil of that way before the multitude, he departed from them, and separated the disciples, disputing daily in the school of Tyrannus. (Acts 19:9)

This brief allusion is all we have to go on. There has been speculation as to who Tyrannus was, but it remains speculation; nothing about this Greek schoolmaster has come down to us. It might be thought that Gary had picked up the reference some-where or other; Sunday school comes to mind. And it is a fact that the boy has a Protestant background.

Jessica recalled vividly that afternoon she found him frozen with fear, staring open-mouthed at something at the top of the stairs. He had spoken of the stairs again. She wondered if they held the key.

'So this Tyrannus was in our house, Gary?'

He nodded, increasing her fears.

'That day? The day you . . .'

'Yeah. He scared me. He was *huge*. A big man, dressed in black, and he was covered in stuff.'

'What kind of stuff?' she asked, not really wanting to hear the answer.

'Rotten stuff. All dirt, like he'd come out of the ground, and he had wounds and big cuts all over him, but he was laughing at—'

'That's enough!' she snapped. 'You've been watching too many horror DVDs at my mother's. By heavens, I'm going over there tomorrow and—'

'No, Mammy!' Gary cried. 'It wasn't the films, it was the ouija board.'

And then he told her of the board, of the entity on the throne, of how it seemed to have followed him home.

The more Jessica heard, the more troubled she grew. She won-dered why Gary would suddenly invent such things. It was not like him. Her good sense advised her not to give his story ap-probation by appearing to believe it. An active imagination was all well and good, but this particular fantasy seemed downright unhealthy. She said as much to Gary, made him a good, nutritious dinner with plenty of vegetables – on the doctor's orders – and banished the entire disquieting affair from her mind.

She consoled herself that the new 'friend' was not the paedo-phile she had feared, but a creature of boyish make-believe.

She wondered if 'Tyrannus' was not a character in *Star Trek*: a 'Borg' – whatever that might be.

Gary returned to school the following week. But he was not the Gary of old; he had altered radically.

Reports began to reach his mother of a change in his behav-iour, indeed in his general demeanour. She learned of bullying, of Gary using bad language, of Gary treating his teachers with gross disrespect. It was as though he had undergone a complete change of personality. She could not understand it, asked herself if she were to blame, if her parenting skills were faulty.

On the Monday following his return to school, he came home late again. It was October and the evenings were longer; it was dark by the time Jessica heard his key turn in the front door. She was torn between anxiety and annoyance. He should have known better.

His excuse was that he had been 'fooling around' by the river. The river again! She demanded to know more but Gary refused to tell her. She had to check him for swearing: 'I won't have that kind of language in this house.' Again he picked a fight with his unfortunate little sister.

Calm was eventually restored. Gary still had a lot of catching up to do, and she left him to his homework. But later that evening, as she was cleaning the bath, she heard Kelly call out from the living-room. She sounded frantic. Jessica wiped her hands and hurried down, thinking that Gary had again attacked his sister. He had not.

He was again lying on the floor. His lips were blue; his eyes were glazed over; his body was locked once more in the mysteri-ous paralysis.

Again she called Dr Flynn, and once again he hurried to her summons. He was in a quandary. He telephoned his brother-in-law at his home and conveyed the news. The neurologist could offer little practical advice; the ECG had, after all, ruled out epilepsy and the other tests showed that Gary was physically healthy.

'I'm afraid I can do nothing more with him, Mrs Lyttle,' the GP confessed. 'I'm going to have to refer him to a psychiatrist.'

He saw her anxious look.

'Don't worry,' he said. 'I wouldn't think there's a serious mental problem. It's probably the onset of puberty. Some boys react to it more strongly than others. All those hormones leaping about in there.' He smiled. 'Enough to drive anybody a little bit batty.'

'But what about medication, doctor? Something to calm him down?'

'That's the very reason why I wouldn't like to prescribe anything of that nature. You never can tell with puberty. The wrong drugs could be disastrous. Besides, I don't believe in sedating children. As far as I'm concerned, parents who go down that road are giving up accountability. Antidepressants are no substitute for love and understanding, which is all a child needs.'

And so began what would prove to be an extended course of psychiatric treatment. The therapist, a child psychiatrist and consultant to Letterkenny General Hospital, embarked on what she called 'gestalt' therapy. Sally wished to focus on Gary's 'self-awareness'. Jessica understood little of what the woman told her; Gary even less. But Sally was persuasive, and the boy seemed to take to her; there was an excellent rapport.

On her advice, Gary saw Sally once a week. Each session lasted a hour, and the therapist was happy with his progress. Jessica noticed the change too. He was returning to his old self, the sweet-natured Gary she knew.

It was therefore with great dismay that Jessica, in early spring, took a phone call from her son's headmaster.

'I'm afraid Gary's had an attack or fit of some sort.'

She feared the worst, sensing what was to come.

'You'd better come over, Mrs Lyttle. It happened midway through a geography lesson.' (Jessica, even in her anxiety, asked herself why the man deemed this an important piece of information.) 'We've alerted his doctor.'

As if that were not serious enough, Gary suffered a second seizure that very week. It came, as did the others, without warning. He was recovering from his ordeal at school, and was stricken in much the same manner as before. With one important difference: this time, neither Jessica nor Kelly witnessed the seizure. It was Carmel Sharkey, the neighbour from next door, who reported it. She had been 'babysitting' Gary while his mother went to the shops.

'Jessica,' she said when Dr Flynn had departed, 'you're not going to like what I have to say to you.'

'Don't tell me any more bad news. I can't take it.'

'No, dear, that isn't it. I think you should take Gary to see a priest.'

Jessica was stunned, as any mother would be. The neighbour was suggesting that her son was somehow *unclean*, in the biblical sense: touched by evil. No mother could countenance such a thing. The stigma is too great.

'What are you saying, Carmel?'

'For his own good. I think you know full well what I'm saying.'

'Well, maybe I do. But Lord save us, Carmel, not a priest. He wouldn't go near a priest.'

'How can you say that? Have you asked him?'

'I just know, that's all. Carmel, you're scaring me.'

'You'll have to face up to it, though. That stuff you told me about the ouija board. I heard about a woman in England who had a lad who was messing around with a ouija board. All sorts of things began to happen. They're bad news, Jessica, so they are.'

'Ah, please, Carmel! Don't start that oul' nonsense with *me*.'

Jessica was accustomed to her friend's pietistic ways. She humoured her, although privately she felt that Carmel Sharkey's devotion to statues was no better than the idolatrous practices of the more primitive African tribes. In the Sharkey home there were more statues to Christ and the Blessed Virgin than Jessica had seen in respectably sized churches. There was a bewildering assortment of effigies of saints, whose identities could only be guessed at. Carmel did not wear her faith on her sleeve; she decorated her home with it. Yet, in all the time that Jessica knew her, she had never once tried to impose any of her beliefs. Until now.

'Half the world doesn't think it's nonsense, Jessica,' she said then, hurt.

'That may be, but I won't have the likes of Father Sheridan putting ideas into my son's head. I don't like that man. He seems to me to be too fond of the good life for his own good. Why would a priest need two cars anyway?'

'I wasn't thinking of Father Sheridan. There's a lovely oul' man I went to before. He's in a Cistercian monastery over in Tyrone. I'm sure you know it.'

'I do.'

'He's a healer. They say he—'

'Ah, please, Carmel!' Jessica cried again. 'It's bad enough I'd take Gary to a Roman Catholic monastery, but to a *healer*. Come on. What is he, some sort of witch doctor, or what's this they call it – a shaman?'

Carmel was shaking her head with vehemence.

'Father Dominic is nothing of the sort. You'd like him, Jessica. He's a kind, gentle soul. And he's genuine.' She took her friend's hand. 'Do it for Gary. What have you got to lose?'

* * *

She made an appointment that day. A two-hour drive took them to the monastery on the shores of Lough Neagh. Gary said nothing as his mother parked the car close to a large and rambling Georgian building. Jessica was nervous as she pushed open a door that seemed to have been built for the passage of giants.

They found themselves in an echoing hall, with a high ceiling, and bare except for a long, pew-like bench, a table, and old oils of popes upon the walls. There was a small room off the hall, and a sign saying RECEPTION.

'We've come for Father Dominic,' Jessica told a smartly dressed young woman.

Minutes later, the monk entered the hall by another door. He was a big man, bearded and dressed in the robe of the Cistercians. Jessica put his age at seventy or more. He barely looked at them as he crossed to yet another door. He pushed it open and beckoned.

But when all were seated in the little sitting-room, Father Dominic showed himself to be the kindly soul described by Carmel Sharkey. He spoke softly, smiled a good deal, and did not pry into areas that were of little relevance. He listened to Gary's tale, eyes shut, nodding from time to time.

To Jessica's surprise, she heard her son speaking of matters he had confided to no one else. In the wake of his third seizure she had sent him to stay with her mother for a few days. She recalled that he returned home if anything more nervous than he had ever been. He refused to be drawn then; now he was telling the priest what had befallen him. Jessica mused that the Catholic confession must work in a similar way.

'I couldn't sleep in Grandma's,' Gary was saying. 'I kept seeing things.'

'What sort of things?' Father Dominic asked.

'Bad things. Shadows. Big, black shadows.'

'In your bedroom?'

'Yeah. I knew there was somebody there but I couldn't see him properly. He kept changing. There were noises too.'

'In your room as well?'

'No,' said Gary with determination. 'They were all over the house. It was—'

'It's an old house, Father,' Jessica said.

'I kept hearing them at night,' Gary went on. 'They were up in the ceiling and in the walls. Real scary stuff. Like there were animals there. But Grandma doesn't *have* any pets. I had to have the light on all the time.'

Father Dominic had gone silent then. Jessica saw that he was staring into Gary's eyes with a look of consternation.

'Tell me about this Tyrannus,' he said.

'He shows me stuff. He showed me what I'll be like when I'm grown up, when I'm twenty-eight or twenty-nine. I'm in an office with a big desk. Tyrannus says that if I come over to him I'll be very rich.'

'"Come over",' the priest repeated quietly.

'He says I'll have great power in the future. And loads of money. But I must do what he wants.'

It may be instructive to pause here and examine Gary's account. He claims that Tyrannus showed him his future, as an adult. Evidently Gary was to become a successful businessman. That, in itself, is most unusual. When small boys dream of their future they do not see themselves sitting in offices. Offices are boring. They see themselves as premier-league footballers, or rock stars, or astronauts: the glamorous jobs. If Gary is fantasizing then it is without doubt a highly unorthodox fantasy.

Having listened to Gary's story, Father Dominic took the boy's wrist firmly in his big hand. From a pocket of his habit he drew out a small object: an oval-shaped silver casket with a glass window; behind the glass a fragment of something old and yellowed was visible. Jessica knew it to be a relic; Carmel had several. The

priest pressed the little casket lightly to Gary's brow and murmured a prayer.

Next, he taught the boy to say another prayer. It was framed
in simple words that a child would have no difficulty remembering. Before they left, he took Gary's mother aside and gave her a
leaflet, a simple prayer to be said daily.

'I think you should know, Mrs Lyttle, that you did well to bring
the boy to me today. I don't like what I see in him. There's evil at
work, I'm afraid.'

Jessica was stunned by his directness. She fumbled for words,
unwilling to accept that Carmel had guessed the truth, and that
the monk was confirming it.

'But he's only a child, Father.'

'Indeed. Children know the difference between good and evil
by an early age. Five or six, mostly – if not before. Your son is
choosing evil. He is entertaining this "demon". I've seen its like
before and I know it for what it is.'

She turned to look at Gary. He was still seated on the chair
that was too high for him, legs swinging in impatience as his eyes
roved the dark panelling of the room and its sombre paintings of
ancient martyrs. Evil? She saw no evil there.

'He's going to have a very difficult and painful life if he doesn't
resist this thing now,' the priest said. 'It's imperative that he fights
it, and you have to help him in that fight.'

His words dismayed Jessica. But she was angry, too, at the ugly
picture being painted for her. In what was becoming a perverse
situation, she felt the need to assert what *she* believed.

'Listen, he's fantasizing!' she said defiantly. 'Nobody believes in
demons any more. We live in more modern times, Father.'

'Indeed,' Father Dominic continued calmly, 'but I assure you
they are not a fantasy. The Devil and his fallen angels exist,
whether you believe in them or not. Not believing in evil means
you are not armed against it. For whatever reason, your son has

become a prime target. God is requesting that you turn back to Him. It is up to you to help Gary come to this understanding.'

Jessica felt defeated, hopeless. She wanted to cry.

'I want you to promise me something,' the priest said gently, sensing her despair.

'Yes, Father?'

'I want you to promise me you'll have him say those prayers to the Blessed Mother every day. She has such great power over the evil one,' he added enigmatically. 'She'll protect you. Prayer is the only way to fight against this. And I want you to bring Gary to see me again. Shall we say this day fortnight?'

Jessica agreed. By the time they got home again, she felt that she needed a strong drink. She had much to mull over, and most of it was decidedly unpleasant.

Under his mother's supervision, Gary recited twice a day the short prayers that Father Dominic taught him. He continued to attend the hospital in Letterkenny, and Sally reported steady progress. She brought him to see Father Dominic again, and continued to do so every other week. After each visit it seemed that a little bit more of Gary's old self was being returned to him. Jessica felt that a bleak period was ending, that whatever it was that had come into the boy's life was leaving him in peace.

But Gary skipped his prayers one day, and another day soon after, and before long he had let the habit slip. Jessica had never held with prayer at the best of times, and perhaps for this reason did not mind too much. And everything was fine again, was it not?

She had lulled herself into a false sense of stability, so much so that when the next untoward manifestation took place, she found herself totally unprepared for it. It happened one evening as Kelly and Gary were doing their homework. Once more, it was Kelly who alerted her.

'Mammy, Gary's going all funny again!'

She turned, to find the boy staring into the middle distance, seemingly oblivious to his surroundings. His left hand was moving rapidly over his copybook. That was the first indication that all was not well.

Gary is right-handed.

Jessica watched in astonishment and a creeping disquiet as her son's pen travelled over the page. The words he was writing – though English they were – made no sense at all. She was reminded of the nonsense poem, 'Jabberwocky'. She could still remember a few lines from somewhere: lines so silly that they stuck in one's head.

> 'And, has thou slain the Jabberwock?
> Come to my arms, my beamish boy!
> O frabjous day! Callooh! Callay!'
> He chortled in his joy.

'What's he writing, Mammy?' Kelly asked nervously, sharing her mother's unease.

'I don't know. . . . Gary?'

Gary did not reply but continued to write frantically. Then all at once he stopped. His body seemed to relax and he calmly turned to the next page. Jessica made to snatch the jotter away, but before she could reach it, his body had tensed again, and the frantic writing continued. She tried to lift his wrist, but was shocked to discover that his arm, and the hand that held the pen, were quite immovable, as if 'made of rock'.

She watched in horror as the writing, clear and then illegible by turns, started pouring out filthy words and phrases that had no place in a ten-year-old's vocabulary. There were drawings too: little designs resembling signs of the zodiac, and five-pointed stars. She knew they were not idle doodles, but had darker connotations.

In such a bizarre situation, she did the only thing she could. Grasping Gary around the waist, she pulled the chair from under him and hauled him away from the table. Incongruously, his body remained in a rigid seated position as though the chair were still in place, while the hand clutching the pen continued to make frantic writing motions in midair. Jessica lowered Gary to the floor. He collapsed, seemingly in a dead faint.

'I was sick with worry,' she says. 'It was too much to take. I never saw the like of it. I couldn't understand any of it; it was crazy. I thought Gary was going to die. But a few seconds later he was all right again. He opened his eyes and looked around. The first thing he said was, "What happened, Mammy?" He didn't remember a thing. Nothing.'

Jessica tore the pages from the jotter, ran into the living-room where a fire burned in the grate, and tossed them onto the coals. She averted her eyes as the pages burst into flame. She could not bring herself to look at the strange lines written by her son's hand. Nor did she wish to know where the garbled words and sinister pictographs had come from. Of one thing she was certain: they had not come from Gary; the words had not been his. More unnerving still: the handwriting had not resembled her son's. It was too elegant, as if from the hand of an artist.

When she returned to the kitchen, Gary was again seated at the table, wearing the same glazed look. She shook him; she was angry. He seemed to come to his senses. But then he looked her in the eye and Jessica will never forget his words, so utterly out of character, and so unexpected, were they.

'F*** *you*,' he spat and ran from the house.

Jessica believes that her mind was fully made up at that moment. She was finally acknowledging that she was up against a very powerful force, one that could induce a sweet, mild-mannered ten-year-old to change utterly. The change was frightening. Jessica had feared it before; now she was in holy terror of it. She asked herself what could happen next.

She thought of God. Her visits to Father Dominic in his monastery had, to an extent, turned her thoughts to the Lord, yet she had to admit to herself that it was a deity unfamiliar to her. The monk's religious world, with its statues and incense, was not the one she knew as a child. She told herself now that it was silliness; that God did not change but His worshippers did. Christ was Christ, whether worshipped in a vast, thronged Roman basilica, or in a plain and unadorned Lutheran chapel.

But these were rational considerations. Her heart told her that she must seek out the help of a priest of her own faith. She withdrew to the quiet of her bedroom, picked up the phone, and called John Ashwood, the Church of Ireland vicar.

He came to visit her that same evening. He was sympathetic on learning of her difficulties, and at once advised the services of an exorcist.

'What!' She was incredulous. 'Are you telling me Gary needs to be *exorcised*?'

'I do. From what you tell me, it sounds as if there's an unclean spirit at work. I'm not saying that it's controlling Gary; I'm saying that it's influencing him in some way. And it's time to send it back to where it came from before it does any more mischief.'

Her son needed an exorcism. She turned the curious word over in her head. Its associations seemed too outlandish by far. But she had to face facts, and take the minister's advice seriously.

'All right, Vicar,' she said at last. 'If you think it'll help Gary. When could you do it?'

'Not me. I haven't the experience. But there's a good man who does: Charles Cartwright. He's retired now but still very active with deliverance.' He patted her wrist. 'Leave it to me. I'll get in touch with him. If anybody can help, it's Charles Cartwright.'

* * *

Jessica and her son arrived by taxi at the Cartwright house in Newcastle on a wet, March afternoon. It was Gary's first visit to the seaside town. From the bus he had seen, in the shadow of majestic Slieve Donard, the high street with its succession of amusement arcades, many open and beckoning him inside. Heaven! He wished to visit them there and then. 'Later, dear,' his mother promised him. There was more urgent business to attend to.

Charles Cartwright studied the boy – perhaps the youngest 'visitor' he had ever welcomed into his home. He hesitated before thinking of Gary Lyttle as a demoniac, one suffering from demonic oppression. During his long ministry he had encountered several such unfortunates. None had appeared as normal – or as bright – as did Gary.

He impressed the rector by his spontaneity and precociousness. He answered all questions put to him seemingly without guile. There was no sign whatsoever of the wilfulness that Reverend Ashwood had spoken about on the telephone, and certainly no trace of the bad language. Gary seemed to him to be a very well-adjusted boy.

'So you haven't been to school lately?' he said.

'No, Mr Cartwright.'

'How long is that now?'

'Three months.'

'Three months tomorrow,' Jessica said. 'I daren't send him back. They think he's a lunatic or something. It's very trying.'

'I've no doubt.' He turned back to Gary. 'Your mother tells me you fight a lot with the other boys.'

'They're always picking on me. They call me names.'

'What names might they be?'

'They call me a devil.'

'But you're not, are you?' the rector said with smile. 'You're a good boy.'

Reverend Charles did not doubt it. What he saw before him

was a lad of ten: dark-haired, good-looking; as normal a young-ster as one could hope to meet.

'I was struck by the way he answered my questions,' he tells us. 'Gary was confident, intelligent, articulate and in no way intimi-dated.' And seemingly guileless, too – until, that is, one looked into his eyes.

The rector finds it difficult to put certain matters into words. Not that he is short on descriptive powers; he is an excellent eye-witness with seemingly flawless recall. Yet he is unable to portray in full what it was he saw that day when he met Gary's gaze. The closest he can come to an adequate description is that the boy's look was 'old beyond his years; older than mine even, and I'm seventy-four.'

The rector can only describe the phenomenon in terms of emo-tion, for he is speaking of something that he believes lies outside the world of rational thought, beyond the human. He is con-vinced that, for a moment at least, it was not *fully* the boy who gazed back at him, but a part of another personality entirely. For want of a better name he calls it 'Tyrannus', and believes that it was the demon that was seeking to dominate the boy. (He is care-ful to avoid the word 'possession', preferring to speak in terms of 'control' or 'affliction'.)

But the moment passed and Gary was 'himself' again. The rec-tor continued as though nothing untoward had occurred.

'Tell me about the ouija board,' he said. 'Where is it now?'

'At the river.'

'Really?' It seemed unlikely.

'I hid it.'

'Do you still play with it?'

'Yeah.'

'Often?'

'Two or three times a week. It tells me stuff.'

'Stuff?'

'Yeah, about how I'll be when I grow up.'

'Tell the Reverend about the Bible, Gary,' his mother prompted.

'It says I shouldn't read it. It says it's rubbish.'

'Mmm. How does it do that? How does it tell you these things?'

The rector had chosen his words with care. He knew as well as anybody that ouija does not make pronouncements of its own accord, but simply replies to questions asked of it. He wondered about the nature of the question that had elicited the condemnation of the Bible. Gary's next words supplied the clue.

'I ask it questions the voice tells me to.'

'Whose voice?'

'The man's. Tyrannus. He says that I shouldn't go near a church. He says bad things'll happen to me if I do. And he says I should stay away from the Bible.'

'Does he indeed? And do you agree with him, Gary?'

'I don't know.'

'Answer me this, Gary: Do you want to be free of this evil?'

'Yes, Mr Cartwright. I do. But Tyrannus doesn't want that. He says if I don't do what he says he'll make me feel so bad that I'll want to kill myself.'

'Never mind what Tyrannus wants, Gary. It's what *you* want that matters.'

'But he can stop me doing what I want.'

'Only if you allow him to.'

Charles Cartwright rose then and crossed to a little table by the window. On it was his Bible and a cross attached to a weighted base. Taking the book, he went to Gary, and stood over him.

'I can take away any power that this "man" has,' he said.

Suddenly Gary shrank back. He looked distressed.

'What is it?'

'He's laughing,' the boy said. 'I can hear Tyrannus laughing.

He's laughing at *you*, Mr Cartwright. He says you're funny.'

'Pay no attention to him, Gary. Put your trust in the Lord Jesus Christ.'

Reverend Charles held his palm aloft. He raised his voice.

'I bind you, in the name of Jesus Christ, and by the power of the Holy Spirit, I strip you of your influence over this child!'

Gary began to shake. His mother, who was well used to his making jokes, at first mistook it for laughter. And in a sense it was. But the laughter was not Gary's; later he would say that it was 'Tyrannus' laughing, and trying to induce Gary to join with him in the laughter, to show him the absurdity of this elderly ecclesiastic with his Bible and his medieval beliefs. But Gary claims that at that point his overriding emotion was one of fear.

The laughing of the demon ceased. The boy had stopped shaking. His eyes were shut.

'It's up to you now, Gary,' the rector said. '*You* have to make the decisions now, you understand? No one else.'

Gary said nothing.

'You must ask Jesus to help you.'

'Say it, Gary,' his mother instructed. 'Do what Reverend Cartwright says.'

It was clear to the rector that Gary was unused to prayer. Nonetheless the boy joined his hands as instructed, shut his eyes and spoke in a loud voice.

'Please help me, Jesus!' he cried.

'Very good,' said the rector. 'Now, repeat after me: I put my trust in you, Jesus . . .'

'I put my trust in you, Jesus.'

' . . . and I invite the Holy Spirit into my heart and into my life.'

'I invite the Holy Spirit into my heart and into my life.'

Gary opened his eyes. Did Charles Cartwright see within them a normal ten-year-old, free of that entity he had witnessed earlier? He is not certain. But there was one more thing the boy must resolve to do, one final act that would serve to ensure his deliverance.

'Gary, I want you to go with Reverend Ashwood and find that ouija board. Will you do that for me?'

The boy nodded.

'Then I want you to burn it. Is that clear? I'll be giving Reverend Ashwood a call next week, and I want him to tell me that the board has been burnt.'

'It will be,' Gary assured him.

But Gary failed to keep his word. When Reverend Ashwood accompanied him to the river, there was no sign of the ouija board. It had either gone missing or Gary had secreted it in another place. Either way, Gary was not saying.

A week later, his grandmother started experiencing paranormal activity in her own home when Gary stayed over. It took the form of strange noises and shadowy manifestations; they were present in his bedroom and in other parts of the house. They caused the grandmother so much distress that she, too, submitted herself to a rite of exorcism with Reverend Charles Cartwright.

At this point in time, Gary's mother seems powerless to effect any change in her son's behaviour. It would appear that she has relinquished control of her son. She prays for him and clings to the one positive note in Father Dominic's assessment. 'Gary is very special. Some of our greatest saints suffered frequent attacks from the Devil, so that their souls might be purified. God is testing him.'

The priest might well have had St Teresa of Ávila (1515–82) in mind when he said that. Certain aspects of the life of the sixteenth-century Spanish mystic, who founded the Discalced, or Barefoot, Order of the Carmelites, have interesting parallels with young Gary's experiences.

She was shown visions of hell, saw demons of 'abominable form', heard voices, suffered severe mental anguish and had frequent seizures which could last longer than an hour. About one such seizure she wrote the following:

> On another occasion the Devil was with me for five hours, torturing me with such terrible pains and both inward and outward disquiet that I do not believe I could have endured them any longer. The sisters who were with me were frightened to death . . . for the Devil had made me pound the air with my body, head and arms and I had been powerless to resist him. But the worst thing had been the interior disquiet. I could find no way of regaining my tranquillity.

When we spoke to Gary, we enquired about his continued use of the ouija board. It is understandable that he should try it once, particularly as he had discovered it in such unusual circumstances; it was less clear why he should have gone back to it again and again, given the mischief it caused. Gary made the same reply each time: 'I was bored.'

Pre-teen boys should not be so jaded by life. Yet Father Dominic suspects that Gary's boredom is a symptom of our times. It is a topic he has touched on more than once.

'In the past, religion created a moral code of ethics and acceptable modes of behaviour in society,' he says. 'Twenty years ago children knew right from wrong. Today, self-interest dominates our thinking, and moral criticism is considered old-fashioned, so that children are allowed to do whatever they please and therefore have no defences against evil. How else do you explain the rise in binge-drinking, drug addiction, teenage pregnancy and violent crime? How else do you explain the anarchy in schools, the lack of respect?'

'Oh, the Devil is very clever in his methods,' he goes on to say. 'By making God look archaic and outmoded, he creates a vacuum in the lives of the susceptible, which he, the Enemy, can then move in to fill.'

The word 'vacuum' is interesting in this context. We never learned what first led Gary to become so frustrated and tired of life. As outsiders, there were only so many personal questions we could ask. But it is clear that his boredom was born of a need for diversion; there was a vacuum that needed filling.

'Grown-ups have no end of diversions these days,' Father Dominic says. He sighs. 'At times I think half the world only wants diversion. I know this sounds like preaching, but I wouldn't be the first priest to say that the Devil makes work for idle hands. I see the truth of that in the rise in drug abuse, alcohol abuse, pornography, violence. It all starts as diversion, a way to relieve boredom.'

'Children don't have these things, but they do have magic,' he says. 'They love magic tricks. Show a boy a bit of magic and his boredom lifts immediately. So what better way to ensnare a little boy than to show him *real* magic?'

When Gary unearthed the board by the river that day, and saw the *planchette* leap into the air, he could have run away. He chose not to. It was magic. By tarrying, to see what would happen next – to see what the conjurer had up his sleeve – he showed himself to be receptive, and thereby exposed his vulnerability.

Father Dominic and Reverend Charles are agreed that the processes of oppression and possession can only be understood in retrospect, and verified by those individuals who have undergone successful exorcisms.

The process of surrendering to evil is twofold. First, the mind must be rendered receptive; the will then becomes amenable to acting upon that which is being offered.

Enter the ouija. Its name, assigned by one of the men who

marketed an early version of the board in the United States, was derived from the Moroccan city of Oujda. But it was not long before a different explanation entered the public domain: that the name was a juxtaposition of the French word *oui* and the German *ja*, translating to 'yes, yes'. It is a fitting interpretation, for it suggests that each time the board game is played, the participant consents to accept whatever may intrude. And he agrees to accept the consequences of having made the invitation – for good or ill. In so 'consenting', Gary Lyttle unwittingly opened the door to Tyrannus. Now he seems unable to free himself of what appears to be a baleful, subjugating influence. Thus are circuits of dependency created.

The longer this state of affairs is tolerated, the harder it is to dismantle it. Often, when attempts are made by the victim to renege on his former decision and escape the nightmare, tremendous pressure is brought to bear by those forces outside or within himself. They frequently take the form of terrifying visions, inner voices, physical torments, and thoughts of death as being the only means of escape.

At the time of *The Dark Sacrament* going to press, Gary appears to have his demons still. He fears them, and appears to be in thrall to them – perhaps in the old, literal sense of the word. To be 'enthralled' meant to be under the control of another; it was sometimes applied to the victims of witches and sorcerers. In exceptional cases it was applied to the victims of demons.

No one but Gary has ever seen – or heard – the demon who calls himself Tyrannus. It would be easy to dismiss him as a figment of a youngster's active imagination, an imagination fed on a diet of cheap Hollywood straight-to-video motion pictures. More difficult to dismiss are Gary's seizures, witnessed by members of his immediate family and his GP. Neither a neurologist nor a gestalt therapist can find a satisfactory reason for them, either physical or psychological.

There are very disturbing signs that point to a problem of a spiritual nature. Gary has now developed a full-blown hatred for anything sacred. Nothing will induce him to enter a church; he has stopped praying. He suffers from depression and has suicidal thoughts. He attacks those closest to him. He seems 'content' to be in the company of his demon, or demons.

Those clergymen involved in the exorcism and deliverance ministries speak with one voice with regard to the amendment of one's life and repentance. 'The most difficult part for me,' an exorcist tells us, 'is not the actual exorcism itself but persuading the delivered person to turn to the Lord for guidance and lead a better life. Someone who hasn't been brought up with God-centred values really cannot appreciate the importance of prayer and repentance. In that sense, they truly are lost souls. In such circumstances, there is nothing much an exorcist can do.'

'Gary must desire to be delivered of his "controllers",' Father Dominic stresses. 'If he chooses to hold on to them, there is little point in prayers said by me or anybody else.'

As long as 'Tyrannus' holds the reins, he concludes, no other power can intervene.

The Woman who Left
her Body at Will

ANGELA BREHEN WAS seventeen years old when she had her first taste of astral travel. At the time she did not call it that; in fact she could not call it anything at all, because throughout the morning following the occurrence she was almost speechless with terror. She imagined that she had died, so frightening was the experience.

It was 1988 and Angela was a pupil at a convent school in Galway City; she was in sixth year, preparing to sit her Leaving Certificate examination. There was little to set her apart from the other girls attending the school; she was bright, but not exceptionally so. She had decided on a career; she planned on pursuing business studies and graduating before her twenty-first birthday, when she hoped to have a full-time job in Dublin – or England perhaps.

On Saturday, 19 March, Angela finished her homework at about eight o'clock, watched some television, and went to bed around eleven. The family home was some two miles from the centre of town, the last house in a quiet cul-de-sac. Her young brothers were already in bed, and she heard her parents retire about twenty minutes later.

She awoke while it was still dark. Angela knew almost instinctively that it was long before getting-up time; she did not even have to look at her bedside clock. She was lying on her back, the position she always found most comfortable. But there was something different about the room.

It was nothing visible. As her eyes grew accustomed to the darkness, she could make out the familiar contents of her room:

the posters on the walls, the dresser with the mirror, her closet, the chair with her jeans draped over it. All was as it should have been. But there was something 'funny' about the room, a sense that a change had taken place since she switched off the light. She closed her eyes again – and within seconds was wide awake, and very fearful.

She describes the sensation as something she 'half felt and half heard', almost impossible to explain. It seemed to her that a force was approaching the place where she lay.

'It was like a storm that was coming,' she says, 'but not a violent one, nothing big or anything. I seemed to sense it coming to the house from a long way off. Something in my head was telling me that this force could go right through walls, and that it was coming for me.'

The 'force' entered Angela's bedroom; it appeared to hover some distance from the foot of her bed and several feet off the floor. She was terror-struck. She shut her eyes tight, afraid of what she might see.

In the next few moments, it seemed to her that something within her was resonating with the force that had entered her room. She felt a wave pulsing slowly up and down her body, travelling from head to toe. The sensation was, again, a heady mix of sound and feeling.

She felt the force inside her quickening, the vibration speeding up and down her body. She was terrified. And when she felt her body being launched into space, she knew the dread of death. Because she was convinced at that moment that she was indeed dying, or had died already. That her soul was leaving her body.

'All sorts of mad ideas came into my head,' Angela recalls. 'I suppose I was a religious girl in a basic sort of way, though I can't remember praying very much outside of a church. But I did believe in God and heaven and the angels, all of that. I believed that when we die we go to heaven. I was convinced that the force

I felt coming for me was the Angel of Death bringing me off to heaven. But the last thing I wanted to do was die. I was seventeen, a kid. I was too young to die!'

In a strange sense, she was conscious of the 'being' that was Angela, as it somehow swept up out of her body at a steep angle. Too fearful to open her eyes, she was asking herself if her soul had eyes at all. Yet her frightened mind was telling her that this new 'body' it was occupying was identical to the one that lay on the bed behind and below her.

And then she was passing through the ceiling and roof of the house, and she could 'see'.

With her new eyes she looked in awe at a sight that was new to her. Spread out below was the estate where her home stood. She saw the roofs, the streetlamps, the trees, roads and swards of grass. She saw it all as if she were a bird.

In other circumstances, Angela would have been enchanted by the whole experience. Which of us has not at some time longed to freely take to the air, to experience the liberation of unassisted flight? And here she was: 'flying'. Not, however, in her physical body, but in something very much different. She was convinced more than ever that she had died.

This conviction shocked her into opening her eyes at last. As in the case of a 'falling' dream, Angela experienced a sudden coming to earth. She was back in her bed, with the yellow sodium light from the street picking out the familiar objects in her bedroom. Her heart was pounding; she was sweating – but she was glad to be alive.

She thought of praying, of giving thanks to God for her safe 'return'. But she did not really believe in the power of prayer. Her family were not devout; each Sunday, the Brehens paid lip-service by attending Mass; for Angela, religion was a school subject and little more.

She told no one about the unsettling experience, not even her best friend Rhoda. Throughout the next day, and in the weeks that followed, Angela puzzled over the bizarre episode. She had no ready explanation, other than that she had been dreaming. And yet, the more she considered that possibility, the more implausible it seemed.

'I think we know when we're dreaming,' she argues. 'Even if it's a really vivid dream we still know it's only a dream. I was convinced that this was something else entirely. What kept on going through my head was that other people must have the same experience – that it wasn't just me. But I'd no one to turn to. I'd have felt like a right eejit even talking about it. My folks would have had me locked up.'

She could not let go of the notion that she had stumbled upon the existence of a hidden faculty, one lying dormant in every human being, its presence unknown and unsuspected to all but a few. She wished she could put a name to this remarkable capability.

The more she dwelt on it, and the more she recalled the wild exhilaration of that night, the less her fear of it became. By and by, she found herself wishing that the strange 'force', that which had plucked her from her bed and transported her into the unknown, would visit her again.

The Leaving Cert was looming. Angela and her friend Rhoda made a trip to Dublin; they needed past papers. Their school had distributed the copies they had, leaving a few pupils short. The girls arranged to visit the educational bookshops and procure the necessary copies; they were going to Dublin anyway, to stay with Rhoda's aunt.

The friends 'got the boring business out of the way' quite quickly. Rhoda wished to visit the clothes shops, but Angela had little interest in fashion. They parted company; they would rendezvous at the bus stop on Nassau Street. Angela returned to her favourite pastime: browsing the bookshops for bargains.

She happened upon the worn paperback in an equally worn shop down a side-street. It had been placed on the wrong shelf. Its jacket showed two men of the East in silhouette and a snow-capped mountain; within the blackness of their forms a universe of stars was visible. The title was *You Forever*, and the author gloried in the unforgettable name of Tuesday Lobsang Rampa. She turned it over.

> Rampa . . . provides step by step instructions for enhancing your psychic abilities. The book is de-signed so you can work at your own pace to develop intuition, see auras, travel in the astral plane, see clairvoyantly, and make your life happier and more comfortable.

She had paused over that curious phrase, 'travel in the astral plane'. It excited her imagination. She wondered if those words might not hold the key to her extraordinary experience that Saturday night in March. She flipped through the book; unfamiliar terms jockeyed for her attention. The author was promising considerably more than 'astral travel'. There was psychometry, self-hypnosis, telepathy. Well, mused Angela, if they're all part of the package, then so much the better. And, in his foreword, the man with the wonderful name appeared to speak to her directly, to flatter her into believing that she was truly somebody special.

> Let's at the outset state definitely that woman is the equal of man in all matters – including those relat-ing to the esoteric and extrasensory realms. Women, in fact, often have brighter auras and a greater ca-pacity for appreciation of the various facets of meta-physics.

Somebody bumped up against her in the narrow confines of the shop. The book slipped from her hands.

'Ah, sorry about that. I can be shocking clumsy.'

The young man ducked to retrieve it. He was perhaps twenty. His long hair, unkempt beard and sloppy clothing marked him out as a student. He was carrying a very worn, leather briefcase. He was studying the book's jacket.

'That's a good one,' he said, handing it to her. 'I have all his books. It's very interesting stuff.'

The young man was earnest and keen. She thought to know the type. They were given to talking too much and smoking foul-smelling roll-ups. All were too opinionated for Angela's liking. Yet this individual seemed not to fit the mould.

'He's actually English,' he said.

'Who?' She had not been listening.

'Lobsang Rampa. Claims he's the reincarnation of some Tibet-an monk or other. And who knows, maybe he is. He sure knows his stuff anyway.' He seemed to blush slightly. 'Are you interested in . . . eh . . . that kind of thing?'

'Depends what you mean by—'

'Meditation, out-of-the-body stuff.' Angela must have betrayed her interest because he followed with, 'Can I buy you a pint?'

'I don't drink,' she said quickly. And, she was thinking, if I did I would not be drinking *pints*. 'And I don't even know you.'

'Barry.' He extended a hand. 'Barry McNulty.'

'Angela Brehen. I'm with a friend though. I'll be—'

'Your boyfriend?'

'No. I haven't got a boyfriend.'

The words were out before she had considered them, and she saw that the young man was interpreting them as an invitation. She was too young then to know how to respond; she had little experience of boys. Besides, Barry was not her type. She wished to end the conversation, get out of the shop somehow.

'Look, I've got to go,' she said impatiently.

He looked hurt. She felt that she had to make it up to him. But he was there before her, with another proposal.

'Why don't I give you my phone number?' he said. 'Next time you're up in Dublin you might give me a ring.'

She nodded. He produced a ballpoint and patted his pockets. He hesitated, began to open his briefcase.

'Oh, write it here,' Angela said, passing him the book.

'But it's not your book,' he said with a grin.

'It will be in a minute.'

And it was. Barry McNulty inscribed both his phone number and address on the half-title page of *You Forever*. She left the shop, left Dublin, and many years would pass before she saw him again.

For three weeks, Angela struggled with the lessons contained in the tattered paperback, following each one to the letter. None seemed to work. She had so longed to reprise her exhilarating nocturnal 'flight'. Dr Rampa had as good as promised that she could release the hidden faculty whose existence she had guessed at. But she could not induce an 'astral' flight through the meditation techniques he recommended. At the end of the three weeks she had concluded that Tuesday Lobsang Rampa was a fraudster. She consigned the book to a back corner of her bedroom closet and forgot about it.

Within a month of her Dublin trip, Angela's life changed utterly. Reality intruded, making her dalliances with the paranormal seem petty and frivolous. Without warning, her mother died. She had been diagnosed with diabetes, but no one had suspected the hypertension that led to the stroke that proved fatal. Nuala Brehen lingered in the hospital bed for six days, and then was gone.

Angela's father never recovered. Nuala had been his childhood sweetheart. On her death he went into a morbid depression that refused to lift. He started drinking heavily – an unusual departure.

His personality seemed to change accordingly. Within six months of Nuala's death he was a wreck. His health had declined; he lost his job; he became a housebound semi-invalid – and a very angry one at that.

'What sort of a God is it,' he would rant, 'who'd take a good woman like your mother, and leave the shower of wasters we have running the country? There's no bloody God at all if you ask me.'

No one – least of all Angela – felt moved to disagree with him. By this time, she had left school and was about to start a course in business studies at University College Galway. She cancelled, put it on hold. She took what was to be a part-time job in a pharmacy in town, and devoted her free time to looking after her father, while keeping the home together. She found herself being a surrogate mother to her brothers, by then aged eight and nine.

The part-time job became full-time. Before she knew it, Angela was in her thirties, holding down a job she had no love for, and caring for a father who was increasingly a burden.

Eventually he, too, died: by his own hand. Life no longer held meaning for him. Angela found him still and cold in his bed, early one February morning. An overdose of prescription drugs had put an end to his misery.

Angela was alone. Her brothers were living in Dublin; both were married with young families. Of the Brehen siblings, only she remained unwed. It was 2004; she was thirty-three, over-weight, prematurely grey – and badly disillusioned. It was not how the bright schoolgirl of seventeen had envisioned her future.

Three events took place in rapid succession towards the middle of July of that year. Angela could not help but conclude that all were in some way linked. The first occurred on a Sunday. Rhoda, her old schoolfriend, whom she had not seen in over a decade, telephoned out of the blue to say that she would be in Galway that afternoon. She was, she explained, 'en route to Chicago', and was looking in on her mother before catching a flight at Shannon the following morning.

'By this time,' Angela recalls, 'Rhoda was "a woman of some importance", as she used to joke. She was a partner in a Dublin investment firm, earning heaps of money and living the life of a high-flyer. She never married either; said she'd no time for it. So there we were, the pair of us, meeting again after all that time. Rhoda bought us lunch and afterwards we went to a hotel for a few drinks.'

The few drinks became a colossal binge. Angela barely remembers the taxi that brought her home that night. But clarity was to come later on, when she had slept for an hour or two.

She awoke in great perturbation. She had had a strikingly lucid dream. It differed in almost every respect from her usual dreams, even the most vivid. This particular dream had all the hallmarks of an experience she recalled from a time long flown – from when she was a schoolgirl preparing for her final examinations. Angela was as certain as she could be that she had undergone, in her dreaming state, an out-of-the-body experience.

'I dreamed that I woke up in my dream,' she says, 'and I was in a strange bedroom. I saw this woman in a white nightdress lying sprawled across the bed, fast asleep with half the bedclothes on the floor. Something about the room told me I'd been there before, and when I looked around me I remembered that I'd spent so many days of my childhood doing homework with my best friend in that very room. The woman on the bed was Rhoda.

'I remember laughing, because she looked so ludicrous lying there, with her mouth hanging open, dead to the world, as they say. "Drunken stupor" were the words that came to mind.'

Then the voice spoke. It seemed to fill not only the bedroom but Angela's head as well, defying her to guess its origin. All the same, it was different, she thought, from the voices we sometimes hear in the course of our day: the imagined voices of our loved ones, voices remembered, voices we manufacture ourselves. We can always tell them apart from the extraneous, unwelcome, voices. This voice was one of the latter. It was female, sibilant but not unpleasant, and it spoke with a strong Galway accent.

'RHODA WON'T SURVIVE THE WEEK,' it said. 'YOU WON'T SEE HER EVER AGAIN.'

Angela was horrified.

'If I'd been in my skin I'd have jumped straight out of it,' she says with a thin smile. 'But of course I wasn't. The next thing I knew I was waking up in my own house, in my own bedroom, wondering what had happened to me. Had I dreamt it? But I knew I hadn't because I'd been in that sort of situation before. I knew it was all real.'

Her first impulse was to telephone Rhoda's house. But after consideration she dismissed the thought. Rhoda would be sound asleep – and no doubt lying in much the same position as Angela had seen her. The clock told her that it was a little before 4 am. Rhoda would not relish being roused at that hour, with a plane to catch later that morning. Her mother, a widow of some years' standing, was elderly and in poor health. Angela could not bring herself to disturb her. And what reason, she wondered, could she provide? 'Mrs Delany, your daughter is in mortal danger; I was in her bedroom in my ethereal body and this voice spoke to me.' It was preposterous. Angela, head already beginning to throb with an incipient hangover, resolved to phone at a 'respectable' hour, turned over and eventually fell sleep.

She was awakened by her bedside telephone ringing shrilly. She cursed aloud on seeing the time. She had overslept by almost two hours. It was the pharmacy, wondering if she was coming to work that day. She assured them she was on her way. And suddenly, as she was hurriedly getting herself ready, the full force of that terrible message, delivered by a discarnate voice, struck her four square.

Rhoda was going to die.

Angela shut her eyes tight, as she would do when a child, 'to make the boogeyman go away'. It never worked then either. She told herself she was being silly, that she was making too much of what was – on reflection, in the sobering sanity of a Monday morning – more than likely an alcohol-induced nightmare. She hauled a brush through her hair, shrugged into her coat, grabbed her bag, and went to start the week.

Three days passed without incident. On Thursday, Angela put in a full day at the pharmacy and was on hand to supervise the late opening. It was past nine o'clock when she arrived home, tired and in need of cheering up. She had a glass of wine and watched half a video.

'I remember feeling terribly depressed; seeing Rhoda again made me realize what a failure my own life had been. There she was, travelling the world in a high-flying job, and there I was: living alone, a lowly shop assistant with nothing to look forward to but old age.'

That night, Angela did not stop at one glass of wine. She drank the entire bottle. She collapsed into bed around one o'clock. She could not know that she was about to have another out-of-the-body dream, more terrifying than the previous one.

The mysterious force came for her as before, lifted her from her bed and propelled her into blackness. As was the case in Rhoda's bedroom, there was no intervening sensation of travel.

'I woke up in what I called "the spirit",' she says. 'I found myself high above a city. It was broad daylight.'

She thought at first that it must be New York. There were skyscrapers and a network of highways linking the strange city with a green and flat countryside. Then she saw what could only have been an inland sea, or indeed a lake. A voice in her head – the sibilant one with the Galway accent – was telling her that the city was Chicago.

She remembers with amazing clarity finding herself above an intersection in what looked like a business district. The light of a summer afternoon slanted between the buildings, casting long shadows. A queue of cars waited for the lights to change.

Some distance away – two blocks away to be exact – there was a flurry of activity. From her vantage point Angela had a bird's-eye view.

She saw a speeding white car approaching the intersection. The lights changed and a yellow taxi moved forward. There was no possibility that the driver of the white car could stop in time. He tried to swerve, and the cab-driver did the same. Had both not attempted the evasive manoeuvre, all might have been well. But the white car struck the cab on the passenger side, sending it spinning across the intersection and into the path of oncoming traffic. There was a pile-up.

Angela found herself being propelled at great speed towards the stricken taxi. She was among the first to examine the wreck. Lying in the back seat was a woman of about her own age. Her eyes were open and staring, her head twisted at an unnatural angle.

It was Rhoda, and she was dead.

Angela woke again in her bed. She was shaking with terror, her heart hammering so fast that she feared for her own life. She stumbled from the room, made her way downstairs, went into the kitchen and poured herself a brandy. She drank it swiftly and poured another.

This time she did not hesitate to ring Rhoda's mother. As it happened, the elderly woman slept very little and was not in the least perturbed; after all, Angela Brehen was an old friend of her daughter.

'Listen, Mrs Delany, would I be able to get in touch with Rhoda? Did she leave a number or anything?'

Rhoda had. It turned out to be that of a hotel in Chicago.

It was after 2.30 in the morning. Angela knew that America was several hours behind but had no idea in which time zone Chicago lay, only that it was farther west than New York. She dialled the number and was greeted at once by a courteous-sounding woman. Yes, Ms Delany was a guest. Could Angela hold?

Angela broke the connection a minute later. She was trying to come to terms with the impossible.

'I couldn't believe it,' she says. 'I still can't. But it turned out that Rhoda was killed that day at the time I saw it happen, allowing for the time difference. I saw it all like it was happening right in front of me. I couldn't have imagined it because it was only later that day that we got word back in Galway. I went round to Rhoda's mother and heard about it. And the horrible thing was, she was somehow holding *me* responsible. God knows why. After the funeral she never spoke to me again.'

Rhoda's remains were flown home and laid to rest in Galway. The funeral took place some eight days after the accident. But before then, on the Saturday following Rhoda's death, Angela was to have her third odd experience. This time, however, there were no paranormal overtones – or so it seemed. It was simply a meeting between two people, in ordinary, workaday circumstances.

Angela went to her job at the pharmacy as usual. She was greatly perturbed by her friend's death and the circumstances surrounding it; she thought that the routine of work would help her cope with the tragedy.

By lunchtime she had recovered some of her equilibrium and could bring herself to chat with the regular customers. At one o'clock she grabbed a sandwich, did some desultory shopping, and was back at her post at a little after two.

To this day she asks herself how it was she recognized the face.

Sixteen years had passed since she last saw the man, in 1988. And she had been no more than a child.

'To crown it all I'd only spoken to him for about five minutes,' she reminds us. 'I wouldn't say I have a great memory for faces. About average, I suppose. But right away I knew it was Barry McNulty. He was much thinner than I remembered and his hair was a lot shorter, but there was something about him that I recognized. Maybe a certain look he had: a kind of intenseness.'

Barry had a little boy with him, of perhaps five or six. The child looked bored and was running a sticky finger along a neat display of hair colourants. Angela saw two boxes topple. She left her station at the back of the shop.

'Angela? It is you, isn't it?'

'It is indeed, Barry: Angela Brehen. That wasn't today or yesterday.'

'You didn't marry then, I take it?'

He had lost none of his forwardness. It was a trait she found unappealing in men. She found herself staring at the child, whom Barry now had by the hand. He must have read her thoughts because he hurried to enlighten her.

'My sister's boy, not mine. He's staying with me a few days. I'm living here now, you know. Moved last month.'

'That's a coincidence.'

'Isn't it?'

There was something about the manner in which he said it that left her wondering.

He was glancing about the shop. 'So this is what you do, eh? Nice.'

He thinks I own the place, Angela concluded. She had no intention of disillusioning him.

'Did you like the book?' he asked suddenly.

'Book . . . ?'

But she had remembered at once, as soon as he walked into the shop. She had given not a thought to it in sixteen years.

'It was okay,' she said. 'Well, not really. If you want to know, I didn't think much of it at all.'

Something in her face must have betrayed her, brought to the surface the terror of the past days. Barry was looking at her intently.

'There's something wrong, isn't there? I've come at a bad time; is that it?'

'No, no. Well . . . yes. A friend died.'

'I'm sorry. Were you very close?'

'We were once.'

He was still studying Angela's face, seemingly trying to find answers there. 'Why do I get the impression there was something very unusual about this friend's death?'

'Maybe you're psychic, Barry.'

'As a matter of fact, I am.' He saw her frown. 'Seriously. I know things. Like that time in the bookshop; I could sense what you were looking for.'

His nephew was betraying an almost intolerable impatience to leave. Angela suggested they meet that evening. She knew a quiet little hotel off Shop Street, where they could talk further. Barry found her there a little after eight.

Over drinks they got better acquainted. She found him an unusually good listener – so good, in fact, that before long she was confiding in him details of the bizarre events surrounding Rhoda's death.

'I read about it in the *Tribune*,' he said. 'One of these freak things. We know not the day nor the hour, as the man said.'

'But *somebody* knew,' she countered.

'What do you mean?'

'A voice told me in a dream.'

'Hmm.'

'Is that all you can say: "Hmm"? I'll tell you something, Barry:

it completely freaked me out, hearing that voice.'

'I can well believe it. But look at it this way, when you're a remote viewer, you're—'

'Remote viewer?'

'A clairvoyant. That's what it is, you know: clairvoyance, remote viewing. When you view a scene remotely, you're entering a different dimension altogether. Time doesn't exist there – at least, not as we know it. So it doesn't matter if something is in what we call the past, present or future; for the clairvoyant it's happening in the here and now.'

'So I can see into the future in the same way I can see the present? I thought the future didn't exist. That we have free will. That we can all make our own future. It isn't written in stone.'

He looked at her keenly.

'That's only someone's theory, Angela. Nothing more. You yourself proved it wrong. You knew that Rhoda wouldn't survive the week. The voice told you so. That's as much proof as you need that you can look into the future.'

'It could have been coincidence.'

He laughed loudly. Heads turned. He lowered his voice.

'That's rich coming from somebody who claims to have visited her best friend clairvoyantly – twice in the one week. Angela, you know as well as I do it was the real deal. You had a premonition of your friend's death, and you travelled to Chicago to see it happen. I believe you, because I've been there myself. You have a gift, just like me: a psychic gift.'

'That's not what I'd call it. I want to be rid of it, if it's all the same to you.'

'No, that's the wrong attitude. You should develop it. That's where I come in.'

Angela did not like the turn Barry's conversation was taking. He was altogether too sure of himself, and too intrusive. She reminded herself that she hardly knew him, much less trusted him with her private affairs. And what, she asked herself, could be more private than your own thoughts, your very dreams?

'I've always been psychic,' he said. 'My mother was, so I think I get it from her. Over the years I've perfected the art. I help a lot of people with my gift, Angela, and you can too.' He sat back in the chair. 'I suppose you could call me a healer.'

'Really! You mean you can heal diseases?' Angela thought it best to humour him.

'I can do anything,' he announced with all the zeal of a Southern Baptist preacher. 'I am what is known as a magician in the great Western Tradition.'

'You mean you're into black magic?'

'No,' he quickly corrected her. 'On the contrary, magic is a powerful tool that can be used for good or evil. Black magic seeks to destroy; white magic seeks to improve and heal. As I say, I use my gift for the betterment of mankind.'

He took up his drink, basking in what he believed was Angela's silent admiration. She, on the other hand, could not help thinking that Barry's speech had been rehearsed, that it was a stock speech kept in readiness to impress the gullible.

'WB Yeats', he said, 'was one as well.'

'The poet? He was a magician too?'

'Yeah, the poet. He was one of the most important members of the Golden Dawn.' He canted forward, his hands clasped together. 'I have to level with you, Angela. Running into you – in the chemist's – it wasn't an accident.'

She felt uneasy. 'Oh?'

'A little bird told me you'd be there. Well, if you must know, it wasn't a bird; it was a voice. You told me about the voice you were hearing. I have one as well. It goes with my psychic abilities. See, I knew you were experiencing this stuff even before *you* did. That's why I'm here.'

She was growing nervous. 'I don't follow.'

'Let me get us another drink, Angela,' he said. 'Then I'll explain the plan to you; see what you think of it.'

The 'plan' turned out to be one of the most audacious ventures that Angela had ever embarked upon. Barry's initial premise was simple: they would 'visit' one another clairvoyantly.

'And that was my biggest mistake,' Angela sighs. 'But I was lonely; I was vulnerable. I'd just suffered the trauma of Rhoda's death. My mind was in turmoil . . . and in a strange way I didn't want to disappoint him. From what he told me, I believed he could help me. When I look back on it now I can see it was mad, but at the time it seemed almost logical. Barry McNulty was very convincing.'

They exchanged addresses and, with the aid of paper napkins, each sketched out a crude map pointing the way. 'Though I doubt if you'll even need a map,' he said with conviction. Barry's home was on the outskirts of the city; in passing, she learned that he was divorced, with three children who lived with their mother. He had joined the civil service on leaving college. Angela found that incongruous, but said nothing.

They met again in the same hotel. They agreed on 'rules'.

'We promised each other that we wouldn't pry,' she goes on. 'That we'd respect each other's privacy. If one of us had some-body round then the other would make themselves scarce.'

Barry had brought along an unusual item. It was a book on meditation techniques. It was photocopied, and she got the im-pression that the original was not in general circulation, but a limited edition, perhaps published by the occult circle to which he claimed to belong. He urged her to study it well. It was, he said, greatly superior to her old Tuesday Lobsang Rampa book.

She was also to discover that he used drugs to help achieve what he called his 'altered states'. He did not come right out and admit it, but rather hinted. He suspected that Angela would shy

away from the very notion of narcotics, and in that he was correct. The idea appalled her.

During that second meeting, they laid down the ground rules
and fixed a date for the first experiment. Angela did not know
what to expect when Barry told her he would visit at a pre-
arranged time.

'Will I be able to see you?' she asked.

'I doubt it. The purpose of the exercise is for *me* to see *you*.'

On the night in question, a Saturday in early August, she stayed
up late, reading without much interest a copy of a woman's magazine. She had made herself comfortable in the living-room; from
time to time she would cast a nervous glance at the clock.

'I was sitting there,' Angela says, 'reading some silly problem
page or other, trying not to get too afraid, when all of a sudden I
felt this presence in the room.'

She put away the magazine and turned in her chair. She saw
nothing.

'I didn't have the feeling it was Barry,' she remembers. 'You
know the feeling you get when you're in a room and there's
someone behind you. It's a "knowing" feeling, comfortable even,
because you're familiar with the person who's there. This wasn't
like that. It was terribly unsettling. For the short time it was in
the room, I had the strongest urge to run out the door and just
keep running. I remember getting up and backing towards the
door, and just as I was doing that, the phone rang.'

'Did I scare you?' At first she did not recognize the voice. The
words were delivered in a curt, clipped manner. It unsettled her
so much that she could not speak.

She thought she heard people laughing in the background.
Then the question came again.

'Did I scare you, Angela?' This time, the tone was deliberately
threatening.

'Barry, is that you?' Her uneasiness growing, she tried to keep her voice calm. She could barely hold the receiver steady.

'Of course it's me! Who the f*** else could do what I've just done? Now, do I have to ask you the question a third—'

'No, no!' Something told her that she must humour him, play his game. She had the unreasonable fear that the consequences of antagonizing him might be terrible. 'Yes . . . yes, Barry, you did scare me. I—I can't describe it.'

'Leave the descriptions to me,' he said brusquely. 'Your house is a semi-detached bungalow,' he continued, in a smooth, matter-of-fact voice, as though reading from notes. 'There's a dining-room with open-plan kitchen on the right and a living-room on the left. You have a dado rail with blue flowery wallpaper and a suite of furniture to match. There are two standing lamps, one next to the TV, the other next to the two-seater.'

Angela, standing in her hallway, clutching the phone, was looking through the doorway into the living-room. The back of her head was tingling as Barry proceeded to describe what she was seeing, as though he were standing right beside her.

'There's a coffee table with two magazines,' he went on. 'The *RTÉ Guide* and *Marie Claire*. The carpet is dark grey with a light blue design running through it. On the mantelpiece there are six or seven photographs. One of them is of you with an older woman in front of Tower Bridge.'

'Stop!' she cried. 'I believe you, Barry. Jesus, it's too weird for words.'

Again she heard laughter in the background.

'I'd call that a very successful experiment, wouldn't you? Tomorrow night it's your turn. I'll be expecting you around ten.'

'Barry, I—'

'Angela, you'd better stick to the plan,' he said abruptly, 'or you'll regret it!'

The line went dead, leaving her perplexed and not a little afraid. She wondered what it was she had got herself into.

* * *

Next day, she tried to reach Barry McNulty, but without success. His phone was off the hook.

'I was so shocked by his manner,' Angela says. 'I think that shocked me more than the weird presence in my living-room. I was in turmoil for the entire day and the awful thing was, I couldn't tell anyone about it. They'd have had me certified. At the same time I tried to rationalize his odd behaviour. If he was a drug user, and there was every indication that he was, then he probably wasn't even aware of having been so rude to me. In the end I decided it was safer to go along with what we'd planned. I'd try to visit him clairvoyantly at the appointed time, then have nothing more to do with him.'

At the same time she was very afraid that her attempt at remote viewing would fail, and she had an irrational dread of such failure.

'Something told me that if I didn't succeed he would make me suffer. I'd read his photocopied book from cover to cover and back again. I knew it like the back of my hand – but only in theory. I started asking myself what would happen if the techniques didn't work.'

She had to make sure. She recalled that prior to her out-of-the-body experiences involving Rhoda, she had been drinking heavily. Convinced that alcohol might hold the key, she bought a bottle of brandy. She settled herself on the living-room sofa, and proceeded to drink enough to make her woozy. She felt her muscles relax. She lay back, and applied the meditation techniques.

They worked. She seemed to pass out, to awaken in an altered state of consciousness. It was not a dream, but not quite reality either; not as Angela knew it. It was a trance.

Barry's map, drawn crudely on the hotel napkin, had proved unnecessary. His home was a cottage, perhaps at one time the gate lodge to a demesne that no longer existed. Even in the gathering dusk she could clearly see that its roof was in disrepair; in fact, the place was little more than a barely habitable shack. Angela entered through the broken slates, rotten battens and rafters – and was dismayed by what she saw there.

'I sort of got an inkling of why him and his wife had split up,' she says. 'It's possible that he was into all this stuff when they were together, but . . . I don't think any woman could have lived there, not without going out of her mind. It was like stepping into Marilyn Manson's den.'

The interior resembled, if anything, a temple. Ranged about the main room were the trappings of magic and mysticism. Angela saw shrines to Eastern deities, statues and statuettes to the gods of antiquity; gold, black and red candles, bowls of incense, ceremonial daggers, and – on the walls and in great profusion – drawings, prints and paintings of characters from legend. The adjoining room was given over to books, hundreds of them. A bedroom adjoined it. Lastly there was a sitting-room; it was a mess, a jumble of furniture and bric-à-brac of every description. Sprawled on a sofa set against one wall was Barry, a can of lager in his hand. He looked up on her entering. Astonishingly, he was aware of her presence. He set down his drink and raised a hand in greeting.

'You made it,' he said, grinning. 'Angela Brehen, you and me are going to have *fun*.'

'I was not prepared for what happened next,' she recalls, grimacing at the mere memory of it. 'But as he spoke, his face began to contort in this horrible way. Like something you'd see in a scary film. And he was coming for me; he looked totally different. I was so scared. All I wanted to do was get out of there. That was when I woke up with a jolt. I was back in my own house, thank God.'

On her return to 'reality', Angela gave herself a few minutes. They had agreed that she should telephone him at once 'while it's all still fresh in your memory', but she had to compose herself first. She was still trembling as she dialled the number, not knowing what to expect – the unpleasant stranger she had seen him become, or his normal self. To her immense relief he was the latter: the customary, self-assured Barry McNulty. She tried hard not to show her fear or slur her words as she gave a description of his home. He was delighted; it all tallied. She had proved to him that his search was over.

Prudently, she made no mention of that 'other' Barry. There was no opportunity to do so, because he did all the talking. He embarked upon a long-winded explanation of what they had experienced. She could follow most if not all of it. He called it TC: transference of consciousness. It was his own designation; he disliked such terms as astral travel and out-of-the-body experiences. 'An OBE,' he joked, 'is something you get from the Queen of England.' She learned that he had sought long and hard for a partner, somebody who shared his facility for TC.

The following weekend he invited himself to her home. He said he had an important experiment he wanted her to take part in.

'I was really shocked at his brazenness,' says Angela, 'but knew I must agree. You're probably wondering why I didn't tell him the show was over, and just end it there. But even when I tried to, I was filled with so much fear, I couldn't get the words out. It was as though he had this hold over me, some kind of power. You know, I used to think that people that fell under the spell of the likes of David Koresh and Jim Jones were just fools, but now I know different. You stay with people like that out of sheer terror. I now know that what I was experiencing were the symptoms of demonic oppression. To Barry, it was business.'

Barry's 'business', as he called it, was the exploration of other dimensions. Angela learned that he had accomplished much on his own, but he needed a partner for what he called the 'tricky stuff'.

'I didn't like the sound of that,' she says, 'but when he explained it, it seemed okay. We would take it in turns looking after each other when one of us was out of the body. It seemed reasonable. Or rather, I kidded myself into believing it was reasonable.'

Barry McNulty required Angela's cooperation in an experiment. It did not, on the surface, appear in any way sinister. In fact, it had at its heart such endearing sentimentality that she was forced to re-evaluate her poor opinion of him. She began to think that her terrible experience – her witnessing his alarming transformation – was simply her imagination playing tricks on her.

With the benefit of hindsight, however, she thinks otherwise: she believes that it was part of his attempt to exert control. Barry seemed to have an uncanny knack of knowing what she was feeling and thinking, and knew how to manipulate a situation to suit his own ends.

It was an idea he had toyed with for years, or so he claimed. Like so many men who never knew their father – or who had lost him at a very early age – Barry greatly missed him, and forever sensed that an important bond had been broken. His greatest wish was that he could meet his father again, to relive those few short years that were little more than hazy memories, and ones that faded unrelentingly with each passing year of adulthood.

For he had loved his father dearly, and his mother continually reassured him throughout his boyhood that his father had loved Barry, his youngest child; loved him if anything more than his other offspring. An industrial accident had killed him, Angela learned. He had clung to life in a hospital bed for forty-two hours before death intervened. He had called out for Barry, but the boy had arrived too late – by mere minutes.

'I was nearly in tears when he was telling me all this,' Angela says. 'I could understand what he'd gone through because it was the same with my mother, though I was old enough to take it better. He was determined to see his father again, and I was the one who was going to help him.'

It was going to be a complicated procedure. It would involve a little more than TC. By this time, Barry was so proficient in inducing TC that he saw it as child's play. Angela had seen how easily he could do it. But this was of a different order.

'Did you ever do LSD?' he asked.

'Barry, I told you what I think about drugs.'

'Sorry, I forgot. Well, I did a lot of LSD. That's what got me started with this other thing. In my first year in Uni a few of us were fooling around with LSD. Brilliant stuff altogether, but Jesus, if you had a bad trip then you knew all about it! But the point I'm making is that you were always warned not to go tripping on your own. You could do stupid things, get into a lot of trouble. Some guys in the States jumped off tall buildings, thinking they could fly.'

'God.'

'So that's why you needed what we called a "buddy". He'd be someone who stayed straight, didn't drop any acid. So if you started freaking he'd be able to take care of you.'

Angela listened as Barry's speech seemed to revert almost effortlessly, and probably unconsciously, to the jargon and narcospeak of decades past. As he spoke, she felt relieved that the drug scene had never fascinated her.

He spoke of spontaneous clairvoyant experiences induced by LSD. They were no hallucinations, he was at pains to point out, but genuine TC. The hallucinogenic drug appears to have triggered in his psyche the same mechanism which caused the release of Angela's etheric double when she was seventeen. Barry had no explanation for this. He did, however, discover that once the drug had facilitated TC, he could dispense with it – or so he said.

'I want to see if time travel is possible,' he told her with an absolutely straight face.

'Oh, come on, Barry; be serious now. Time travel!'

But he hastened to assure her that he was using the term in an innovative sense. He was not foolish enough to believe the nonsense one came across in books on the subject of astral travel, he said: the wild claims people made of their ability to travel back in time to, say, ancient Rome, or the building of the pyramids, or even the Crucifixion. That was impossible, he said; Einstein had said so, and that was good enough for Barry. His method involved what he called 'awakening in consciousness in your own past'. He explained.

'I was seven when my dad died,' he reminded her. 'So I was conscious in the sense that I could reason, work things out for myself. There's this memory I have of being with him; it's so clear I can remember every detail. He loved sailing, had his own boat, kept it moored down at Bullock Harbour in Dalkey. It was only a tiny thing, a cheap fibreglass job, but to me it was a huge yacht. I kept begging him to take me sailing with him but he never would. He'd take one or two of the others, and sometimes my mother even, but he never took me because I was hopeless at swimming. "But I'll wear a life-jacket," I used to say, but he still thought it was too dangerous.

'Until one Saturday morning, very early, he boots me out of bed and tells me we're going sailing. I'm telling you, Angela, that was just about the happiest day of my life. I'd just turned seven, I was on my school holidays, it was a fabulous summer – and I was sailing in Dublin Bay with my dad!'

Angela recalls Barry's expression of rapture as he recounted that wonderful day of long ago.

'I can still remember the wind on my face, the sea-spray coming up over the boat and my father teaching me how to maintain a starboard tack. Then he let me take the tiller. It couldn't have been for more than five minutes but by God it felt like an hour. "Hold that heading on the Bailey, hold that heading on the

Bailey," he kept saying, meaning I had to keep the bow pointing at the Bailey lighthouse off Howth. And that's the image that's stayed with me all these years: me in my life-jacket gripping that tiller, my arms on fire, my dad grinning at me and giving me the thumbs up. He must have been as proud as I was. I want to use that as my focal point.'

Barry's audacious plan was to TC into the mind of his seven-year-old self. In effect: time travel.

'I knew the idea was totally off the wall,' Angela says. 'But I couldn't tell him what I really thought. I was afraid of what he might do. It was safer to humour him. I kept thinking he'd overdosed on something. I was checking his eyes to see if they were normal. You know: that the pupils weren't dilated or anything. But he was serious.'

'He told me that he nearly made it once or twice,' she says. 'He told me he was very close. He would use the mantra – he called it that – of his father saying over and over, "Hold that heading on the Bailey." He said he was nearly there but at the last minute he chickened out. He didn't know if he'd be able to come back.'

'Then he told me about something that made me prick up my ears,' she says. 'He told me that a *voice* came to him the last time he attempted it. He was just about to give up when he heard the voice. It said: "You can do it."'

Unlike Angela's mysterious voice, heard in Rhoda's bedroom shortly before her death, the voice Barry heard was male.

'I had him describe the voice, and what he told me corresponded with what I experienced that time. It seemed to come from outside and from inside his head, all at the same time. He had an explanation – Barry always had explanations. He said it was his *oversoul* speaking to him.'

Listening to Angela Brehen is sometimes akin to attending a talk given by a psychic or some such dabbler in the paranormal.

No sooner has one digested the one arcane belief than another presents itself. Angela's 'oversoul' appears to have much in common with Jung's concept of the collective unconscious. In some respects, it also seems to correspond to the Judeo-Christian idea of the soul: both are eternal, both survive the death of the body.

Barry McNulty had yet another interpretation. He likened the oversoul to the Eastern concept of 'masters' – masters in the sense of a group of individuals (or advanced souls, to employ the esoteric terminology) – who watch over humankind and guide the soul along the 'proper' spiritual path.

'You heard your oversoul speak to you,' Barry told Angela. 'I heard mine.' The gender was unimportant, he assured her. Her oversoul or master communicated with her using a female voice because it judged that she would be 'more comfortable' with this.

It appeared to make sense.

In the quiet of Angela's home, the two embarked on a series of experiments which even she is prepared to concede were bizarre. Barry would be the 'traveller' and Angela his 'minder'.

The traveller would attempt to TC with the younger self; the minder would be on hand to deal with possible emergencies. Barry's fear was that, were he to TC for a prolonged period, a stranger – or perhaps some busybody of a neighbour – might think he was in a coma and seek medical assistance.

Barry's talk and his desire to be reunited with his father had a profound effect on Angela.

'Up until that point I hadn't thought very much about my mother,' she says, 'but then one morning I woke up in floods of tears, and I knew that what I was experiencing was the grief of my eighteen-year-old self . . . of the young girl I'd been when my mother died. God, it was terrible! I was going through the whole grieving process, but this time it was worse, ten times worse.

Barry came to the rescue, of course. What he said made so much sense. It was something like: "There's only one way to heal your pain, Angela. Your mother's calling you. You must visit her on the astral plane and prove to her that you're all right."'

Angela confesses that at that point a 'reunion' seemed the answer. She felt that a meeting with her mother – however unorthodox – would lift her out of the desolation she was feeling.

'I knew I had to see her again,' she says. 'I'd convinced myself that talking to her, if only for a minute or two, would put things right. I wanted to tell her I was happy, even if things hadn't worked out the way she hoped they would. I suppose I wanted her to be proud of me.'

So Barry and Angela each fixed their 'golden moment', the target they would aim for. He went first. Angela had prepared the room, her old bedroom, where she had her first experience of astral projection at the age of seventeen. She felt that there might be something 'special' about the room. She cleared it of everything except the bed, a chair and the bedside locker. They drew the curtains and Barry made himself comfortable on the bed. It gave her a strange sensation.

'I couldn't help thinking what my mother would make of me having a man in my old bed – well, *on* the bed at any rate. But, as I said, there was nothing between Barry and me. He was strangely asexual; there was always something very cold about him.'

Barry assured her he would give a sign of some description if his 'transfer' was successful. He could not be more specific.

'You'll know,' was all he said.

'What if it goes wrong? What then?'

They had discussed this at length, yet she needed to be sure she understood him. After all, his sanity – if not his life – might depend on her correctly interpreting his signals.

If I'm not back – if I'm not awake – within two hours, then I want you to wake me gently, okay? No rough stuff. Don't shake me; don't press. Just call my name softly. Keep calling until I wake up.'

'And if you don't?'

'I'll leave that to your own discretion.'

Barry need not have worried, however, because he did not succeed. He tried that night, and the next. He even tried the day after, in broad daylight. 'Maybe I need to be able to visualize the sun on Dublin Bay,' he said. But, day or night, nothing worked. He was sorely disappointed. Or so it seemed.

It was Angela's turn.

She began in good faith and high spirits. The thought of meeting her mother had eased her grief-stricken depression considerably. Now she was determined to succeed.

She lay down on the bed, shut her eyes, and made herself comfortable, secure in the knowledge that Barry was on hand, should anything go wrong.

'By that stage I trusted him,' she says. 'All my earlier fears gave way to . . . awe, I suppose. Yes, awe is the best way to describe it. He became my guru. I believed that if he could help me see and speak to my mother again it would change everything.'

Angela had never before even entertained the possibility of communicating with her dead mother. She had always considered spiritualism and séances to be somehow unhealthy, if not downright wrong. She had no wish to disturb the dead. But what Barry was exploring was not the same thing at all, she reasoned; it was not a matter of contacting the dead, but returning to a time when Nuala Brehen was fully alive and vital. Surely there was nothing wrong with that.

For an hour long – Barry was keeping track of time – nothing happened. Angela, as relaxed as she could will herself to be, tried to recreate that tableau from her past. The kitchen. The kitchen in 1988; not so very different from the kitchen in 2004, yet sufficiently altered to interfere with her visualization. She had had it renovated in 1998, had replaced the table and chairs, had new fronts put on the drawers and cupboards. The walls were canary yellow now; magnolia then.

She tried to picture her mother seated with her back to the window, as she had been sitting that day. She would be nursing a cup of tea – a cup, never a mug – with a small plate of chocolate digestives to hand. She would be wearing the minimum of make-up. She needed her hair done; Angela had made the appointment for her the previous day. She had taken off her apron and was wearing her dowdy old beige house-dress. She was stirring her tea; when thinking hard about something, she would spend a ridiculously long time stirring her tea.

'Don't make the same mistake I did, love,' she was saying. 'Don't make the same mistake I did.'

It was Angela's 'mantra', her equivalent of Barry's father's nautical instruction. Over and over she had imagined her mother saying it, had concentrated on the lips moving, on the workworn fingers gripping the spoon as she stirred her tea; on the pale yellow blind on the window; on the metronomic tick-tocking of the old kitchen clock. She had become very proficient at it.

'Don't make the same mistake I did, love.'

Somebody coughed softly. Angela thought for an instant that the sound came from her own throat, but knew then it was Barry. So caught up had she been in her visualization exercise that she had blanked him out entirely.

She sat up, annoyed.

'Why did you do that?' she demanded.

'Look,' Barry produced a pill box from his pocket. He held out a tiny white tablet. 'Take this,' he said. 'Acid.'

'Barry, I told you before: I don't do drugs!'

'But you drink, don't you!' he shouted, his face contorting with rage. 'It's the same bloody thing. And it's only half a tab.'

'I was so shocked,' she recalls. 'The calm Barry had turned into that awful creature again, the one I hoped I'd never have to see again. He just wasn't himself. I know people say that about guys who do awful things, but in Barry's case it was literally true. I was scared of him. I knew that if I didn't take the LSD, something terrible was going to happen. I'd no option.'

She lay back down on the bed again, trying not to show how frightened she was. She applied the meditation techniques, but it was hard to relax. Barry had unnerved her.

Then, perhaps a half-hour later, the LSD began to take effect. It was like nothing she had ever experienced. It was as though she was stepping outside reality, entering a place that obeyed other laws. . . .

And all at once she was *there*. It was no dream, no figment of her imagination, no restored memory. Angela had awakened in the kitchen of 1988. There sat her mother, Nuala Brehen, looking remarkably youthful – incongruously youthful, until Angela remembered with surprise that, in 1988, Nuala was about the same age as she herself was in 2004. She could very well have been looking across at herself.

'Don't make the same mistake I did, love.'

'What mistake is that, Mammy?'

Angela could not believe that she had spoken the words. Yet her own larynx had formed them; she had heard and felt them emerging from her lips. Except that the lips did not belong to her; not really. They were those of a seventeen-year-old schoolgirl. She looked at her hands. They were slim and svelte, the skin smooth and as yet unblemished by 'liver spots', and damage the Greek sun would wreak. She raised a hand to her hair and felt it long and lank; the trips to expensive hairdressers would come later.

She was really there. She had done it. She had achieved the inconceivable: she had transferred her consciousness to the person she once had been.

'WELL DONE,' a voice said. 'OH, VERY WELL DONE, ANGELA. AND THERE IS SO MUCH MORE TO BE DONE. SO MUCH YOU CAN ACCOMPLISH HERE.'

It was the woman's voice again, the one with the Galway City accent. It was coming from everywhere and nowhere, speaking with that same sibilance and breathy quality. Her master, her guide, her oversoul.

But her mother was speaking again, cutting across the words of her spirit guide.

'I don't want you to go wasting your life, love,' Nuala Brehen was saying. 'Me, I didn't really have a say in the matter. But times were different then. My mother was a slave all her life, you know. She slaved for her husband and she slaved for us. She took me aside one time, the same way I'm doing now with you, and—'

'Angela!'

'—gave me the same advice I'm—'

'Angela! Angela, come back now.'

Her mother's face was blurring, her words growing indistinct and garbled. Angela was hearing them as though they were being transmitted through a tank of water. The contours and colours of the kitchen were giving way to blackness. A voice was speaking softly at her ear.

She opened her eyes to find Barry McNulty's face swimming above her own, pale in the semi-darkness of the room. She was back. She felt betrayed.

'For heaven's sake! Couldn't you wait?'

As soon as the words were out, she was regretting her folly. Now she would have to face his dark side. She felt strange, too; the drug was still exerting its power. She was not herself.

But Barry showed no anger; only concern.

'Wait?' he said. 'I waited nearly three hours! We agreed on a limit of two, Angela. But you looked so normal lying there. I didn't want to spoil anything.'

'It *can't* have been three hours. It felt like ten minutes.'

'Trust me – it was three hours.'

'I want to go back.'

'Angela, it's one o'clock. Maybe we should call it a night.'

'To hell with that. I was doing so well, and you ruined it.'

'Well, thanks very much. I was just sticking to our agreement.'

'I want to try again. I may not get this chance again. I *saw* her, Barry. I spoke to her. She was as real as you are now.'

'Your mother?'

'You were right all along. It *is* possible. Oh, Barry, this thing is huge! This has to be about the most important breakthrough of its kind. I have to go back there.'

Angela did go back, though not that night. Try as she might, she could not recapture the circumstances of that first excursion into her past. A week went by, then another, before Barry returned to her home.

'I thought he was making me suffer, because I'd been successful and he hadn't. But it was all part of the game. *I* knew and *he* knew that the LSD had enabled my transition. In the end I had to ask him to let me have more, and stay by me while I made a second attempt.'

When he did come again, it was with the stated objective of returning Angela to the point at which she had left off. He said that he was going to learn from her. She was the pioneer, the one who had opened the door to untold possibility.

As before, Angela took the drug and entered into that state of 'other' consciousness. Barry sat by the bed in the darkened room, on hand, as it were, to help in case of unexpected difficulties.

'Don't make the same mistake I did, love.'

She was there in less time than it took before – so rapidly, in fact, that the 'transfer' left her slightly dazed and disorientated.

The selfsame tableau presented itself, as though she had never left it. There was her mother endlessly stirring her tea, like some fragment of film endlessly looping. And in a sense it was a good analogy; Angela was indeed returning to a moment that would always be there, to be played back endlessly by she who had discovered the secret mechanism. Now she wished to go beyond that moment.

'I didn't, Mammy,' she said, through the mouth of her younger self.

Nuala Brehen stopped her stirring and frowned.

'You didn't what, Angela?'

'I didn't make the same mistake. I never married, you see. I never had children. I went out and got a job.'

'What are you talking about, love? Sure you're not making any sense at all.'

Angela was going to make the most of the situation; she was going to exploit her new-found power to the full. She left the table, revelling in the feel of a body that was at once alien and somehow familiar. She was moving with youthful grace and lack of effort, could feel the potency of the energy in her limbs. She had forgotten how it felt to be that age – and yet the tragedy of being that age, she knew, was that only in later life, when it is much too late, does one appreciate it.

She turned back to the woman seated at the table.

'What's got into you, Angela? You're acting very strange.'

Should she tell her? Would her mother believe her? No, of course not. It was insane. She sat down again and looked long at Nuala Brehen. She felt such a surge of love for this middle-aged woman who had once been her darling mother. She could sense her thoughts and emotions, because in her 'other', older, existence she shared a great many of them.

For the first time ever, she sensed how it must have been to be her mother. Pregnant at seventeen-and-a-half, married at eighteen, Nuala had never known the freedom of carefree, unattached young womanhood.

'Mammy, I want you to know that I love you. You're a wonderful woman.'

Nuala stood up, hands automatically brushing her skirt for stray crumbs. Angela could sense that she had embarrassed her.

'I'll put the kettle on,' she said. 'Would you like another cup?'

'I'll do it. You sit down there now. You never relax, Mammy. You're always on the go.'

Angela went to the AGA, reached for the still-warm kettle and brought it to the sink. She was smiling to herself as she allowed the tap-water to gush into it. It felt so extraordinary to be there, at that time, in that place. She glanced left and right, seeing the sun come slanting in at the window, illuminating the old, worn cupboards. . . .

But – wait a minute. The cupboards were not old and worn; they were her own modern ones. She looked to the left of the window where the sepia-tinted picture of her grandfather used to hang. It was no longer there.

Angela stopped what she was doing, perplexed, the ghost of a suspicion forming. She turned off the tap and set the kettle down. She looked again at the wall.

It should have been magnolia, not canary yellow. In 1988 the kitchen walls were magnolia; gone dull in places, grease-spattered in others, smoke-darkened above the cooker.

But she was seeing yellow walls. A decade would pass before she had them painted yellow.

She turned and studied the back of the woman seated at the table. Nuala Brehen was reaching for a digestive biscuit: a chocolate digestive.

Two years before her death, Nuala Brehen was diagnosed with diabetes. She was immediately prohibited from eating chocolate.

'I felt a tingling all over my face right then,' Angela says. 'I knew there was something desperately wrong.'

A moment later she heard the mysterious voice again, that

which she had identified as belonging to her 'oversoul'. It was speaking soothingly, coming from all corners of the kitchen, even from the ceiling.

'LOOK AGAIN, ANGELA; LOOK AGAIN,' it was saying.

She looked, and the walls were no longer yellow, but magnolia – good old safe magnolia. The cupboards were once again old and worn, and her grandfather's picture was hanging in its rightful place. But she was having no more of this. She sensed a terrible threat of danger.

'I was panicking,' she says. 'I was afraid of what might happen to me. Maybe I felt I might die or something horrible. I started to shout. I was shouting things like "Jesus help me! Let me out of here!" I saw my mother turn to look at me and then I was shown the most horrifying vision.'

Angela falters, on the verge of tears as she tries to describe the indescribable.

'I was shown what the progression of death had done to my poor mother's body. It was done in a kind of time-lapsed sort of way, and no matter what I did, I could still see it. I could even *smell* it. I squeezed my eyes shut, but I could still see everything. Then I heard that voice again and it said . . . I'll never forget the words. It said, "SEE, ANGELA: NO SOUL, NO GOD, NO AFTER-LIFE. ONLY DEATH, ONLY DEATH!"

'I remember screaming "no!", over and over.'

Through her own frantic shouts she heard a third voice, a male voice, close at hand. It was derisive, mocking. She heard laughter and words she could not comprehend.

The bright kitchen was darkening, as though it were sinking slowly to the bottom of a murky pond. With it went her mother's eyeless corpse, still standing there, its head cocked at an angle, the ravaged lips mouthing silent words.

She felt her body grow heavy, as though it were filling up with water or some other liquid. She opened her eyes to see Barry

McNulty. He was sprawled in the chair, head thrown back, laughing insanely.

Angela stumbled from the room, down the stairs, and out into the safety of the street. To this day she has no memory of what happened after that. Later, she was told that a neighbour had found her wandering barefoot, shouting and screaming that the Devil was in her home.

She was taken by ambulance to the local hospital.

Angela spent three days in care. They had pumped her stomach. They told her that she had overdosed on drugs; that she was lucky she had not harmed herself, that she might have died. She was discharged with a caution, and a lecture.

'I didn't dare tell them the real story. They would have had me locked up. But Barry McNulty was the one who needed locking up, not me. The first thing I did when I got home was to sit down and write him a letter, telling him in no uncertain terms that if he ever came anywhere near me again, I'd have him arrested for stalking.' Angela sighs heavily. 'God, I was so naive to think it was that simple. I overlooked the fact that his powers went way beyond the physical.'

Her problems began soon after she posted the letter.

'It started with little things,' she says, 'very subtle at first, so that I thought it was just my own forgetfulness. I'd keep losing or misplacing things, like my keys or handbag. One day I found my make-up bag in the cutlery drawer . . . and I really got worried. Was I going mad? Another day I came home from work to find the front door unlocked. I always double-locked it. Always.

'My first thought was Barry McNulty. Everything kept building and building. After that the nightmares started. In my dreams I kept being returned to that awful scene in the kitchen. One night I thought I saw that terrible image of my mother standing beside my bed. Then the phone would ring at all hours. Sleep became impossible. God, it was a living hell. I just wanted to die – to end it all. My work suffered; everything suffered. There was no way I was going back to the doctor. I knew that medication and a spell in hospital were no cure for what I was suffering. Oh, how I regretted ever having dealings with Barry McNulty! He was grinding me down, so that I'd come to him for help.'

Matters came to a head before too long. When they did, Angela was to discover just how powerful Barry was, and how potent were the forces he had at his bidding. She was getting ready for bed one night. All seemed normal – until she sensed that there was something in the room with her.

'I was pulling my nightdress over my head, when all of a sudden this . . . *thing* was behind me.' She struggles to describe it. 'God, I really can't put into words how awful it felt. It didn't feel human; it felt like it was going to swallow me up. I knew, *I just knew* that if I turned around to look, something terrible would happen.'

There were three other bedrooms in the house. She would sleep elsewhere. But, no matter where she went, the menace followed her.

'I knew it was Barry who was doing it. He was taking his revenge for the letter and showing how he could control me. So I started pleading with him to take it away, whatever it was he'd sent to my house. I was convinced he could hear me. I told him I hadn't meant to send the letter. I was crying, and screaming for him to help me. I would have done anything at that point to be rid of that thing.'

It seemed that her pleas were answered. Within minutes, as Angela lay slumped on the bed, sobbing, she sensed the presence departing.

The telephone rang. She suspected who the caller was, and knew she had to answer it.

'Barry? Is that you?'

For a moment or two there was silence. Then the laughter started. It erupted from the receiver: hysterical laughter that grew louder and louder, until it filled her head and – it seemed to Angela – the house itself.

She slammed down the phone. She went upstairs, took two sleeping pills, lay down, and soon fell into a groggy half-sleep.

But her ordeal was far from over. Sometime later, she was awakened by noises outside the bedroom door. She sat up in alarm. Somebody was pacing up and down the landing.

'Pacing is maybe the wrong word,' Angela explains. 'It was more like someone dragging their feet . . . a stocky man with a gammy leg. There was wooden flooring on the landing, so I could hear these heavy boots echoing through the house.'

She was distraught. She dared not put the light on, lest the sliver of light coming from under the door betray her whereabouts. In the circumstances, she did the only thing she could do. She groped her way to the door and quietly locked it.

The dragging feet could be heard at the far end of the corridor. Angela got back into bed and sat in the darkness, holding her breath. She heard the heavy boots turn and begin the slow trudge up the corridor again. She prayed that the footfalls would somehow stop at the staircase and continue down the stairs.

They did not.

'Oh, Jesus, help me!' she whispered over and over to herself.

The dragging footsteps approached her bedroom door. They stopped.

Angela clamped a hand over her mouth. Inwardly she was screaming, but she must somehow contain her fear. Whatever it was that stood on the other side of the door seemed to know how to induce the utmost terror in her.

She waited. And waited, trembling.

All at once, there came a frenetic scratching and scraping at the door. She describes it as being 'like the paws or claws of an animal trying desperately to get in.' It was the last thing Angela heard.

'I passed out,' she says. 'Now I know what's meant by the phrase, "I nearly died of fright." That night I came as close as anyone could to doing just that.'

'You do know', Father Ignatius McCarthy said, 'that it's a bad idea to try to communicate with the dead? That's why I advise people not to attend séances or that sort of thing. Jesus warned against it. You're taking a risk.'

He had received her in a book-lined study in the monastery. The room with its faded antiques and heavily polished furniture seemed an appropriate setting for the elderly exorcist, who had made himself comfortable in a leather wing chair.

Angela confesses that she has the greatest difficulty with people's ages, but to her, Father Ignatius was as old a priest as she had ever come across still fulfilling his ministry. She had travelled a fair distance to visit him. At first she considered going to see somebody in Galway; but she was known there, because of her job in the pharmacy. She thought it wiser to seek help farther afield. She needed anonymity. A relative suggested that Father Ignatius could help. In some circles he was known to have experience of 'troublesome' cases.

Angela was at pains to communicate to the priest her need of his services without delay.

'My home was under siege,' she tells us. 'I was a refugee in my own town. Since that terrible night, with the "visitor" from God knows where, I'd been forced to live in a B and B. I dared not go home again. I went back during the day to grab some things, but I couldn't stay more than a minute. The place gave me the creeps – even in daylight.'

At first, she could not come straight out and confide in this kindly stranger details of the insane enterprise – and yes, she thought of it then in those terms – that had brought her to such a pass. She cursed herself hard and long for being a fool. Her gullibility had exposed her to unknowable danger. She had come to know the nature of such danger. But, for the time being, she was content in wrapping it in terminology that only hinted at the truth. Angela was at pains to point out that she had not been a willing participant in Barry's scheme. She was the victim. She was a little vexed that he seemed not to understand that.

'I hear what you're saying, Father,' she told him. 'But I never went to any séances or that sort of thing. And I never *asked* for those strange out-of-the-body experiences that started this. They just happened.'

'Did they now?' The priest looked at her intently. 'Fair enough. But I'm not so interested in what happened to you at seventeen. At that age we all have fantasies about flying and being astronauts and heaven knows what else. No, I'm more interested in the present. Tell me something: that first time you found yourself "in the spirit", as they say, in your friend's bedroom, and then looking down on her body at the crash scene, what kind of state were you in – prior to all that?'

'What d'you mean, Father?' She laughed nervously, but saw that he was not amused. 'I was in bed asleep of course.'

'That's not quite what I mean. Would there have been drugs or drink involved?'

'Well . . . yes.' She hesitated. 'I'd been drinking both times.'

'To the point where you blacked out?'

Angela could only nod a response, too ashamed to say anything more.

'I thought as much. Now, please don't take this the wrong way, Angela, but I'm wondering if you appreciate how foolish that is – that drinking to the point where you black out. Most people don't, you see. Most don't give it a second thought. But *I* do. And here's the thing: when you're out of your mind with drink, or indeed drugs – they're all the same in my book, Angela – you actually leave yourself open. And anything can come in.'

Angela had never heard the like of it. It was ludicrous and she told him so. If that were the case, she argued, then a sizable swath of the population of Ireland was possessed. That was what Father Ignatius was implying.

'If you drink to excess,' he countered, 'to the point where you forget who you are, you leave yourself vulnerable. That's all I'm saying. More evil acts are carried out under the influence of drugs and drink than most of us like to think about.'

She could not fault him on that. She hesitated. The full import of his words had registered.

'My God, Father, are you saying I'm *possessed*?' It was an appalling prospect.

'No, not possessed, but you certainly left yourself open to the possibility. You see, Angela, Satan is very clever. Not only can he use our weaknesses to fool us, he can also use our ignorance and vanity to lull us into believing falsehoods. That's the trap. Your weakness was believing you needed to contact your mother, and your ignorance in the area of occult practices led you to think it was actually possible.'

'But I really *did* see my mother, just as I remember her.'

'Exactly! Just as you remember her. We all carry around memories of people close to us who've passed on. I get people coming to me from time to time with that sort of story. They'll have been to this or that clairvoyant or medium, and they all come out with the same sort of nonsense. "Oh, such-and-such told me something that only my dead husband or wife or whatever would have known." And I tell them what I'm going to tell you now. Satan knows all about us as well. And there's nothing to stop him looking inside our heads and using the memories we have of our loved ones to fool us.'

'He can do that?'

'He can do many things. He could even appear to some of our greatest saints in the guise of Our Lord or the Blessed Virgin. Why do you think the Vatican is so cautious when they hear of yet another sighting of the Virgin Mary across the world? They have to be cautious; they know the score. Out of the many hundreds, only a handful have been officially recognized.'

She had to ask. It was the question that had gnawed at her for days. It would not let go of her.

'The thing that's in my house, Father . . . is it . . . Is it the Devil?'

Father Ignatius gathered his thoughts before replying.

'That friend of yours: Barry. He sounds to me like he's involved in the occult in a big way. Very dangerous territory, black magic and all of that . . .'

Angela was opening her mouth, intent on explaining her naïveté, but Father Ignatius held up a hand.

'Oh, no doubt he told you it was white magic?'

The priest's perceptiveness astonished her. 'Yes, he did. He said he was a healer, and he used white magic to help people.'

'Ah yes, he would say that, wouldn't he? "White" sounds very proper; more acceptable, you might say. That's the trap, you see. That's how the gullible get sucked into these things.' Father Ignatius looked at her steadily. 'There's no such thing as white magic, Angela. There is only black, and all forms of magic are practised with recourse to Satan.' He leaned forward. 'Now, I don't want to alarm you, my dear, but I'd say that Barry has called up something of that nature to attack you.'

'When you say "something" . . .'

'An evil spirit, a demon. It sounds like it to me. Those noises you heard in the night; that inhuman presence you felt. This is done to frighten you, to cause great fear. But let me assure you that there's no more to fear; the good Lord will deal with it. We can get rid of it.'

'Do you mean, Father, that you'll do a . . .' She was hesitant in voicing the word.

'An exorcism. That's what you're trying to say. Well, no, Angela, I don't expect we'll be doing a full exorcism. Not in the sense I think you mean it. Nothing as dramatic as that. But we shall see.'

The priest patted her shoulder.

'By the sound of it, it's your friend Barry who really needs the exorcism,' he said. 'Not that he'd ever submit himself to one – more's the pity.'

Angela had not been a practising Catholic since her teens. For her, prayer was a distant memory; prayers recited to ward off evil belonged to a distant past. She did not know what to expect that Friday. It was 8 October 2004.

Father Ignatius was due to arrive at seven o'clock. Angela, still too afraid to venture into her home, was sitting outside in her car when the blue Vauxhall pulled up. She was surprised, and slightly uneasy, to see that he was accompanied by two others. He had given her to understand that he would come alone.

The driver was a burly priest who introduced himself as Liam Mulryan. He would assist Father Ignatius, Angela learned, as would the third member of the party: Sister Immaculata, a soft-spoken, elderly Carmelite.

They entered the house.

The two priests excused themselves at once, explaining that they would 'have a look around the place'. In truth, they were ascertaining where 'presences' might be strongest.

Yet all seemed tranquil on that particular evening; Angela had half-expected to sense something, but the house gave off nothing more sinister than the disused feeling houses do when left vacant, even for a short period. All the same, she was nervous. Sister Immaculata kept her company in the kitchen as she prepared tea.

She was grateful for the nun's cheeriness. She seemed intent on keeping the atmosphere light.

'People come to Father Ignatius all the time,' she said, 'with stories about disturbances in their homes. A lot of the time it's a case of an old house settling on its foundations, or air in the water pipes, that sort of thing. On the odd occasion it's something else entirely, and we come along to help out.' She smiled.

Angela did not like the sound of that.

Presently, tea having been drunk, the two priests began their preparations. A Mass would be said in the living-room. The table would serve as the altar.

Father Ignatius lit the candles and draped a purple stole about his shoulders. Sister Immaculata and Father Mulryan produced printed prayer sheets and knelt down to one side. Angela joined them. The service was about to begin.

It was nearing eight on a mild autumn evening. All was quiet both inside and outside the house at the end of the cul-de-sac. The curtains were drawn against the darkness. The main light in the living-room was on.

The celebration of the Mass passed off without incident. Angela was relieved, thinking all was over.

'Far from it,' she says. 'Little did I know it was about to begin. Father Ignatius said that he wouldn't be doing an exorcism, but that was before he saw the house. I don't know what him and the other priest saw, but it must have been enough to convince them there was something seriously wrong.'

After the closing prayers, Father Ignatius announced that what he enigmatically referred to as 'the blessing of the house' would commence. All made the Sign of the Cross. The celebrant opened his book and proceeded to read aloud.

'In the Name of Jesus Christ, God and Lord; through the intercession of the Immaculate Virgin, Mother of God, Mary, and Holy Michael the Archangel, the blessed apostles Peter and Paul, and all the saints; and relying on the holy authority of our office, we are about to undertake the expulsion of any evil spirits that are present here.'

There followed a respectful silence as Father Ignatius placed his book upon the table and joined his hands.

'May God rise up and may His enemies be dissipated,' he entreated.

'And let those who hate Him flee before Him,' the nun and the younger priest said in unison. Sister Immaculata held her prayer sheet closer to Angela and indicated the responses. They would be given by three voices.

'Let them be dissipated like smoke,' Father Ignatius continued in a strong voice.

'As wax flows before fire, so let sinners perish before God,' the trio answered from the text.

'Look on the Cross of the Lord. Be defeated, all enemies!' The exorcist's voice was gaining in volume.

'The ancient strength will conquer, the King of Kings!' The words of the nun and young priest rang out with the certitude of the faithful. Angela strove to keep up.

The strange-sounding, medieval words were affecting her. As she spoke them, it seemed to her that they were charged with power, and that she was to some degree partaking of that power. The solemnity of the occasion, and the earnestness with which the three religious prayed, caused her to dwell on the gravity of her situation. She was uneasy.

'Let your mercy be with us, o Lord!'

'According to our hopes in you,' said Father Ignatius, concluding the prayer. All bowed their heads in silence.

From upstairs came the unmistakable sound of a door opening. Angela gasped and looked at the others, but they did not stir.

Father Ignatius took up his prayer book again.

'We exorcise you, each unclean spirit, each power of Satan—'

The words were cut short as the same door was, quite audibly, banged shut.

'. . . each infestation of the enemy from hell, each legion, each congregation, each satanic sect—'

Heavy footsteps, sounds produced by a number of booted feet, were crossing the landing. Several moved quickly and as one, as if marching to some ethereal command; others dragged behind as if they belonged to the wounded. They paused abruptly at the head of the stairs, marching on the spot. Angela bit her lip in fright; she tasted her own blood. Sister Immaculata laid a comforting hand on her arm.

Father Ignatius glanced at the ceiling and waited for the commotion to cease.

Presently, it did. He looked back at his text and continued, unperturbed.

'In the name and by the power of our Lord Jesus Christ! Be uprooted and put to flight from the Church of God, and—'

The phantom footsteps began descending the stairs, tramping out a slow, ordered rhythm. And it seemed that they paused and marked time on each and every tread. Their determined marching was like that of a platoon of battle-weary soldiers advancing in a final push. With each tread gained, the marching grew louder.

Tramp, tramp, tramp.

'Be uprooted and put to flight from the Church of God—'

Tramp, tramp, tramp.

The footsteps were drawing ever nearer. Angela let out a little cry. Of the company, she seemed to be the only one who was showing fear.

'. . . and from the souls that were made in the image of God and redeemed with the blood of the divine lamb.'

Tramp, tramp, tramp.

The phantom army had reached the bottom of the stairs. The measured tramping of so many pairs of boots now filled Angela's

hallway. All that separated the group from the horror was the living-room door. Father Ignatius took up the crucifix and pressed
it to his lips. Father Mulryan remained kneeling with his head
bowed in prayer. The nun passed her prayer sheet to Angela. She
spread her arms wide and gazed heavenward. She was about to
speak. Abruptly, the din in the hallway ceased.

The nun seized her chance. She spoke out into the tense silence,
in a voice that was loud and confident.

'Father, in your goodness, come to us now,' she implored. 'Now
in our hour of need. O good Jesus, hear us. Save us, o Lord. Save
us, your servants, from every threat or harm from the evil one.
We beg you, we beg you!'

Angela's hands began to tremble. The prayer sheet fell from
her grasp. Father Mulryan calmly retrieved it and handed it back
with a reassuring smile.

Sister Immaculata continued.

'We beg you, Father, through the intercession of the archangels St Michael, St Raphael, and St Gabriel, to protect us now.
To protect us now in our hour of need. Come, o Lord; come, o
Holy Spirit; come, o Holy Virgin Mother; hear our call. Deliver
us from the evil that is present here.'

Father Ignatius lowered the crucifix. Sister Immaculata placed
an arm about Angela's shoulders. The young priest raised his
head and looked towards the door as if in expectation.

All waited. As if on cue, the next manifestation presented itself.

The sinister scratching and scuffling – that which had driven
Angela from her home – started up on the other side of the door.
She began to shake and sob in terror. She was unprepared for any
of this; it was to have been a simple 'blessing of the house'.

Father Ignatius took up the crucifix and held it aloft, facing
into the danger.

'Do not dare further!' he commanded in a loud, authoritative voice. 'Do not dare further to defile this place, most cunning Serpent. Do not dare further to deceive the human race.'

The scratching noises grew louder.

' . . . to persecute the Church of God, to strike and shake the chosen of God like chaff. God the Father commands you. God the Son commands you. God the Holy Spirit commands you.'

The scratching began to lessen.

'Christ orders you: He who is the eternal word of God become man. He who destroyed your hateful jealousy against the salvation of our race.'

There came a frantic pounding as if a dozen heavy boots were kicking against the door, drowning out the words of Scripture. But Father Ignatius would not be deterred. His voice soared above the cacophony.

'He who humiliated Himself, making Himself obedient to death. He who built His Church on a firm rock and provided that the strength of hell would never, *would never* prevail over that Church. He who will remain with His Church for all days, even up to the end of human time.'

The door flew open. All heads turned. Just as suddenly, it banged shut again. This action was repeated twice more in rapid succession, sending tremors through the room. The candles guttered wildly, then died, the bottles of holy oil and water fell over.

Angela made to stand up. She was terrified. She wanted to escape, out through the back door. The nun tightened her arm about her shoulders.

'We're nearly there,' she whispered. 'Have faith, child. God is good.'

Father Mulryan righted the bottles and relit the candles. The exorcist took up the holy water and began sprinkling it about the room.

'The sacrament of the Cross commands you! The virtues of all the mysteries of the Christian faith command you. The most exalted mother of God, Mary the Virgin, commands you. She, though lowly, trampled on your head from the first instant of her Immaculate Conception.'

Angela felt her fear dissipating under the comforting arm of the nun and the words spoken so commandingly by the priest.

He laid aside the holy water and unstoppered the bottle of holy oil. Sister Immaculata helped Angela to her feet. She and Father Mulryan placed a hand on each shoulder. Father Ignatius anointed Angela's forehead with the oil.

'I command you and bid all powers who molest this servant of God, by the power of God Almighty, in the name of Jesus Christ our Saviour, through the intercession of the Holy Virgin Mother, to leave this servant of God for ever, and to be consigned to the unquenchable fire, to that place that the Lord God has prepared for you.'

The blessing being accomplished, he went to the door. It was time for the banishing. Father Ignatius moved through the hallway and the downstairs rooms, sprinkling holy water as he went. His voice, charged as it was with authority, could be heard throughout the house.

'Go now from this place! Death is your lot, impious one. And for your angels there is an endless death. For you and for your angels the unquenchable flame is prepared. Because you are the prince of cursed homicides, the author of incest!'

They heard him ascend the stairs.

'The head of all the sacrilegious, master of the most evil actions, the teacher of heretics, the inventor of all obscenity. Go out, therefore, impious one. Go out, criminal. Go out with all your falsehoods. Leave, therefore now. Go away, seducer! The desert is your home. The serpent is your dwelling. Be humiliated and cast down. Behold, the victorious Lord is near and quick. All things are subject to His power.'

Returning to the living-room, he went to Angela and, making

the Sign of the Cross on her brow, said: 'May your servant Angela be protected in soul and body by this sign of your name.' On her chest he made the Sign of the Cross again: once, twice, thrice.

'Preserve what is within this person,' he intoned. 'Rule her feelings. Strengthen her heart.'

All present again bowed their heads in silent prayer. As she prayed, Angela felt her fear drain from her. In those moments, she did indeed sense that her heart was strengthened.

Father Ignatius motioned for them, his little congregation of three, to kneel again. He extended his hands over them.

'Father,' he intoned, his voice gentle, no longer that of the bane of demons, 'we pray you, all-powerful God, that evil spirits have no more power over this servant of yours and in this place, but that they flee and not return. Let the goodness and the peace of Our Lord Jesus Christ enter here at your bidding, Lord. For through Jesus we have been saved. And let us not fear any ill, because the Lord is with us. He who lives and reigns as God with you in the unity of the Holy Spirit, for ever and ever. Amen.'

Father Ignatius then led Angela through a profession of faith. The ceremony ended with the Lord's Prayer, the Anima Christi, and a final prayer of deliverance. The work was completed.

'It was a long night,' Angela recalls. 'But a long and miraculous night, that's for certain.'

And, after her visitors had gone, she did something she had not planned on. She went to sleep in her own bed. She sensed that she could do so without fear, without a thought for unseen and unwelcome forces.

'Before they came, I thought I'd be leaving with them to stay at the B and B,' she says. 'That wasn't the case. My fear had vanished completely. I fell asleep immediately from the exhaustion, and woke up knowing – simply knowing – that I'd never be bothered again.'

* * *

Angela Brehen still lives in Galway City. Her new home is on the other side of the Corrib, and a considerable distance from the house of her birth. She moved there shortly after the exorcism, in the spring of 2005.

'It wasn't because I was afraid of being "invaded" again,' she assures us. 'No, I certainly didn't move for that reason. It was because Barry McNulty still knew where I lived, so I thought it safer to move, and I gave up my job in the chemist's as well. I just needed to make a clean break. My job seemed to belong to that time as well, when I was foolish and naive. I've grown up a lot since then. You know, the positive part of all of this was that it brought me closer to God. He saved me; I know He did. I'm sure of it. And the irony is that evil brought me to goodness. I had to come face to face with the one to find the other.'

She later learned that Barry McNulty's home was found abandoned. She has not seen him since.

Father Ignatius believes that he may have fled the country. Having received us in the book-lined study of the abbey, he speaks frankly about the case. And Barry.

'She'll never be bothered by him again,' he declares with confidence. 'She's safe now, thank God.'

We wonder about Barry's psychic gifts; if he can still call on them to help him work his mischief.

'Oh, he might have the Devil on his side,' the priest says, 'but Angela has God on her side now, and he's no match for God.'

Was it coincidence then, his running into Angela after all that time? In Galway, in the same city.

'I don't hold with coincidence. Barry had a purpose in mind when he bumped into Angela as if out of the blue. He knew what he was doing; I'm sure of that. Someone in the grip of demonic control feels compelled to act, to do the most objectionable things to others in order to somehow save themselves. There's a hierarchy of evil spirits. The minor ones, the foot-soldiers, do the dirty work, to prepare the way for the generals. Their job is to enslave. Barry was attempting to enslave Angela, make her suffer so much fear that she'd have to turn to him to take the "thing" away. If she hadn't sought out God's help, heaven knows how she might have ended up.'

'I pray for Angela,' he says later. 'I pray for Barry as well. Now *there's* a man who's in sore need of prayer! I hope and pray that wherever he is, he'll receive the help he needs.'

We ask him his opinion of Barry's TC, the transference of consciousness. He shrugs.

'I'm not saying it's not possible. Of course it is. If you read up on a number of saints, you'll come across that kind of thing. Except in Angela's case it wasn't what she thought it was. Barry probably started out innocently enough, then got deeper and deeper into it until he'd gone too far. We know so little about ourselves, how our minds work, that we can be easily fooled. And Satan and his minions are out there, just waiting for a chance to fool us. That's how it's always been, ever since Eve was tempted with the apple.'

He chuckles.

'We aren't half as advanced as we think we are,' he concludes. 'We know so little. When you reach my age, that's the time you'll come to realize how little you really know.'

EXORCISM OF THE POSSESSED

ROMAN CATHOLIC RUBRICS ON EXORCISM

A rubric is a liturgical direction or guideline. One of its more common uses is in the Christian missal. The word derives from late Middle English *rubrish*, which referred to a heading or section of text printed in [ruby] red for distinctiveness.

There are three types of rubric governing the office of priest: those of the breviary, the missal and the ritual.

What follows are the guidelines governing exorcism as laid down by the Vatican.

1. A priest – one who is expressly and in special wise authorized by the Ordinary – when he intends to perform an exorcism over persons tormented by the Devil, must be properly distinguished for his piety, prudence, and integrity of life. He should fulfil this devout undertaking in all constancy and humility, being utterly immune to any striving for human aggrandizement, and relying not on his own, but on the Divine power. Moreover, he ought to be of mature years, and revered not alone for his office but for his moral qualities.

2. In order to exercise his ministry rightly, he should resort to a great deal more study of the matter (which has to be passed over here for the sake of brevity) by examining approved authors and cases from experience; on the other hand, let him carefully observe the few more important points enumerated here.

3. Especially, he should not believe too readily that a person is possessed by an evil spirit; but he ought to ascertain the signs by which a person possessed can be distinguished from one who is suffering from melancholy or some other illness. Signs of possession are the following: ability to speak with some facility in a strange tongue or to understand it when spoken by another; the faculty of divulging future and hidden events; display of powers which are beyond the subject's age and natural condition; and various other indications which, when taken together as a whole, pile up the evidence.

4. In order to understand these matters better, let him inquire of the person possessed, following upon one or the other act of exorcism, what the latter experienced in his body or soul while the exorcism was being performed, and to learn also what particular words in the form had a more intimidating effect upon the Devil, so that hereafter these words may be employed with greater stress and frequency.

5. He will be on his guard against the arts and subterfuges which the evil spirits are wont to use in deceiving the exorcist. For oftentimes they give deceptive answers and make it difficult to understand them, so that the exorcist might tire and give up, or so it might appear that the afflicted one is in no wise possessed by the Devil.

6. Once in a while, after they are already recognized, they conceal themselves and leave the body practically free from every molestation, so that the victim believes himself completely delivered. Yet the exorcist may not desist until he sees the signs of deliverance.

7. At times, moreover, the evil spirits place whatever obstacles they can in the way, so that the patient may not submit to exorcism, or they try to convince him that his affliction is a natural one. Meanwhile, during the exorcism they cause him to fall asleep, and dangle some illusion before him, while they seclude themselves, so that the afflicted one appears to be freed.

8. Some reveal a crime which has been committed and the perpetrators thereof, as well as the means of putting an end to it. Yet the afflicted person must beware of having recourse on this account to sorcerers or necromancers or to any parties except the ministers of the Church, or of making use of any superstition, nay any sort of forbidden practice.

9. Sometimes the Devil will leave the possessed person in peace and even allow him to receive the Holy Eucharist, to make it appear that he has departed. In fact, the arts and frauds of the Evil One for deceiving a man are innumerable. For this reason the exorcist must be on his guard, lest he fall into this trap.

10. Wherefore, he will be mindful of the words of our Lord (Matthew 17:20), to the effect that there is a certain type of evil spirit who cannot be driven out except by prayer and fasting. Therefore, let him avail himself of these two means above all for imploring the Divine assistance in expelling demons, after the example of the holy fathers; and not only himself, but let him induce others, so far as possible, to do the same.

11. If it can be done conveniently, the possessed person should be led to church or to some other sacred and worthy place where the exorcism will be held, away

from the crowd. But if the person is ill, or for any valid reason, the exorcism may take place in a private home.

12. The subject, if in good mental and physical health, should be exhorted to implore God's help, to fast, and to fortify himself by frequent reception of penance and Holy Communion, at the discretion of the priest. And in the course of the exorcism he should be fully recollected, with his intention fixed on God, whom he should entreat with firm faith and in all humility. And if he is all the more grievously tormented, he ought to bear this patiently, never doubting the Divine assistance.

13. He ought to have a crucifix at hand or somewhere in sight. If relics of the saints are available, they are to be applied in a reverent way to the breast or the head of the person possessed (the relics must be properly and securely encased and covered). One will see to it that these sacred objects are not treated improperly or that no injury is done them by the evil spirit. However, one should not hold the Holy Eucharist over the head of the person nor in any way apply it to his body, owing to the danger of desecration.

14. The exorcist must not digress into senseless prattle nor ask superfluous questions, or such as are prompted by curiosity, particularly if they pertain to future and hidden matters, all of which have nothing to do with his office. Instead, he will bid the unclean spirit keep silence and answer only when asked. Neither ought he to give any credence to the Devil if the latter maintains that he is the spirit of some saint or of a deceased party, or even claims to be a good angel.

15. But necessary questions are, for example: about the number and name of the spirits inhabiting the patient, about the time when they entered into him, the cause thereof, and such like. As for all jesting, laughing, and nonsense on the part of the evil spirit, the exorcist should prevent it or condemn it, and he will exhort the bystanders (whose number must be very limited) to pay no attention to such goings on; neither are they to put any question to the subject. Rather they should intercede for him to God in all humility and urgency.

16. Let the priest pronounce the exorcisms in a commanding and authoritative voice, and at the same time with great confidence, humility, and fervour; and when he sees that the spirit is sorely vexed, then he oppresses and threatens all the more. If he notices that the person afflicted is experiencing a disturbance in some part of his body or an acute pain or a swelling appears in some part, he traces the Sign of the Cross over that place and sprinkles it with holy water, which he must have at hand for this purpose.

17. He will pay attention as to what words in particular cause the evil spirits to tremble, repeating them the more frequently. And when he comes to a threatening expression, he recurs to it again and again, always increasing the punishment. If he perceives that he is making progress, let him persist for two, three, four hours, and longer if he can, until victory is attained.

18. The exorcist should guard against giving or recommending any medicine to the patient, but should leave this care to physicians.

19. While performing the exorcism over a woman, he ought always to have assisting him several women of good repute, who will hold on to the person when she is harassed by the evil spirit. These assistants ought if possible to be close relatives of the subject, and for the sake of decency the exorcist will avoid saying or doing anything which might prove an occasion of evil thoughts to himself or to the others.

20. During the exorcism he shall preferably employ words from Holy Writ, rather than forms of his own or of someone else. He shall, moreover, command the Devil to tell whether he is detained in that body by necromancy, by evil signs or amulets; and if the one possessed has taken the latter by mouth, he should be made to vomit them; if he has them concealed on his person, he should expose them; and when discovered they must be burned. Moreover, the person should be exhorted to reveal all his temptations to the exorcist.

21. Finally, after the possessed one has been freed, let him be admonished to guard himself carefully against falling into sin, so as to afford no opportunity to the evil spirit of returning, lest the last state of that man become worse than the former.

Appendix Two

Prayer to Archangel Michael

The name Michael means in Hebrew 'He who is like God'. The Archangel Michael is traditionally seen as the arch-foe of Satan, since it was he who fought Lucifer and his angels when they challenged God. The Revelation of St John the Divine (12:7–9) recounts how 'there was war in heaven'.

> Michael and his angels fought against the dragon; and the dragon fought and his angels, and prevailed not; neither was their place found any more in heaven. And the great dragon was cast out, that old serpent, called the Devil, and Satan, which deceiveth the whole world: he was cast out into the earth, and his angels were cast out with him.

Pope Leo XIII had a curious experience in 1884, towards the end of his reign. In conclave with his cardinals, he suddenly fainted. They feared him dead, but he recovered consciousness with the words: 'I have had a terrible vision.' He told of the legions of the Devil overrunning the world, yet repulsed in the end by Michael and his forces. The pontiff took the vision to be a sign that the importance of the archangel should be acknowledged, and to this end composed a prayer, to be included at the close of all 'low' Masses. It is a bone of contention for many Catholics, both clerics and laity, that this prayer – a powerful petition in the fight against evil – was dropped in 1970, during the reign of Pope Paul VI.

Two translations follow. The first is the full prayer, complete with responses, as written by Leo XIII. The second is the shorter version, designed to be easily memorized.

371

PRAYER TO ARCHANGEL MICHAEL
Full Version

Most glorious Prince of the Heavenly Armies, Saint Michael the Archangel, defend us in our battle 'against principalities, against powers, against the rulers of the darkness of this world, against spiritual wickedness in high places' (Ephesians 6:12). Come to the assistance of men whom God has created to His likeness and whom He has redeemed at a great price from the tyranny of the Devil. Holy Church venerates thee as her guardian and protector; to thee, the Lord has entrusted the souls of the redeemed to be led into heaven. Pray, therefore, the God of Peace to crush Satan beneath our feet, that he may no longer retain men captive and do injury to the Church. Offer our prayers to the Most High, that without delay they may draw His mercy down upon us; take hold of the dragon, 'the old serpent, which is the Devil, and Satan'; bind him and cast him into the bottomless pit, 'that he should deceive the nations no more' (Revelation 20:2–3).

In the Name of Jesus Christ, our God and Lord, strengthened by the intercession of the Immaculate Virgin Mary, Mother of God, of Blessed Michael the Archangel, of the Blessed Apostles Peter and Paul and all the Saints, we confidently undertake to repulse the attacks and deceits of the Devil.

'Let God arise, let His enemies be scattered: let them also that hate Him flee before Him. As smoke is driven away, so drive them away; as wax melteth before the fire, so let the wicked perish at the presence of God.' (Psalm 68:1–2)

V. Behold the Cross of the Lord, flee bands of enemies.

R. He has conquered, the Lion of the tribe of Juda, the offspring of David.

V. May Thy mercy, Lord, descend upon us.

R. As great as our hope in Thee.

(At the ✠ make the Sign of the Cross.)

We drive you from us, whoever you may be, every unclean spirit, all satanic powers, all infernal invaders, all wicked legions, assemblies and sects; in the Name and by the power of Our Lord Jesus Christ, ✠ may you be snatched away and driven from the Church of God and from the souls made to the image and likeness of God and redeemed by the Precious Blood of the Divine Lamb. ✠ Most cunning serpent, you shall no more dare to deceive the human race, persecute the Church, torment God's elect and sift them as wheat. ✠ The Most High God commands you. ✠ He with whom, in your great insolence, you still claim to be equal, He 'who will have all men to be saved, and to come unto the knowledge of the truth' (1 Timothy 2:4). God the Father commands you. ✠ God the Son commands you. ✠ God the Holy Ghost commands you. ✠ Christ, God's Word made flesh, commands you. ✠ He who to save our race outdone through your envy, 'humbled Himself, and became obedient unto death' (Philippians 2:8); He who has built His Church on the firm rock and declared that the gates of hell shall not prevail against Her, because He will dwell with Her 'alway, even unto the end of the world' (Matthew 28:20). The sacred Sign of the Cross commands you, ✠ as does also the power of the mysteries of the Christian faith. ✠ The glorious Mother of God, the Virgin Mary, commands you. ✠ She who by her humility and from the first moment of her Immaculate Conception, crushed your proud head. The faith of the Holy Apostles Peter and Paul and of the other Apostles commands you. ✠ The blood of the Martyrs and the pious intercession of all the Saints command you. ✠

Thus, cursed dragon, and you, diabolical legions, we adjure you by the living God, ✠ by the true God, ✠ by the holy God, ✠ by the God who 'so loved the world, that He gave His only begotten Son, that whosoever believeth in Him should not perish, but have everlasting life' (John 3:16); stop deceiving human creatures and pouring out to them the poison of eternal damnation; stop harming the Church and hindering her liberty. Begone, Satan, inventor and master of all deceit, enemy of man's salvation. Give place to Christ in whom you have found none of your works; give place to the One, Holy, Catholic and Apostolic Church acquired by Christ at the price of His Blood. Stoop beneath the all-powerful Hand of God; tremble and flee when we invoke the Holy and terrible Name of Jesus, this Name which causes hell to tremble, this Name to which the Virtues, Powers and Dominations of Heaven are humbly submissive, this Name which the Cherubim and Seraphim praise unceasingly repeating: Holy, Holy, Holy is the Lord, the God of Armies.

V. O Lord, hear my prayer.

R. And let my cry come unto Thee.

V. May the Lord be with thee.

R. And with thy spirit.

Let us pray.

God of Heaven, God of Earth, God of Angels, God of Archangels, God of Patriarchs, God of Prophets, God of Apostles, God of Martyrs, God of Confessors, God of Virgins, God who has power to give life after death and rest after work, because there is no other God than Thee and there can be no other, for Thou art the Creator of all things, visible and invisible, of whose reign there shall be no end, we humbly prostrate ourselves before Thy glorious Majesty and we beseech Thee to deliver us by Thy power from all the tyranny of the infernal spirits, from their snares, their lies and their furious wickedness; deign, o Lord, to grant us Thy powerful protection and to keep us safe and sound. We beseech Thee through Jesus Christ Our Lord. Amen.

From the snares of the Devil, deliver us, o Lord.

That Thy Church may serve Thee in peace and liberty, we beseech Thee to hear us.

That Thou may crush down all enemies of Thy Church, we beseech Thee to hear us.

Holy water is sprinkled in the place where we may be.

PRAYER TO ARCHANGEL MICHAEL
Short Version

St Michael, Archangel, defend us in battle. Be our protection against the wickedness and snares of the Devil. May God rebuke him, we humbly pray; and do thou, o Prince of the Heavenly Host, by the Divine Power, thrust into hell Satan and all the other evil spirits who prowl about the world, seeking the ruin of souls. Amen.

St Patrick's Breastplate

or

The Lorica of St Patrick

Much of what we know of Ireland's patron saint derives from his *Confessio*, a document comprising a little over 10,000 words and written in Latin – probably his first language. It is part memoir, part meditation.

In later life he wrote in Irish, his adopted language. The 'Lúireach Phadraig' may or not be from his hand and there are a number of variations in existence. Though commonly known as 'St Patrick's Breastplate', 'Lorica' is perhaps a better translation, since the lorica was segmented Roman upper armour, offering protection on *all* sides. This would be in keeping with the spirit of this beautiful prayer, of which a new translation is given here.

I armour myself today
With the power of the Trinity.
I believe in the Trinity,
In the Oneness of God,
Creator of the universe.

I armour myself today
With the grace of the Nativity,
With the Baptism of Christ,
His Crucifixion and Entombment,
His Resurrection and Ascension,
His glorious Second Coming
Upon the Judgement Day.

I armour myself today
With the grace of the seraphim,
The submissiveness of angels,
The attendance of archangels,
The prospect of resurrection,
And everlasting life.
The prayers of patriarchs,
The predictions of prophets,
The preaching of apostles,
The faith of confessors,
The purity of the Virgin,
The deeds of righteous men.

I armour myself today
With the majesty of heaven,
The splendour of the sun,
The brightness of the moon,
The radiance of fire,
The flashing of lightning,
The swiftness of the wind,
The deepness of the ocean,
The vastness of the earth,
The solidity of rocks.

I armour myself today with:
God's power to direct me,
God's might to sustain me,
God's wisdom to instruct me,
God's eye to watch over me,
God's ear to hearken to me,
God's word to give me speech,
God's hand to direct me,
God's way to lie before me,
God's shield to protect me,

God's army to defend me,
Against the snares of demons,
Against the lure of vices,
Against the lusts of nature,
Against all who plot to harm me,
Be they far, or near at hand,
Be they few or be they many.

I invoke today all these virtues
Against every hostile, merciless power
Which may assail my body and my soul,
Against the incantations of false prophets,
Against the black laws of heathenism,
Against the false laws of heresy,
Against the deceits of idolatry,
Against every art and spell that binds
The soul of man and woman.

Christ, guard me today
Against poison,
Against burning,
Against drowning,
Against fatal wounding,
That just reward be mine.
Christ be with me,
Christ be before me,
Christ be behind me,
Christ be within me,
Christ be beside me,
Christ to win me.
Christ to comfort and restore me.
Christ be beneath me,
Christ be above me,
Christ be at my right,

Christ be at my left,
Christ guard me in the home,
Christ be my transport,
By land and by sea,
Christ be in quietude,
Christ be where danger threatens,
Christ be in the hearts
of all who love me,
Christ be in the mouth
of friend and stranger,
Christ be in every eye that sees me,
Christ be in every ear that hears me.

I armour myself today
With the power of the Trinity.
I believe in the Trinity,
In the Oneness of God,
Creator of the universe.

The Lord is salvation,
The Lord is salvation,
Christ is salvation,
May your salvation, o Lord,
be ever with us.

Translated from the Irish
by David M Kiely

FURTHER PRAYERS OF EXORCISM

PRAYER AGAINST MALEFICE
From the Greek Ritual

God, our Lord, King of Ages, All-powerful and Almighty, you who made everything and who transformed everything simply by your will. You who in Babylon changed into dew the flames of the 'seven-times hotter' furnace and protected and saved the three holy children. You are the doctor and the physician of our soul. You are the salvation of those who turn to you.

We beseech you to make powerless, banish, and drive out every diabolical power, presence, and machination; every evil influence, malefice, or evil eye and all evil actions aimed against your servant [name here]. Where there is envy and malice, give us an abundance of goodness, endurance, victory and charity.

O Lord, you who love mankind, we beg you to reach out your powerful hands and your most high and mighty arms and come to our aid. Help us, who are made in your image; send the angel of peace over us, to protect us body and soul. May he keep at bay and vanquish every evil power, every poison or malice invoked against us by corrupt and envious people. Then under the protection of your authority may we sing, in gratitude: The Lord is my salvation; whom should I fear? I will not fear evil because you are with me, my God, my strength, my powerful Lord, Lord of Peace, Father of All Ages.

Yes, Lord our God, be merciful to us, your image, and save your servant, [name here], from every threat or harm from the Evil One, and protect him by raising him above all evil.

We ask you this through the intercession of our Most Blessed, Glorious Lady, Mary ever Virgin, Mother of God, of the most splendid archangels and all your saints. Amen.

PRAYER AGAINST EVERY EVIL

Spirit of our God, Father, Son and Holy Spirit, Most Holy Trinity, Immaculate Virgin Mary, angels, archangels, and saints of Heaven, descend upon me.

Please purify me, Lord, mould me, fill me with yourself, use me. Banish all forces of evil from me, destroy them, vanquish them, so that I can be healthy and do good deeds.

Banish from me all spells, witchcraft, black magic, malefice, ties, maledictions, and the evil eye; diabolical infestations, oppressions, possessions; all that is evil and sinful, jealousy, perfidy, envy; physical, psychological, moral, spiritual, diabolical ailments.

Burn all these evils in hell, that they may never again touch me or any other creature in the entire world.

I command and bid all the powers who molest me – by the power of God All Powerful, in the name of Jesus Christ our Saviour, through the intercession of the Immaculate Virgin Mary – to leave me for ever, and to be consigned into everlasting hell, where they will be bound by St Michael the Archangel, St Gabriel, St Raphael, our guardian angels, and where they will be crushed under the heel of the Immaculate Virgin Mary. Amen.

SELECT BIBLIOGRAPHY

Alexander, William Menzies, *Demonic Possession in the New Testament : Its Historical, Medical and Theological Aspects*, Eugene : Wipf and Stock Publishers 2001

Allen, Thomas B, *Possessed : The True Story of the Most Famous Exorcism of Modern Time*, New York : Doubleday 1993

Amorth, Gabriele, *An Exorcist Tells His Story*, San Francisco : Ignatius Press 1999

— *An Exorcist : More Stories*, San Francisco : Ignatius Press 2002

Clark, Stuart, *Thinking with Demons : The Idea of Witchcraft in Early Modern Europe*, New York : Oxford University Press 1997

Cornwell, John, *Powers of Darkness, Powers of Light : Travels in Search of the Miraculous and the Demonic*, London : Penguin 1991

Crabtree, Adam, *Multiple Man : Exploration in Possession and Multiple Personality*, London : Grafton Books 1988

Cuneo, Michael, *American Exorcism : Expelling Demons in the Land of Plenty*, New York : Doubleday 2001

Curran, Robert, *The Haunted : One Family's Nightmare*, New York : St Martin's Press 1988

De Certeau, Michel, *The Possession at Loudun*, Chicago : University of Chicago Press 2000

Ferber, Sarah, *Demonic Possession and Exorcism in Early Modern France*, London : Routledge 2004

Finlay, Anthony, *Demons! : The Devil, Possession and Exorcism*, London : Cassell Illustrated 1999

Klass, Morton, *Mind Over Mind : The Anthropology and Psychology of Spirit Possession*, Lanham : Rowman & Littlefield 2003

Lewis, IM, *Ecstatic Religion : Anthropological Study of Spirit Possession and Shamanism*, London : Penguin 1971

Lutzer, Erwin W, *Serpent of Paradise : The Incredible Story of How Satan's Rebellion Serves God's Purposes*, Chicago : Moody 2001

— *Seven Snares of the Enemy : Breaking Free from the Devil's Grip*, Chicago : Moody 2001

Martin, Malachi, *Hostage to the Devil : The Possession and Exorcism of Five Contemporary Americans*, San Francisco : HarperSanFrancisco 1992

McAll, Kenneth, *Healing the Family Tree*, London : Sheldon Press 1982

McConnell, Brian, *The Possessed : True Tales of Demonic Possession*, London : Headline 1995

McNutt, Francis, *Deliverance from Evil Spirits : A Practical Manual*, Grand Rapids : Baker 1995

Oughourlian, Jean-Michel, *The Puppet of Desire : Psychology of Hysteria, Possession and Hypnosis*, Stanford : Stanford University Press 1991

Peck, M Scott, *People of the Lie : The Hope for Healing Human Evil*, New York : Simon & Schuster 1983

— *Glimpses of the Devil : A Psychiatrist's Personal Accounts of Possession, Exorcism, and Redemption*, New York : Simon & Schuster 2005

Pelton, Robert W, *Confrontations with the Devil : Arts of Exorcism*, New York : Yoseloff 1980

Pocs, Eva and Klaniczay, Gabor (eds), *Communicating with the Spirits : Christian Demonology and Popular Mythology : Demons, Spirits and Witches, Vol. 1*, Budapest and New York : Central European University Press 2005

Richards, John, *But Deliver Us From Evil : An introduction to the demonic dimension in pastoral care*, London : Darton, Longman & Todd 1974

Seymour, St John D, *Irish Witchcraft and Demonology* (1913), New York : Causeway 1973

Van der Toorn, Karel, *et al* (eds), *Dictionary of Deities and Demons in the Bible*, Leiden & Grand Rapids : Brill 1999

NOTES

Exorcism in Our Time

12 <u>BURNING LAKES AND CAVERNS</u>: The Christian conception
of hell has an intriguing history. The notion of a flaming
pit dates from biblical times, when the inhabitants of Jeru-
salem burned their rubbish in the Valley of Hinnom, to the
south of the city. In Hebrew the name was rendered as Ge
Hinnom, which came to be corrupted to Gehenna. Fires
burned day and night in Gehenna, as the city disposed of
its detritus – which included, rather brutally, the corpses
of those who had been executed, i.e. those condemned to
death.

The metaphorical step from 'the condemned' to 'the
damned' was an easy one for the ancients to make, particularly because the Valley of Hinnom was also the site of an
old temple to Moloch, the malevolent solar (or fire) deity
of the Canaanites. Moloch's enormous bronze statue was
hollow and a fire burned perpetually within. The Israelites
sacrificed their first-born to him. The victims were placed
in the idol's hands and raised to the mouth by a system of
pulleys, thereby simulating their devouring by the fire-god.
The practice continued into the sixth century BC.

<u>VAST HOSTS OF DEMON ARMIES</u>: Milton was relying for
the most part on *Pseudomonarchia daemonum*, a catalogue of demons compiled in 1583 by the German nec-
romancer Johann Weyer (1515–88). Derived from earlier
works of magic, it lists 7,405,926 demons, all under the

command of 69 Princes of Hell, each of whom commands legions of lesser demons. The Englishman Reginald Scot published a translation the following year in his *The Discoverie of Witchcraft*. In 1904 SL McGregor Mathers, who co-founded the Hermetic Order of the Golden Dawn, a magical society based in London, published a new translation of *The Goetia: The Lesser Key of Solomon the King*, with the addition of a further three chief demons, bringing the total to 72.

ADMONISHMENTS OF THE BESTIARY: Bestiaries were medieval books illustrating mythical creatures such as the unicorn and the manticore. Each drawing was accompanied by a morality lesson. The earliest form dates from second-century Greece, and they were extremely popular in twelfth-century France and England. The bestiary often served as a legitimate zoological guide, but towards the close of the seventeenth century its influence was waning as science overtook myth and superstition.

14 TIMOTHY LEARY: The son of an Irish-American dentist, Timothy Francis Leary (1920–96) was educated by the Jesuits in Massachusetts. He took degrees in psychology in Alabama and California, becoming a lecturer at Harvard. Having taken magic mushrooms in México, he went on to explore the therapeutic benefits of hallucinogens such as psilocybin and lysergic acid (LSD). He was dismissed from Harvard for allowing his students to experiment with the latter. Leary would protest that his work had importance in the treatment of alcoholism and in criminal reform, but he is remembered chiefly for his advocacy of 'mind-expanding' drug use, as encapsulated in his catch-phrase: 'Turn on, tune in, drop out.'

15   THE MOMENT THE FILM WAS SHOWN: *The Exorcist* was never banned in Ireland, but screened with some of the more lurid scenes, and those containing blasphemy, deleted. The uncut version was re-released for Irish cinemas in 1998. In 1995, twenty-five years after the film's debut, it was finally allowed on video and DVD in the UK. The delay was caused by a number of allegations, such as claims that its showing had led to the suicides of young people, and the 'satanic' child-abuse scandals of 1989.

19   PSYCHIATRIST DR KENNETH MCALL: Robert Kenneth McAll (1910–2001) was born in China and worked as a doctor in a mission hospital when the country was under Japanese occupation. When the Americans entered WWII, he and his family were interned and suffered great hardship. After the war the McAlls moved to Britain and Kenneth went on to qualify as a psychiatrist, eventually progressing to private practice. A devout Christian, he came to perceive the spiritual dimension in many cases of mental illness. His first book, *Healing the Family Tree* (1984), advanced the revolutionary – and hotly disputed – proposition that the deeds of one's ancestors can have a bearing on contemporary mental problems.

Dr McAll relates the case of a patient whom he calls Margaret. After her mother died, the seventy-three-year-old began having outbursts of aggression, which took the form of unprovoked attacks on Violet, her younger sister. Margaret would go wild, breaking things and being uncharacteristically abusive. Afterwards she would be genuinely remorseful, but unable to explain her behaviour. The doctor learned that her mother had behaved in much the same way throughout her life.

With the help of Violet, Dr McAll drew up a family tree,

covering six generations. They found that in 1750 a murder had been committed in the family and that subsequently the eldest daughter died from alcoholism, but not before she had destroyed much of the family property.

From that time on, the eldest female in each generation presented similar disturbing behaviour. This continued on down to Margaret, who was born in 1904.

Moreover, Margaret's thirty-two-year-old niece Rhonda, the eldest daughter of her youngest sister, was undergoing psychiatric treatment for a similar malady. Her husband had threatened divorce when, on returning home on several occasions, he found the house trashed – an eerie echo of the ancestor's destructive bouts.

Dr McAll, together with two clergymen and Violet, offered a Eucharist for Margaret and Rhonda, and for the eldest females of the previous six generations. The service was held in private and without the knowledge of Margaret and Rhonda. The doctor records that, with the conclusion of the service, neither woman required any further psychiatric care. Rhonda's husband dropped his threat of divorce and Margaret became the loving, quiet sister that Violet had always known.

22   THE CURÉ D'ARS: Jean Baptiste Marie Vianney (1786–1859) is perhaps France's most celebrated saint. He was born in Dardilly, near Lyons, of poor farming stock. He started school at the age of twenty and proved to be a below-average student. It took him ten years to struggle through his exams (he failed Latin twice) and so realize his ambition of becoming a priest.

In 1815 he was given his first parish. The parishioners were not impressed, believing him too stupid for the task, and they circulated a petition to have him removed. When the petition reached Jean he agreed that he was indeed inadequate and duly signed it too. On reading the list of signatories, the bishop was amused but took Jean's side.

In 1818 he was sent to Ars to be parish priest, or curé. Soon word spread about the holy man's ability to 'see into people's souls' and his extraordinary healing ability. By 1855, thousands were flocking to him for healing.

He would fast for days, hear confessions for eighteen hours a day and get by on only one or two hours' sleep. For thirty-five years Satan is said to have attacked him, trying constantly to break his will. The abuse took the form of severe beatings and strident noises – singing in a deafening voice and shouting, 'Vianney! Vianney! Potato Eater!' This last was a reference to what the Curé d'Ars would eat after days of near starvation.

The Devil allegedly told him, in frustration, that if there were just three men on earth like him, Satan's kingdom would be at an end.

26   A 'SUITABLE' EXORCIST: In *Hostage to the Devil*, the former Jesuit Malachi Martin offers a more elaborate definition of what constitutes the ideal exorcist.

> Usually he is engaged in the active ministry of parishes. Rarely is he a scholarly type engaged in teaching or research. Rarely is he a recently ordained priest. If there is any median age for exorcists, it is probably between the ages of fifty and sixty-five. Sound and robust physical health is not a characteristic of exorcists, nor is proven intellectual brilliance, postgraduate degrees, even in psychology or philosophy, or a very sophisticated personal culture. . . . Though, of course, there are many exceptions,

the usual reasons for a priest's being chosen are his qualities of moral judgement, personal behaviour and religious beliefs – qualities that are not sophisticated or laboriously acquired, but that somehow seem always to have been an easy and natural part of such a man. Speaking religiously, these are qualities associated with special grace.

28 THE FAITH MOVEMENT: Michael Cuneo is bringing together the various strands of evangelism operating in America today. They are the successors to preachers of earlier decades like Oral Roberts and AA Allen. Their leaders include charismatic individuals such as Benny Hinn, the team of Robert Tilton and Marilyn Hickey, Kenneth E Hagin, Kenneth Copeland, and Paul Crouch and his wife Jan, whose Trinity Broadcasting Network has assets exceeding $600 million.

EXORCISM AND HISTORY

31 SANSKRIT: One of the oldest Indo-European languages, written Sanskrit is some 3,500 years old. Today in Asia it occupies a similar position as Latin in the Christian Churches, being the liturgical language of Hinduism, Buddhism and Jainism. There have been recent attempts to revive it as a vernacular.

34 BOOK OF TOBIT: From 6:8. Protestantism regards this biblical book as apocryphal. In older Catholic Bibles it is known as the Book of Tobias, Tobias being the son of Tobit, a Jew who was exiled in Ninevah, Mesopotamia.

37 POPE CORNELIUS: The emperor Caius Messius Quintus Decius reigned in Rome from AD 249 until his death in 251.

This was a time of great Christian persecution, enthusiastically continued by his successor, Caius Gallus, who it seems died in the same year as the exiled pontiff. Although Cornelius was declared a martyr, there is no evidence that he suffered a violent death. Novatian, the theologian who took his place in 251, thereby creating a schism, was also exiled, and was said to have died a martyr.

EAGLE MOUNTAIN: The god Lugh, father of Cúchulainn, had his place in all the Celtic pantheons. The Welsh knew him as Llew Llaw Gyffes, 'Lew of the Versatile Arm'. To the Gauls he was Lugos. In ancient Ireland he was known as Lugh Lámhfada, or 'Lugh of the Long Arm'. He was a solar deity possessed of many skills, including medicine and brewing. He was also a shape-shifter, his favoured animal being a raven, sometimes an eagle. This last might account for the old name of Croagh Patrick.

38   MOSES IN THE SINAI: 'Now Moses kept the flock of Jethro his father in law, the priest of Midian: and he led the flock to the backside of the desert, and came to the mountain of God, even to Horeb' (Exodus 3:1). The biblical Horeb, where Moses communed with God, was renamed Mount Sinai by Greek Orthodox monks in the fourth century AD. There is some confusion today when identifying it; Gebel Mûsa (Moses' Mountain) is taken to be the original Horeb, although the nearby (and smaller) Mount Serabit seems a better contender, it being the site of an ancient Egyptian temple to Hathor.

    The temple site was excavated in 1904 by Sir William Matthew Flinders Petrie. Mount Serabit (Serabît el-Khâdim) lies some twenty miles east of the Gulf of Suez and nearly one hundred miles from the border with Israel.

ST ANTHONY ON HIS MOUNTAINTOP: Sometimes known
as St Anthony the Great, he was born in upper Egypt in AD
251 to wealthy parents, became a hermit and wandered
in a mountainous desert region some sixty miles west of
Alexandria. His hagiographer Athanasius recorded how
Anthony was subjected to a bewildering gamut of dreams,
hallucinations and temptations. These last have had an enduring influence on Christendom, becoming the inspira-
tion of several painters, from Hieronymus Bosch to Dalí.

In 1874 the French philosopher Gustave Flaubert published his masterpiece, *The Temptation of St Anthony*. It is
in the form of a drama and features a bewildering cast of
players, from ancient kings to the Devil, all of whom try to
tempt the hermit away from the spiritual path. The dream
aspect of the work influenced the young Sigmund Freud.

Flaubert's translator, Lafcadio Hearn, summarized the
more lascivious temptations: 'His thoughts wander . . .
he dreams of Amonaria, his sister's playmate. . . He be-
holds the orgies, the luxuries, the abominations . . . and
the Queen of Sheba descends to tempt the Saint with the
deadliest of all temptations. Her beauty is enhanced by ori-
ental splendour of adornment; her converse is a song of
witchcraft.'

LUGH NA DEAMHAIN: It is unfortunate that the name of
the Celtic deity Lugh is so close to the old Irish word *lug*,
which means 'hollow' or 'valley'. The word has survived
unaltered in other Irish place names that have undergone
a crude anglicization, e.g. Lugnaquilla or Lug na Coille,
'The Wooded Hollow'. The addition of the aspirative 'h'
may well have been an attempt by the early Church to de-
monize Lugh. Interestingly, his name is also cognate with
the Latin *luceo*, 'to be bright', from which the name Lucifer,

or 'Shining One', is derived. Lugh was the Celtic solar god, the bringer of light, and, as such, an important heathen deity. It would have been natural for the early churchmen, in their efforts to supplant the 'false' gods, to identify him with an evil entity.

39   AN DIABHAL: The Devil has an intriguing etymology. Linguists trace the word's origin to the Sanskrit *deva*, meaning 'god', or 'giver of light'. (Intriguingly it is also close to 'diva', the leading light of the opera.) Via the Greek verb *diabalein*, meaning 'to oppose', the word entered Latin as *diabolus*, Italian as *diabolo*, French as *diable*, and occurring in English as 'diabolic'. German and Dutch rendered the consonantal sounds as *Teufel* and *duivel*, the latter becoming 'devil' upon reaching Britain. It is possibly no more than coincidence that the Irish version, *diabhal*, contains within it *dia*, meaning 'god'. This is derived from the Latin *deus* and has another root entirely. The word 'god' seems to be largely a late European innovation. It appears in German, Dutch, Danish and Swedish as respectively *Gott*, *god*, *gud* and *gud*. There have been attempts to trace the root back to the Sanskrit *hu*, meaning 'to invoke'. It seems a weak argument. That root has indeed come down to us, though in a different context: the 'hue' of 'hue and cry'.

43   FIRST IRISH WITCH TRIAL: One would expect that Ireland, given its reputation as the 'natural' home of all things paranormal, had more than its fair share of witches and sorcerers. Not so, according to St John D Seymour who, in 1913, published *Witchcraft and Demonology in Ireland*, an exhaustive work, which examined the phenomena from 1324 to 1808. He concluded that witchcraft was far less prevalent here than in England and Scotland, and offered a curious explanation. He noted that fairy lore was largely

confined to the 'Celtic' section of the community, whereas the 'English' in Ireland – the descendants of the Anglo-Norman colonists – were more likely to practise witchcraft. In short: witchcraft and sorcery were principally Protestant phenomena. He wrote:

> In England after the Reformation we seldom find members of the Roman Catholic Church taking any prominent part in witch cases, and this is equally true of Ireland from the same date. Witchcraft seems to have been confined in the Protestant party, as far as we can judge from the material at our disposal, while it is probable that the existence of the penal laws (active or quiescent) would deter the Roman Catholics from coming into any prominence in a matter which would be likely to attract public attention to itself in such a marked degree.

45   MADE THE SIGN OF THE CROSS: The symbolism of this minor ritual has a colourful history. Obviously, it represents the cross upon which Christ was crucified and which came to symbolize the Christian Church. It is used by Roman Catholics, Anglicans, Eastern Rite Catholic Churches and the Orthodox Churches.

Reverend Kenneth W Collins notes a curious interpretation of the Western style. He believes that the movement from left to right represents Jesus' descent into hell, or Hades (the left side), and His ascension into heaven (the right side). This is consistent with the tradition which holds that all matters demonic, including black magic and satanism, belong to the 'left-hand path'.

The Sign of the Cross was not exclusively Christian. In

the ancient world, Indian Buddhists as well as members of Hindu sects used it when anointing the forehead.

46 ARCHBISHOP JAMES USSHER: Also written Usher (1581–1656). He was born in Dublin, and was Anglican Archbishop of Armagh from 1625 to 1656. His scholarship was legendary, as was his fervent anti-Catholicism, this despite his mother being Catholic. He is best remembered for his having dated the Creation, a date that is still recognized by many Christians as being the true one. Ussher was able to narrow it down not only to the year but to the very time of day: dusk on 22 October 4004 BC.

49 HOLY FATHER'S INTERVENTION: Pope John Paul II, during a visit to the Temple of Saint Michael in Perugia, Italy, in 1987, spoke of 'the battle against the Devil, which is the principal task of St Michael the Archangel.' He reminded the faithful that it is 'still being fought today, because the Devil is still alive and active in the world.' He spoke of evil in the modern world and its causes. 'The disorders that plague our society,' he declared, 'man's inconsistency and damaged state, are not only the results of original sin, but also the result of Satan's pervasive and dark action.'

EXORCISM IN IRELAND

54 CATHOLICS ATTENDED MASS: A 2003 poll conducted by RTÉ found that roughly half of those aged eighteen and older attended weekly Mass; in 1998 the figure was closer to 60%. The traditional urban-rural divide was still in evidence in the new poll, yet showed a sharper decline in rural areas: down from 77% to 60%. In the towns and cities, on the other hand, the decrease had been 5% – from 48% weekly Mass attendance in 1998 down to 43%.

1. Devilry on the Dingle Peninsula

72   DEAD, BLACK FLIES: Flies seem to figure in an inordinate number of hauntings that have unpleasant overtones. In this regard it is intriguing to note that the arch-demon Beelzebub is sometimes known as Lord of the Flies. Indeed, this appears to be a Hebrew-Aramaic translation of the name itself, in earlier texts rendered as Baalzebûb. It is also cognate with the Philistine god Ba'al, who may or may not have been a malevolent entity.

99   DEALING WITH THE PRETERNATURAL: It is often thought that the terms 'preternatural' and 'supernatural' are interchangeable. In fact 'supernatural' should be used only in reference to God and that which is of God. A preternatural entity, such as an evil spirit, is considered to be superior in power to a human being, but inferior to the divine.

102   HOLY WATER AND INCENSE: The use of incense predates Christianity by many centuries, if not millennia. There are countless references to it in the Old Testament, for example: 'And Aaron shall burn thereon sweet incense every morning . . . a perpetual incense before the Lord throughout your generations' (Exodus 30:7–8). The New Testament also mentions it, as in Revelation 8:3–4: 'And another angel came and stood at the altar, having a golden censer; and there was given unto him much incense, that he should offer it with the prayers of all saints upon the golden altar which was before the throne. And the smoke of the incense, which came with the prayers of the saints, ascended up before God out of the angel's hand.' However, there is no record of its Christian use until the fifth century. The symbolism of incensation is threefold: the burning zeal of the faithful, the fragrance of virtue, and the ascent

of prayer on high. The cloud it produces may also symbolize the incorporeal nature of the Divine.

2. THE HOUSEWIFE AND THE DEMON DUBOIS

108   CASES OF DEMONIC ATTACK: Possession or infestation is usually defined as the appropriation of a person's psyche by a preternatural entity. Most commentators are of the opinion that such an entity can only gain access when the person chooses to allow it. Julie on the other hand fought against the entity and it was never able to possess her to any extent. It goes without saying that it is far more difficult to banish an entity that has gained full or partial control of its victim.

116   ONE WHO LIES UPON: Incubus has the same root as 'incubation', originally the process by which a bird hatches her eggs, i.e. by sitting on them. With the naming of the hospital 'incubator', the device that assists a premature infant, the idea of lying or sitting upon was lost. It is perhaps significant that the Latin *incubito* means 'to defile'.

The word 'nightmare' has curious origins. In fact it has nothing at all to do with horses. We can trace the root of 'mare' to the Anglo-Saxon verb *merran* or *myrran*, meaning 'to obstruct' or 'to impede', which is related to Old Icelandic *merja* (pronounced 'mer-ya'), meaning 'to bruise' or 'to crush'. According to Nordic folklore the *mare* or *mara* was an evil spirit known to visit women at night and paralyze them. Often there was a sexual dimension to the haunting but certainly not in all cases. It was believed that other demons actually had sexual intercourse with humans while they slept; the entity that attacked women was known as the incubus, while the succubus molested sleeping men.

IN THE NAME OF JESUS CHRIST: It will be seen that the uttering of the Lord's name is a common feature of the cases covered in this book. From earliest times it was held that the name of Jesus contained great power, and could be used for the subjugation of demons. In Acts of the Apostles 16:18 we read: 'But Paul, being grieved, turned and said to the spirit, I command thee in the name of Jesus Christ to come out of her. And he came out the same hour.'

See also APPENDIX TWO, p. 374.

3. THE TEMPTATION OF FATHER FINTAN

137 TRANSITIONAL DIACONATE: This is the final preparatory period, generally lasting six months or more, before ordination. In the Catholic Church there is a distinction between this and the 'permanent diaconate'. In the former, a man will go on to become a priest; in the latter he remains a deacon but takes a vow of celibacy.

141 THROWS HIMSELF ACROSS GOD'S PLAN: The existentialist psychologist Rollo May (1909–94) had a different explanation. Writing in *Love and Will*, he stated that the Greek word *diabolos* literally means

> 'to tear apart' (*dia-bollein*). Now it is fascinating to note that this diabolic is the antonym of 'symbolic'. . . . There lie in these words tremendous implications with respect to an ontology of good and evil. The symbolic is that which draws together, ties, integrates the individual in himself and with his group; the diabolic, in contrast, is that which disintegrates and tears apart. Both of these are present in the daimonic.

162   DRIVEN A DEMON FROM A CAMEL: Taken from *Vita sancti ilarionis* or *The Life of St Hilary*, a fourth-century manuscript said to have been written by St Jerome, who was a contemporary admirer of the holy man of Poictiers, France. It is sometimes attributed to Fortunatus, a bishop of Gaul.

     The notorious biblical episode involving the Gadarene swine perhaps gave rise to the belief among early Christians that animals could also become possessed. Certainly in the Middle Ages, when witches were being hunted down, their luckless pets suffered burning and other means of 'execution', in the belief that the animal was the witch's 'familiar' spirit. Goats also fell victim, doubtless because of their unfortunate likeness to the traditional portrayal of Satan as a goatlike entity.

     The superstitions pertaining to 'demonic' cats have not died out entirely. In parts of England cats born at the end of the blackberry season are considered tainted by evil, due to a belief that Lucifer was expelled from heaven at that time of year, and that he fell among brambles. Even the three hairs at the tip of a cat's tail are considered demonic, and in parts of the American south it is held that Satan will punish anyone who drowns a cat, the animal being under his protection.

4. THE UNQUIET SPIRIT OF CHILD SARAH

173   EVIDENCE OF 'PSYCHOKINETIC' ENERGY: It is also known as telekinetic energy. The most celebrated pioneer in the field of parapsychology and related research was Joseph Banks Rhine (1895–1980). In 1966 he and a number of colleagues, including J Gaither Pratt and Charles E Stuart, published the definitive work on PK: *Extra-sensory Perception after Sixty Years: A Critical Appraisal of the Research*

in Extra-Sensory Perception. This was based on results first published in 1940.

Recent research into the PK phenomenon itself – as purportedly demonstrated by groups of people who lift heavy objects with the power of the mind alone – was led in recent times by British psychologist Kenneth J Batcheldor, who believes that 'unconscious muscular action' is the basis for telekinesis, which relies to a great extent on the faith of the participants. He holds that fear is the key: that it is the fear of the power itself that inhibits the successful application of PK.

5. MR GANT AND THE NEIGHBOUR FROM HELL

204   THERE'S NO GOD HERE: This is strikingly similar to the utterance of the demented nun in the case entitled 'The Temptation of Father Fintan'. In the one instance, the site of the manifestation was Lourdes; in the other, Luxor, ancient Thebes of the Egyptians. Both are/were sacred sites. The two instances seem to give the lie to the common supposition that such sacred places are out of bounds to demonic influences.

210   THE SMURL FAMILY OF PENNSYLVANIA: The case is the subject of *The Haunted: One Family's Nightmare* by Robert Curran (1988). It details the extraordinary manifestations that terrorized the Smurls, infestations that could only be banished after four exorcisms. Ed and Lorraine Warren – who collaborated in the writing of the book – conducted the most extensive investigations into the phenomena, and were themselves apparently the target of demonic attack. Ed Warren has the distinction of being the world's only lay demonologist trained by the Vatican.

213 My name is Legion: Some believe that the notorious New York serial killer who called himself Son of Sam was demonically possessed. Sam Berkowitz, who embarked on a horrific murder spree in the 1970s, was asked his name when arrested. He replied: 'My name is Legion, for we are many,' the precise words contained in Mark's Gospel (5:9). It remains a puzzle as to why Berkowitz, an orthodox Jew, should have quoted the New Testament, a collection of books normally read only by Christians. As with the demoniac of Scripture, cemeteries held a curious fascination for Berkowitz; he liked to spend time among the tombstones, especially those of the women he murdered.

Interestingly, Peter Sutcliffe, the Yorkshire Ripper, also worked in a cemetery. It was while he was digging a grave there, that he claimed a voice spoke to him from the grave of a Polish man. The voice told him that his mission in life was to rid the streets of prostitutes. Between 1975 and 1981, Sutcliffe attacked twenty women, not all of whom were prostitutes. Only seven survived his savage assaults.

It is understood that Sutcliffe underwent several exorcisms conducted by a Catholic priest, while awaiting trial in Armley jail, Leeds.

223 St Benedict medal: The saint was born in Nursia, near Rome, ca. 480, and went on to found the monastic order that bears his name. This particular medal features a cross with the letters CSPB, signifying *Crux Sancti Patris Benedicti*: The Cross of Father Benedict. The cross was a favourite Benedictine emblem. Inscribed also are the initial letters of a Latin prayer, which translates as May the holy cross be my light. May the dragon never be my guide. Just why this saint came to be associated with exorcism is not clear. Many miracles were

attributed to him, some of Christ-like proportions, such as enabling a follower to walk on water. Such miracles would have identified Benedict in the minds of the faithful as one possessing superior power over Satan.

6. Little Lucy and the Phantom Family

245   Residual haunting: Peter Underwood, Britain's foremost researcher into the paranormal and author of *The Autobiography of a Ghost-Hunter* (1983), broadly categorizes ghosts thus:

1. Elemental (or primitive or racial-memory) manifestations. They are mainly seen in rural areas and in particular sites. They are rare and appear to be malevolent.

2. Poltergeists, which include death-bed visions and manifestations triggered by crises or traumas.

3. Traditional or historical ghosts. They usually dress in period clothing and follow old floorplans of houses and other buildings, thereby appearing to 'walk' several inches above the floor. They neither speak nor interact with the observer. Often it is found that they are the ghosts of those who suffered trauma during their lifetimes.

4. Mental imprints. They are some kind of imprint upon the atmosphere and resemble holographic images. Often they must be viewed from a specific angle and at a given time. The manifestation they produce never alters, as though a film sequence is being played back over and over.

5. Time distortion and cyclic ghosts. They seem to

be replays of past events, often the re-enactment of famous battles.

6. Ghosts of the living, which may be a part of the phenomenon known as bilocation, or the result of clairvoyance and telepathy. Observers claim that the apparition is all but indistinguishable from the real person.

All the ghosts seen by Lucy Gillespie seem to fall into more than one of these categories, in particular the third and fourth.

7. THE GOOD PRESBYTERIAN AND THE SUCCUBUS

258   A GROUP OF SPIRITISTS: The terms 'spiritualist' and 'spiritist' do not mean the same thing. Spiritualism is the belief in the spiritual or non-material world. Technically speaking, all religions are spiritualistic, since they are founded on a belief in the ethereal realms. Spiritualism (with a capital S) is the name given to a religious movement which has a strong basis in Christian morality. Sometimes called Survivalism, it is generally accepted that it began in 1846 when the Fox sisters of Hydesville, New York, allegedly communed with the spirit of a dead man. The Foxes and their followers channelled spirits chiefly by means of table rapping and talking boards (ouija).

Spiritism was the name coined for a similar religious movement founded by a Frenchman calling himself Allan Kardec, who was a scientist and academic, not a medium. In 1857 he published *Le Livre des Esprits* (*The Spirits' Book*) in which he claimed that Spiritism was the 'Third Revelation'. Among its tenets are reincarnation and the transmigration of souls, ideas not embraced at the time by

the Spiritualist movement. Today across the world Spiritu-
alists greatly outnumber Spiritists.

APPARENTLY INVOLVING AN 'APPORT': An apport is a
physical object produced, as if from nowhere, during a
séance. It can be, but is not necessarily, produced by the
medium. An object which is made to disappear is called a
deport. Such materializations seldom prove to be genuine
but owe their appearance to sleight of hand. Notable ex-
ceptions seem to be apports produced by the Scole Experi-
mental Group, a team of researchers who conducted paranormal experiments in Norfolk between 1992 and 1999.
One such apport was a copy of the *Daily Mail*, dated 1
April 1944. As reported in *The Scole Experiment: Scientific Evidence for Life after Death* (1999), the paper was

> in almost mint condition (apart from folds),
> with no sign of the yellowing that would have
> been expected from the impurities in the fifty-
> year-old newsprint. (Much later a piece of
> this newspaper was sent off by investigators
> to be analysed by the Paper Industry Associa-
> tion. It was tested and found to be genuine
> wartime paper.)

8. THE BOY WHO COMMUNES WITH DEMONS

286 A MILD FORM OF EPILEPSY: There are a number of mis-
conceptions surrounding epilepsy, not least being the belief
that it is a mental illness. In fact it is a form of physical
dysfunction which takes the form of a seizure, which can
occur (and recur) at any time. Epilepsy is caused by abnormal electrical activity in the brain and can be treated
with medication and/or surgery, although not all sufferers

respond equally well. It is more common than many people imagine. Dr John Wilkinson, author of 'The Bible and Healing: A Medical and Theological Commentary' in *Review of Biblical Literature* (2000), is among those who have researched the historical incidence of epilepsy and a possible link to possession. 'If demon possession is a fact there seems no reason why it could not be the cause of some cases of epilepsy,' he argues. 'We do not know enough about the spirit world to disprove demon possession nor enough about epilepsy to deny that it may be caused by such possession.'

287   COMMONLY CALLED A SEIZURE: In brief, a seizure is a sudden and erratic firing of neurons that effects a change in behaviour. The so-called myoclonic seizure would be the first suspect in Gary Lyttle's attack, as it results in muscle spasms on both sides of the body. It is, however, of short duration, in contrast to Gary's attacks or 'spells'.

Epileptic seizures were undoubtedly one of the causes of the persecution of Europe's witches in earlier centuries, as frequently the seizures suffered by epileptics were identified as the mark of a witch.

In 1494, two German monks, at the behest of the Vatican, produced the definitive handbook on witch-hunting, *Malleus Maleficarum*, the Hammer of Witches, which made the link between seizures and diabolic control.

Apart from Hitler's *Mein Kampf* and the *Thoughts of Chairman Mao*, there can hardly have been a more incendiary book in the history of mass murder. The *Malleus* was largely responsible for the deaths of hundreds of thousands of innocent people, mainly women.

We have no way of knowing how many of its victims were actually epileptics.

9. The Woman who Left her Body at Will

315 TUESDAY LOBSANG RAMPA: Cyril Henry Hoskins (1911–81) made a spectacular literary debut in 1956 with *The Third Eye: The Autobiography of a Tibetan Lama*, in which he claimed to be a Buddhist master. Millions of copies were sold around the world. The writer was in fact a plumber's son from Devon; this was among the facts uncovered by a private detective hired by a group of academics who grew more than a little suspicious of 'Dr' Rampa's teaching, and by extension his bona fides. By way of explanation Hoskins revealed that the real Lobsang Rampa had taken over his body as a means of continuing his teaching. Hoskins went on to publish many more books, sustained by a gullible public. Eventually, however, mounting allegations of fraud forced him to flee to Canada, where he died in obscurity.

326 CLAIRVOYANCE, REMOTE VIEWING: The two terms are cognate, though the latter has come to be associated with, among others, the US military, who sought to develop this 'gift' in groups of volunteers. The research went by different titles, beginning in the 1970s as a response to reports of Soviet investigation into so-called 'PsyOps'; the final phase was Project Star Gate, which was abandoned in 1999. Although more than $20m was spent, it is not known if any success was achieved, and sceptics cast doubt on the claims made by the participants. Clairvoyance should not be confused with astral projection, which appears to be an altogether different phenomenon, related to the near-death experience reported by many.

327 MEMBERS OF THE GOLDEN DAWN: This was the Hermetic Order of the Golden Dawn, a magical society

founded along Rosicrucian lines in London in 1887 by three Freemasons. Aside from WB Yeats, its membership included Maude Gonne and the notorious Aleister Crowley. Several of its rituals were based on ancient documents translated by SL MacGregor Mathers, one of the founders, including the fearsome *Goetia, the Lesser Key of Solomon the King* and *The Book of the Sacred Magic of Abra-Melin the Mage.* The Golden Dawn drew on the philosophies of ancient Egypt and Greece, combined with threads of Gnosticism and the Jewish Qabalah. It inspired many of the magical lodges found throughout the world today.

333 DAVID KORESH AND JIM JONES: James Warren Jones (1931–78) set the precedent for the charismatic cult leader who induces mass-suicide in his followers. Jones was born in Indiana to a father who was a member of the Ku Klux Klan, and from an early age seemed determined to make reparations. On becoming a minister he actively sought to embrace black America and promote racial equality. He founded the Peoples Temple in Indianapolis, but in 1977 moved it to Guyana, South America, when he was accused of tax evasion. Most of his 1,000 followers joined him, where they established a commune in the jungle.

Jones was becoming increasingly delusional, claiming to be an incarnation of Jesus Christ, the Buddha and others, and to be capable of performing miracles. He ruled his 'people' with an iron fist, demanding total obedience. When the US authorities moved to arrest him, his men fatally ambushed the party, including a Senator. Jones then induced his remaining disciples – 914, including 276 children – to commit suicide by consuming a soft drink laced with cyanide.

David Koresh (1959–93) was born Vernon Wayne How-ell in Houston, Texas. He never knew his father and was sexually abused by his stepfather. He went to California to become a rock guitarist, but failed. He returned to Texas and joined a breakaway sect of Seventh-Day Adventists calling itself the Branch Davidians. Soon after, Koresh proclaimed himself leader. There were growing reports of brainwashing and child-abuse at the Davidian ranch near Waco, and also that Koresh was demanding sex from any female member he chose. Eventually the FBI raided the farm in 1993. The fifty-one-day siege resulted in the deaths of four agents and seventy-six sect members, including Ko-resh. It was found that several adults had killed their own children before shooting themselves.

338   THE COLLECTIVE UNCONSCIOUS: Carl Gustav Jung (1875–1961) was born and spent most of his life in Switzerland. As a pioneering psychiatrist he collaborated with Sigmund Freud for many years until they had a notorious falling out after WWI, owing to Freud's fixation with sexuality as the root of numerous psychological problems. Jung became immersed in spirituality and the symbolism of dreams. He developed many theories on the subconscious mind, including the notion of the collective unconscious (which he later referred to as the objective psyche) and the archetypes: symbols common to all human beings, and arising in that part of the psyche 'shared' by all.

The New England Transcendentalists, a group of writ-ers led by Ralph Waldo Emerson, perceived a similarity to the concept of the oversoul, believing it to be a force per-vading the universe upon which all individual human souls may draw, thus enabling one to communicate with God. It transcends the individual soul or consciousness.

Index